THE WEST

An illustrated history

THE WEST

An illustrated history

Edited by
Henry Steele Commager
with
Marcus Cunliffe
Maldwyn A. Jones

Promontory Press
New York

THE EDITORS: Henry Steele Commager has taught history at
Columbia, Cambridge, Oxford, and other universities, and at
Amherst College, for over forty years. He is the coauthor
(with S. E. Morison) of *The Growth of the American
Republic*, and author of *Theodore Parker, The American
Mind, Majority Rule and Minority Rights,* and many other
books. He is the editor of *Documents of American History*
and, with Richard B. Morris, of the fifty-volume *New
American Nation Series.* Professor Commager was recently
awarded the Gold Medal of the American Academy of Arts
and Letters for his historical writings.

Marcus Cunliffe is Professor of American Studies at the
University of Sussex. He has been a Commonwealth Fellow
at Yale and has taught at Harvard and other American
universities. Professor Cunliffe's books include *The
Literature of the United States, The Nation Takes Shape,
Soldiers and Civilians,* and *The American Presidency.*

Maldwyn A. Jones is Commonwealth Fund Professor of
American History at the University of London. He has been
a visiting professor at Harvard and at the universities of
Chicago and Pennsylvania. Professor Jones has written
extensively on American ethnic groups and is the author of
American Immigration, a volume in the *Chicago History of
American Civilization.*

© 1976 by Grolier Enterprises Inc.
This edition published by Promontory Press, New York.

Printed in the United States of America.
ISBN 0 88394 995 4
Library of Congress Catalog Card No: 80 80521

Introduction

The westward expansion of the United States was one of the greatest movements of peoples in history. It had begun as soon as the thirteen colonies of the eastern seaboard won their independence, and the aspirations of the American people were not to be satisfied until the national domain stretched from the Atlantic to the Pacific. Thus the 1840s witnessed a fresh wave of expansionist sentiment. It resulted in the annexation of Texas, the occupation of Oregon and, in consequence of war with Mexico, huge new territorial gains. By the Treaty of Guadalupe Hidalgo (1848) the United States acquired the Mexican provinces of New Mexico and Upper California (which included the present states of California, Nevada, Utah, Arizona, New Mexico, and parts of Colorado and Wyoming). By mid-century, therefore, the task of rounding out the nation's continental boundaries was complete. Yet only half a century earlier the Mississippi had formed the western boundary of the United States.

The desire for more territory which came to a head in the 1840s had more than one source. It owed something to the notion, fostered by early explorers, that the region between Missouri and the Rockies, already under American jurisdiction, was too arid for agriculture. Map-makers labeled the area the "Great American Desert" and until after the Civil War there was a general disposition to leave it to the Indians. Hence land-hungry pioneers came to look longingly at the empty or sparsely-settled tracts lying beyond the nation's borders. Commercial interests provided a further stimulus. Eastern businessmen, their eyes on the rich trade of the Far East, were anxious for harbors on the Pacific coast. The American appetite was further sharpened by the chronic fear of European, especially British, intervention in the western borderlands. But what gave the expansionist drive its distinctive character was that it possessed a romantic and idealistic ideology summed up in the phrase "manifest destiny." This term, coined by a newspaper editor in 1845, implied the inevitability of westward expansion and proclaimed that the special mission of the United States was to extend its political institutions and way of life throughout the entire North American continent.

A series of independent American thrusts into the Far West during the preceding generation had already prepared the way for annexation. In response to Mexico's liberal colonization policies American settlers, largely from the South, swarmed into Texas in the 1820s, carrying slavery and cotton culture with them. Twenty years later, thousands of adherents of the Mormon faith, finding themselves persecuted in the United States, sought a new Zion in an isolated part of the Mexican borderlands—the arid and inhospitable Great Salt Lake Valley. Meanwhile smaller bands of pioneers had braved the perils of the long overland journey by covered wagon across the Plains and over the Rockies. Some of these overlanders settled in the sleepy province of California; others, fired by stories of a land of unexampled fertility, took the Oregon Trail to a distant region still in dispute between the United States and Britain.

The election to the presidency in 1844 of an avowed expansionist, James K. Polk, was the signal for the consolidation of these scattered empires. Texas, which had been seeking admission to the Union ever since becoming independent in 1836, was finally annexed in 1845. Then, in May 1846, a border skirmish near the Rio Grande gave Polk the pretext he needed to go to war with Mexico. His object was to despoil Mexico of half her territory. At almost exactly the same time—perhaps because he wanted to avoid war on two fronts—Polk settled the Oregon dispute by abandoning the extreme American claim to the line of 54° 40'.

For the United States the Mexican War was a succession of triumphs. Her largely volunteer army occupied New Mexico and California with ease, defeated the numerically superior Mexicans in a succession of pitched battles and finally captured the enemy capital, forcing Mexico to surrender. The peace treaty gave the United States all the territory for which she had gone to war—in all half a million square miles—as well as the coveted outlet to the Pacific. And even before the treaty could be ratified a further gain materialized. Gold was discovered in California, an event which, by attracting a motley army of fortune-seekers from all over the United States and elsewhere, transformed a peaceful, pastoral province almost overnight into one of the gaudiest and most lawless places on earth.

Ever since the first white settlers set foot on the eastern shore of the great shaggy continent at the beginning of the seventeenth century, the sweep toward the West—or, more accurately, toward a succession of Wests—had gone on inexorably. Yet at the close of the Civil War the settlement of the continent was far from complete. One bridgehead had been established beyond the Mississippi; another existed some 1,500 miles farther west, along the Pacific littoral. Separating these two frontiers there was a vast, sprawling region that still awaited settlement and political organization. It was occupied by roaming bands of red men, belonging to many different tribes. Almost as many white men were scattered throughout the region, but except for the Mormons in Utah, few had struck roots. Comprising traders, prospectors, trappers, guides, cowboys, and sheepherders, these men were as nomadic as the Indians and almost as far removed from the ways of white civilization.

During the decades after the Civil War the Wild West, as it was known, established a powerful hold on the imaginations of eastern Americans. Its existence brought both a touch of romance and a sense of boundlessness into national life. Popular conceptions of the region were shaped by stories of stagecoaches and outlaws, mining rushes and cattle drives, six-shooters and branding irons, buffalo herds and council fires. Easterners eagerly devoured yarns set in such notorious centers of western lawlessness as Tombstone and Deadwood and featuring such legendary characters as Wild Bill Hickok, Calamity Jane, Wyatt Earp, and Billy the Kid. The popular image was often inaccurate but for Americans the myth was more significant than the reality. The western scene was destined to implant itself permanently in the American consciousness.

Yet ironically the period in which the Wild West came to enjoy such a vogue was also the period in which it was tamed. Between 1865 and 1900 the last and most romantic chapter was added to the great American epic of settlement. Two factors paved the way: the removal of the Indian barrier and the building of the great transcontinental railroads. Though the Plains Indians were formidable foes, their bravery was no match for the numerical and technological superiority of the whites. The mass slaughter of the buffalo, on which the red men had depended for food, shelter, clothing, and fuel, was the final blow. The construction of the great transcontinental lines was a stupendous engineering feat. The railroads not only opened up wide areas to settlement but played a leading part in shaping the entire western economy.

Two picturesque but transitory episodes started the transformation of the West. A succession of gold and silver strikes, beginning with the rush to Pike's Peak in 1859, sent fortune-hunters swarming all over the western mountains and brought a mining kingdom into existence. Simultaneously the Great Plains became cow country. The open range and the railroad combined to make the long drive northward to shipping points like Abilene and Dodge City a practicable and profitable proposition. But the day of the miner and of the cattleman was brief. The generous land policies of the federal government, together with the colonization efforts of the railroads, brought a flood of settlers into the Great Plains from the eastern states and from Europe. Agriculture in the arid, treeless West was a difficult and hazardous venture, but it was made possible by new methods of cultivation, new strains of disease-resistant wheat, new inventions like barbed wire, and the large-scale adoption of farm machinery. By such means the whole expanse of the Great Plains was brought under cultivation and by 1890 so much of the public domain had been pre-empted that the frontier was officially declared closed.

Political organization kept pace with settlement. Nebraska was admitted to the Union as a state in 1867, Colorado in 1876. Then in 1889, Montana, Washington, and the two Dakotas were admitted together; Idaho and Wyoming followed the next year. For the first time there was now a continuous band of states extending from the Atlantic to the Pacific.

The closing of the frontier was a momentous event in American history. It brought to an end a process which had spanned three centuries. Yet it produced no dramatic changes. Its most important immediate consequence, perhaps, was to sharpen popular awareness of the extent to which America's natural resources had been wasted. Thus at the end of the century the first tentative steps were taken toward a program of conservation that would save what was left of the vanishing West.

Contents

Chapter I

WESTWARD TO THE PACIFIC

By the early 1800s the American people were showing an active interest in the territory to the west of the established areas of settlement. They had won their independence; now it was time to consolidate their hold on the continent. Soon American trade had spread south into Mexico; overland routes had been discovered to California; and an attempt had been made to challenge the primacy of the Hudson's Bay Company in the Northwest. But it was the fur trade which hastened American knowledge and commercial penetration of the Far West. This became the domain of the mountain men, whose hardy individualism and legendary feats of exploration quickly made them American folk-heroes.

Exploring the Interior

"Motion was in their days," sang England's great poet Lord Byron as he described Americans on the frontier in the nineteenth century. It was a time when America, recently born into nationhood, took stock of its inward dimensions. It was like a young man feeling the muscle and tissue of his growing body, sensing, knowing, with every nerve preciously alive. Byron went on: "Serene, not sullen, were the solitudes of this unsighing people of the woods." In this adolescent spirit they turned to the engulfing of their continent, calling into their service all manner of idealism, practicality, hard-fisted greed, grubby commercialism, racial prejudice, violence, and grandiloquence.

Much was already prepared for them. In the Treaty of Paris after the American Revolution, Britain surrendered far more land than the seaboard colonies had a right to expect. The compact stretched their public domain to the Mississippi River, about one-third of the breadth of North America. President Thomas Jefferson believed that the nation then possessed "room enough for our descendents to the thousandth and thousandth generation." Within one generation, however, Jefferson capitalized on French circumstances to double the area, pushing the nation's borders as far west as the Rocky Mountains and the Continental Divide.

From the beginning American colonists had been interested in the West. Through symbols as well as political decisions they thought of themselves as a westering people. In the 1840s naturalist Henry David Thoreau captured this feeling when he wrote, "Westward is heaven, or rather heavenward is the west," and "I must walk toward Oregon, and not toward Europe." Of all the early western dreamers since 1607, however, Jefferson, the sage of Monticello, may have been the most scientific and broad-minded. He had supported botanical expeditions and other scientific ventures into the West. He had long sympathized with John Ledyard, a wild schemer who foresaw grand ropes of trade tying America with Russia and China. And Jefferson's plans for the famed Lewis and Clark expedition predated the purchase of Louisiana.

Following the model set by Lewis and Clark, Jefferson and subsequent presidents down to the Mexican War frequently mounted similar explorations. In fact the United States Army had another survey in the field before Lewis and Clark returned. With little of the drama of its famed predecessor, this expedition was dispatched under the command of a twenty-two-year-old from a military family, Lieutenant Zebulon Pike. In 1805 he led a small group of men to seek the headwaters of the Mississippi River, a task which would occupy surveyors and geographers for a generation. On the upper Mississippi

"Westward is heaven," wrote Thoreau. To the American people the West held out the promise of individual opportunity—and national destiny. This painting, Westward the Course of Empire, is by Emanuel Leutze.

Thomas Gilcrease Institute, Tulsa, Oklahoma (detail)

Zebulon Pike (below left) explored the Mississippi in 1805, and in 1806 he was sent by General James Wilkinson (below right) to spy out the defenses of New Spain. Pike strayed into Spanish territory and was arrested in Santa Fe (above).

the American army sought also to assert control, especially over British fur traders. The following year Pike was assigned a more significant task, or at least a more risky one. With twenty-three men he was to ascend the Arkansas River to the region of the present city of Denver. He made a stab at climbing the peak which now bears his name. After touching the Rockies, he led his men southward. Claiming to be lost, he crossed the border into New Spain. As an officer leading an army

expedition into foreign territory without permission, he was arrested by the Spanish authorities in Santa Fe, the old adobe capital in the northern borderlands. The Spaniards moved him further south to Chihuahua where his papers were confiscated before he was escorted to the border.

Pike was implicated in a far more serious game than that of a young lieutenant mistakenly stumbling across a boundary. He was probably involved in the Aaron Burr-James Wilkinson conspiracy to proclaim an independent state in the West, spying out the defenses of New Spain. How different his position in history might have been had the conspiracy not been scotched by Burr's arrest in the fall of 1806.

The report that Pike presented to the army and the nation had none of the personal interest of the Lewis and Clark journals, and was noticeably devoid of the detail which a scientific expedition should pursue. Stripped of its military importance, however, the Pike expedition did unwittingly affect the westward movement. Pike brought back to the settlements along the Mississippi descriptions of Santa Fe, its people, its color, and above all, its economic opportunities. Serenely nestled in the foothills of the southern tip of the Rockies, Santa Fe lay closer to St Louis than to the centers of Mexican production. As an isolated frontier post, it needed mules, guns,

cloth, iron kettles, sugar, and coffee. It could offer in exchange furs from the Rocky Mountains and silver from the mines of northern Mexico. Some of the competitive Yankee types in St Louis understood, and the Santa Fe trade was born.

The first American traders into northern Mexico found themselves, like Pike, either behind bars or brusquely deported. In 1821, Mexico proclaimed its independence from Spain. With eased regulations the impatient Santa Fe traders again tried their luck. William Becknell was the most serious of the group, and from a five-month venture he reaped profits so large that he repeated the effort in 1822. That year he found the most effective route, and his path—along the Arkansas, Cimarron, and Canadian rivers to Taos and Santa Fe—became the well-trodden Santa Fe Trail. By 1824 one caravan along the trail had returned with furs and silver worth $190,000.

The army's role in the penetration of the wilderness continued with the expedition of Major Stephen Long in 1819–20. Long was not only a better engineer than Pike, but he undoubtedly had a better mind. Phi Beta Kappa at Dartmouth College, he secured an appointment as assistant professor of mathematics at West Point. Abandoning the classroom for the field, he transferred to the Topographical Corps in 1816. The next year he made the customary trek to the headwaters of the Mississippi. Two

After his release from prison, Pike wrote a report of his explorations which pointed out the advantages of trade with the Spanish. Before long, Americans were traveling the Santa Fe Trail (above).

years later he sharpened his surveying skills on an expedition to the Yellowstone country. On the way he proved his engineering bent by drawing designs for boats to ascend the upper Missouri River. Later in 1819 he set out on his most important assignment: further exploration of the Great Plains, the high, semi-arid plateau lying east of the Rocky Mountains. His expedition returned in 1820, having tramped and mapped the central plains between the Platte and the Canadian rivers.

Pike had already likened the Arkansas River country to African deserts, good only to prevent the "ruinous diffusion" of population. Long agreed with him and carried the concept further. He described the plains as the "haunt of bison and jackal," the chief beneficiaries of a wasteland whose "sole monarch" was the prickly pear. "In regard to this extensive section of the country," he wrote, "I do not hesitate in giving the opinion, that it is almost wholly uninhabitable by a people depending upon agriculture for their subsistence." Certain indirect results might, however, be foreseen. This regional barri-

Major Stephen Long (above) explored the Great Plains in 1819. He believed the region unsuited for settlement. Titian Peale, who accompanied Long on his journey, painted Sunset on the Missouri *(right).*

cade could well check national disintegration. As James Madison had shrewdly contended in the *Federalist Papers*, a republic that was too large would shatter from regional factions. Long thought the Great Plains would so thwart further expansion to the West that the nation would remain small enough to survive. It was the doctrine of the "Great American Desert," a buffer between the settled parts of the country and what lay beyond. Wild animals and Indians, yes, but the white man and settled agriculture, no. Twenty years later, another generation of explorers would dispel this notion.

The Fur Kingdom

By the time of Long, another group was far advanced in grappling with the wilderness. They too were explorers, but their maps lay only between eye and brain. These were the mountain men of the Far West, living a moment of freedom in an unspoiled wilderness. The roots of their occupation lay deep in the past. In the sixteenth century the French colonists in the North, finding no gold, contented themselves with the development of a fur trade. Down through the nineteenth century, the French origins of the trade were revealed by the terms applied to the adventurers who roamed the lakes, rivers, and frontiers of the area in search of furs—coureurs-de-bois and voyageurs. It was even two renegade Frenchmen who

organized the Hudson's Bay Company, the great English rival of the French. From then on, the English were destined to place their own special mark on the trade. In the eighteenth century the Hudson's Bay Company became so genteel and established that its initials were often said to represent "Here Before Christ." After the British gained control of Canada in 1763, other English fur companies emerged. By 1821 the Crown forced the largest of these, the North West Company, to merge with its rival. So the Hudson's Bay Company posts rested supreme. They were flung across the continent with handfuls of Englishmen and Scotsmen brewing tea in baronial halls and supervising the trade while the actual labor was done by Indians and Frenchmen. As far as the Columbia River and Fort Victoria on Vancouver Island, the British strode the continent and laid claim to its wealth in fur.

As late as the 1840s, the urbane Peter Skene Ogden with his colleague John McLoughlin commanded the company's trade along the Columbia River. Ogden's trapping expeditions ranged far inland toward the place which now bears his name—Ogden, Utah—and as far south as northern Nevada and California. The British presence was indeed formidable, and it was against such economic power that the Americans had to compete.

John Jacob Astor made a good start in the struggle. Born in Germany, he emigrated first to London and then to New York in 1783. He parlayed his meager assets into a fortune which by 1808 made him a millionaire. Soon after

Above: John Jacob Astor tried without success to dispute British monopoly of the Northwest's fur trade. Left: Jedediah Smith—trapper and explorer. Frederic Remington's painting shows Smith leading a party from Green River to San Diego in the 1820s.

The British dominated the fur trade in the Northwest. Peter Skene Ogden (left) and John McLoughlin (right) headed the Hudson's Bay Company operations on the Columbia River.

that his American Fur Company dominated the American trade. Sensing the expansionist meaning of the Lewis and Clark expedition, he hoped to spread the Astor influence all the way to the Pacific. Consequently, in 1811 he set up a post at the mouth of the Columbia River and called it Astoria. It was an ill-starred venture. Two expeditions left to strengthen the fledgling outpost—one by sea under Captain Jonathan Thorn in the *Tonquin* and one by land under Wilson Price Hunt. Both ultimately reached their goal, but at such a cost as to prove disastrous. The War of 1812 also posed serious diplomatic problems, so Astor

sold his post and left the field to the British.

In contrast with Astor's corporate approach, the free trapper or mountain man came to typify the most rugged brand of individualism the continent ever produced. In the stereotype, he sought unrestrained freedom. He was, in William Brandon's words, "the freedom fantasy made flesh." His way of life was suggested by an old trapper's advice to a greenhorn:

. . . one soon learns to say nothing, and do less, but for himself; and the greenhorn is often reminded, amid showers of maledictions, to confine his philanthropic deeds and conversations to his own dear self. . . . If you see a man's mule running off, don't stop it—let it go to the devil; it isn't yourn. If his possible sack falls off, don't tell him of it; he'll find it out. At camp, help cook—get wood and water—make yourself active—get your pipe, an' smoke it—don't ask too many questions, an' you'll pass!

Jedediah Strong Smith was not a typical mountain man. In the free-wheeling life of the trappers, the shy Smith was paradoxically moralistic, even prudish. Clean shaven, he seldom drank, smoked, or swore, and he was reputed never to have slept with an Indian woman. Perhaps his straight ways made it possible to perform prodigious feats of tramping and trapping. In one season, for example, he began near the Great Salt Lake, trapped southward to the Colorado River, west into the San Joaquin Valley, north as far as the Columbia, and back along the Snake to the Rockies. He had trapped at least

Oregon Historical Society

*Astoria, John Jacob Astor's trading outpost on
the Columbia River, was sold to the British after
only a year in 1812. This painting was executed
in 1845 when Astoria was known as Fort George.*

2,000 miles. On such excursions he, like most trappers, learned the western continent intimately. These experiences guided later surveyors and settlers. Smith is credited with the discovery of the South Pass in Wyoming, the most feasible passage through the central Rockies.

Smith was free, but he was also beset by doubts and uncertainties. "O, the perverseness of my wicked heart," he wrote. "I entangle myself altogether too much in the things of time. . . . I find myself one of the most ungrateful, unthankful creatures imaginable." His letters home reveal this sense of guilt, based on a desire to assist his fellow man. "It is that I may be able to help those who stand in need that I face every danger—it is for this, that I traverse the mountains covered with eternal snow." Why he so persisted in returning to the wilderness, not the most obvious place to engage in humanitarian service, is hard to explain. Still, Smith's frustrations and vague anxieties may make it easier to understand his restlessness, and by implication, some of the restlessness of the frontier American.

William Ashley illustrated a different aspect of the fur trade—its organization. Ashley was a dignified, respected citizen of St Louis, the heart of western commerce, a likely place for a man to seize opportunity. In Washington Irving's words, the city was expanding with the "hectoring, extravagant, bragging boatmen of the Mississippi" and "the gay, grimacing, singing, good-humored Canadian voyageurs."

Amid this amalgam, Ashley commanded the militia and was elected lieutenant governor of Missouri. Ashley was not involved with the earlier Missouri fur trade but in the 1820s he and Andrew Henry organized ventures into the Rockies and set up a post on the Yellowstone. Ashley abandoned the idea of a permanent station, however, and in 1824 conducted the first "rendezvous." At a time and place designated in advance, but changing from year to year, men like Ashley representing the corporate side would meet with free trappers. Each season some high meadow rocked with the boisterous clamor of the rendezvous. The mountain men came—as many as 600 at one gathering—their mules laden with peltry. They were ripe for gambling, drunkenness, brawling, and sex. Indians raised teepees, ready for the fun and the trading. Long company caravans brought guns, knives, blankets, foodstuffs, and news from home. Weeks later the wagons returned east, creaking under their loads of furs. The profits from such a fair could reach $50,000, as they did for Ashley in 1825, or over 1,000 per cent for the companies. The rendezvous over, the fires extinguished, and

The rendezvous brought trapper and trader together, with Indians joining in. Held each year between 1825 and 1840, it was the market-place of the Far West. The most frequented sites were on the Green and Wind rivers, at Pierres Hole, and the Cache Valley in the present states of Idaho, Utah, Wyoming, and Montana. From throughout the West, mountain men and Indians flocked to the meeting place. They traded, drank, and gambled. W. H. Jackson's painting above records a rendezvous on the Green River, Wyoming. Left: A Hudson's Bay trapper, the American's main competitor. Far left: Mountain Man by Albert Bierstadt. Essentially a solitary figure, the mountain man lived a freewheeling life in territory that few whites had seen.

With a pet bear cub tethered to the bow of their canoe, fur traders glide peacefully down the Missouri with a supply of skins. The journey was not always as romantic as portrayed here, but moments of tranquility under a soft sky lent an idyllic touch to the homeward trip. This painting by George Caleb Bingham—one of his finest—was executed in 1845.

the wagons gone, the trappers dispersed to the streams and forests, dreaming of their exploits during the magnificent debauch. William Ashley had indeed created an institution to match the free spirit of these men.

Freedoms and Hazards of the Frontier

In two ways the fur trade carried forward the westward push of America. First, men wove a curtain of myth about freedom and individualism as they poked into every corner of the wilderness. Second, its organized corporate units economically exploited the resources of an underdeveloped land. The trapper's life mixed loneliness and danger. Through snow and icy waters he found his prey and earned his livelihood. He might take an Indian squaw for a companion, bedfellow, and help-mate. But he abandoned her when it suited his purposes. He seemed more attracted to the roaming life than to material rewards. He bartered a year's catch for whatever he could get at the rendezvous, squandered most of it on whiskey for himself and beads for his woman, and then disappeared into the mountains he cherished. As one observer has said: "They were masters of their own lives. When they felt like it, they pulled down their lodges, packed their possessions on their animals and moved to another place which pleased them, and their home was there so long as they wished." Motion, indeed, was in their days.

As for dangers, none was more dreaded than the grizzly bear. This monstrous animal often towering eight feet tall was widespread in the West. It was said to be as prodigious in bad temper as in size. A comrade once described a fearful encounter between Jedediah Smith and such a creature. Smith was working with a small group of men, and while single-file on the trail a grizzly attacked. Smith took the brunt and the two sprawled on the grass together. Smith's ribs were broken and his head badly mauled before the bear could be driven off. One of the trappers took some scissors and cut away hair to reveal a gash across the skull. Smith remained conscious, and directed his friend to get needle and thread and start sewing up the wound. From the edge of his left eye to his right ear the needle secured the skin back in place.

One of his ears was torn from his head out to the outer rim. After stitching all the other wounds in the best way I was capable and according to the captains directions the ear being the last, I told him I could do nothing for his Eare. O you must try to

The Metropolitan Museum of Art, Morris K. Jesup Fund, 1933

Jim Bridger-Mountain Man

Of all the mountain men of the West, Jim Bridger was the best known. The son of an innkeeper, he was born in Richmond, Virginia, on March 17, 1804. At thirteen he was orphaned and soon after took up an apprenticeship to a St Louis blacksmith. Then in 1822 he was told about a newspaper advertisement placed by fur trader William H. Ashley. It sought "one hundred young men to ascend the river Missouri to its source, there to be employed for one, two, or three years." Bridger replied, and so began the forty years he spent in the vast expanses of the West.

That first beaver-trapping expedition took him into the Yellowstone country, up the Yellowstone, Powder, and Sweetwater rivers and over the Continental Divide. And in 1824 he discovered Great Salt Lake. But Bridger was keen to enter the fur trade on his own account; he knew he had the makings of a competent explorer and trapper. Self-reliant and a "loner," he felt at home roaming the plains and mountains and there he wanted to spend his days.

Accordingly in 1830 with four others, he purchased Ashley's Rocky Mountain Fur Company. In the first two years they trapped for themselves, and bought from others, furs worth $80,000. But the cost of goods given in exchange for furs and transportation to and from market cut heavily into revenue and gave each partner only a modest return. Personal friction added to difficulties and after four years the company was wound up.

Bridger saw that the fur trade was declining and that the West was being

Jim Bridger knew the West perhaps better than any man. During his forty-odd years on the plains and in the mountains he was trapper, trader, and guide. He built Fort Bridger (bottom) on the Oregon Trail in 1843.

The Kansas State Historical Society, Topeka

opened up to settlement. In 1843 therefore he built Fort Bridger on Black's Fork of the Green River. Here with a store, a workshop, and a forge he catered for the needs of travelers on the Oregon Trail and, later, the wave of Mormons moving to Great Salt Lake through the pass that Bridger established.

In the 1850s he settled for a time on a farm he had bought near Kansas City. But the pull of the West was strong and soon he returned as a guide in government and private service on exploration and surveying assignments.

Bridger's knowledge of, and acceptance by, the Indians was due in large part to the fact that he took in succession three Indian wives. During his life he explored and traveled the area covered by the present states of Idaho, Wyoming, Montana, Utah, and North and South Dakota. Bridger became blind in the early 1870s and on July 17, 1881, he died on his farm.

In the mid-1860s, an acquaintance left a vivid picture of Bridger. "Straight as an Indian, muscular and quick in movement . . . with an eye piercing as the eye of an eagle that seemed to flash fire when narrating an experience that had called out his reserve power, there was nothing in his costume or deportment to indicate the heroic spirit that dwelled within, simply a plain, unassuming man."

State Historical Society of Wisconsin

stitch up some way or other said he. Then I put my needle stitching it through and through and over and over laying the lacerated parts together as nice as I could with my hands. Water was found in about a mille when we all moved down and encamped the captain being able to mount his horse and ride to camp where we pitched a tent the onley one we had. . . . This gave us a lisson on the character of the grizzly Baare which we did not forget.

Far more, it was a lesson on the character of the mountain man and the life he led.

Decline of the Fur Trade

The fur companies were extensions of the established economy, providing the trapper with a market, supplies, and some contact with civilization. In the heyday of trapping, western firms rose and fell and were reorganized with different combinations of men. But on the whole the fur trade, both men and companies, remained the agent of empire.

By the 1840s, Green River, Pierre's Hole, and the glades once wild with rendezvous were quiet again. Two changes signaled the end of the great day of western trapping—the advent of the silk hat which brought a sudden decline in the demand for beaver skins, and a depletion in the supply of animals. In some regions the beaver had literally been trapped out of existence. In the great San Joaquin Valley of California, for example,

Bears were among the West's many lethal perils.
This mountain man, one S. E. Hollister, fought
off the animal but his arm was badly mauled. Grizzly
bears averaged eight feet in height and 800 pounds.

Courtesy The Bancroft Library, University of California, Berkeley

they were practically eliminated. Whole valleys which once rang with the sounds of slapping beaver tails were now silent. But at least the animal was not exterminated. The new fashion for silk hats helped save it from that sad fate.

The Rockies and the Sierra Nevada, their tallest peaks rearing over 14,000 feet, were lures rather than barriers to the mountain men. But for settlers and merchants the mountains had to be either overcome or avoided. An alternative route by sea around Cape Horn was two or three times as long, and it too involved dangers, like the fog and ice in the Straits of Magellan. In the 1820s and 1830s, the sea lanes were better known than the overland passes. Because the American Revolution had blocked the sailing trade with England, Yankee ships had conceived of the Pacific as a substitute. Ships from Boston rounded the Horn, followed Drake's course up the Pacific shoreline, and eventually reached the northwest coast where the Columbia and Fraser rivers pour into the sea. Here they traded with the Indians, mostly for sea otter skins which they then carried to the Far East. The mandarins of China were fond of otter fur and paid well.

Whaling was another lodestone for the Pacific trade. Hundreds of whalers sailed out of New Bedford, Nantucket, and Boston. They were fitted out for three or four years, and when they returned to Massachusetts their hulls trailed yards of weed and their holds bulged with oil. By 1806 they were bringing back half a million gallons of whale oil a year.

By the late 1820s the supply of sea otter on the northwest coast was playing out, and Yankee merchants began to look farther south for business. A few New Englanders like Abel Stearns, Alfred Robinson, and Thomas O. Larkin already lived in California in the 1830s. When Richard Henry Dana arrived in 1835, taking notes for his novel *Two Years Before the Mast*, California already had an established Spanish culture.

The basic economy revolved around cattle, and hence the most sizable exports became hides and tallow. So the Yankee merchant ships, which once carried packs of sea otter pelts to China, now sailed to California with all manner of manufactured goods—needles and thread, cloth, pans, cutlery, shoes, and food. They returned with great packs of leather and casks of tallow to shoe the feet and light the tables of New England.

The Americans, however, were not the only invaders of California, and certainly not the only foreigners to think of plucking its delights. The Russians pushed their fur interests along the chilly Aleutian chain and down the coast, competing for sea otter. In 1812 just north of San Francisco Bay they built Fort Ross with its Orthodox steeple and brass cannon. The English, in the form of the Hudson's Bay men, had trapped as far south as the waters of the Sacramento River, and frigates of the Royal Navy were not unknown in Monterey Bay.

The Movement West

The story of infiltration into California was not appreciably different when viewed by land rather than by sea. California was the last step toward the Pacific for each brand of frontiersman. Just as the fur trade had earlier penetrated the Rocky Mountains, so it would represent the earliest overland push into California. If the American presence was ultimately to lead to political imperialism, then the trappers were unwitting pawns in the expansionist game. Jedediah Smith, for example, came to California in 1826 to trap beaver. He ran into trouble with local officials, then moved into the San Joaquin Valley. When leaving the province the following year, he made the first crossing of the Sierra Nevada by a white man.

Farther south in 1828, a father-son team of trappers, Sylvester and James Ohio Pattie, were brought into San Diego to be jailed. When the mother had died in Missouri, Sylvester Pattie and his oldest son abandoned the eight other children and took off for the fur trade in Santa Fe. They were good trappers; along the Gila River they killed 250 beaver in a two-week period. James Pattie was as egotistic as he was enterprising. He quarreled with Indians, unlike those mountain men who took so naturally to Indian life. After a skirmish with Mojaves on the way to California, he committed unmentionable atrocities on the dead. But once in California the Patties' arrogance alienated the Mexicans, and since they had no permission to trap there they ended up in jail. In these difficult surroundings Sylvester died. James effected his own release solely because he was able to inoculate victims

Beaver skins were widely used in hat manufacture until the 1840s when silk became popular. This 1820s watercolor shows a New York City warehouse displaying "fashionable beaver hats."

of smallpox, then raging in the region.

Another trapper by the name of Isaac Graham was a boasting Tennessean. When he came to California he abandoned the fur trade in favor of a "still house" for making whiskey. His adobe east of Monterey became a rendezvous for a motley, drifting crew of trappers and sailors. Thirty of them fought with Graham in a local revolution in 1836. It is not known whether they had a principle in mind. They may have simply enjoyed, like so many frontiersmen, the leveling of rifles on moving targets. Yet it may not have been coincidental that they supported the cause of greater independence for California from Mexico City.

Without realizing it, all of these men were paving the way for others. In 1841, American settlers began to trickle over Smith's trail through the Sierra Nevada. By 1845, 500 settlers came that way and this was not the only route identified by trappers. Joseph Reddeford Walker found a good course through the southern spur of the Sierra Nevada into the San Joaquin Valley. The Patties had pointed out the Santa Fe-Gila River-Mojave Desert passage towards San Diego and Los Angeles. So the lines were drawn for the great migrations of the 1840s on which would rest the imperialist thrust.

Frémont and the Expansionist Dream

No one combined the fur trade, the California dream, and the overland routes as dramatically as John Charles Frémont. He took what the mountain men knew and the explorers had recorded and went into the field himself. He then drew up the maps and reports which would illuminate the last stage of the westward march to the Pacific. He found few paths, but he marked a multitude. Jedediah Smith had discovered the South Pass, but John Frémont reduced it to accurate longitude and latitude.

Frémont was a thin, slight, headstrong, ambitious man. In his youth he had used parental acquaintances to secure positions, first, in the navy where he managed to sharpen his mathematical skills and, second, in the army's Topographical Corps. The latter agency, charged with the mapping and exploration of the new western lands, was a good place for an energetic young engineer. His work with the Topographical Corps followed systematically the more isolated efforts of Pike and Long. It allowed Frémont to throw his destiny with the westward movement.

While still in his twenties, he courted and eloped with Jessie Benton, "a rose of rare color," he wrote. She was the "effervescent" daughter of Senator Thomas Hart Benton of Missouri, the most influential legislator in Washington. The senator was not impressed with his daughter's choice. He was reconciled only when the two confronted him after the marriage. In a defiant

Above: Sylvester Pattie is wounded by Indians. Sylvester and his son James were fur trappers whose activities took them into Mexican California in the 1820s. Highly successful trappers, the Patties stirred up more trouble than most and, unlike the great majority of mountain men, ran foul of Indians. Left: Joseph Reddeford Walker opened up an overland route through the southern Sierra Nevada into California in 1834. The mountain men pointed the way for American infiltration into the region.

gesture to her father, Jessie held her husband's arm while quoting Ruth of the Old Testament: "Wither thou goest, I will go; and where thou lodgest, I will lodge; thy people shall be my people, and thy God my God!" Senator Benton's acceptance of the marriage cemented an alliance charged with the expansionist forces of the 1840s. From then on whatever Frémont did was tied to key councils in Washington.

Frémont's first venture to the West in 1838 was the traditional one, sharpening his skills on the mapping of the upper Mississippi Valley. In the summer of 1842 he led his first survey of the Rocky Mountains. His father-in-law had a special desire to have Frémont map Jedediah Smith's route through the South Pass, in order to make an easier passage for Oregon immigrants. Kit Carson, mythical mountain man, guided the party. They traveled up the Missouri and Platte rivers to the South Pass, then into the Wind River Mountains where Frémont raised a flag on the peak which now bears his name. With typical bravado, though mistakenly, he thought it the highest peak in the entire Rockies.

His next expedition lasted over a year, from 1843 to 1844, and took Frémont over the Oregon Trail to the Pacific. From the mouth of the Columbia, he turned southward into California and completed the tour via northern Nevada and the Great Salt Lake. On his return he closeted himself with his wife, Jessie, and the two of them produced a striking report. It was a vivid, detailed account of the beauties and values of the Far West veneered with enough science to lend credibility. Published in a large edition, it was widely distributed. The narrative dispelled the notion of the Great American Desert, claiming the fertility of the plains for agriculture and laying to rest Stephen Long's warnings. But, more important, it stimulated in its young readers the desire to go west, to see the glories of the Rockies, to sense the pulse of the Columbia, and to revel in the flowery fields

of California. The colored lithographs illustrated Indian teepees by Fort Laramie, the white glacial slopes of Pike's Peak, and the teeth of the Wind River peaks above spruce trees. When the young engineer, now "the beau ideal of all that was chivalrous and noble," announced a third expedition, he was deluged with applications.

The party gathered at Westport, near St Louis, in the spring of 1845. The sixty members had been carefully selected—scientists, artists, guides, and hunters (former mountain men). They regularly held exercises in marksmanship, which led skeptics to wonder if the expedition had more than scientific mapping in mind.

The skeptics were right. This expedition did document the best routes for future migrations westward, but it was also a military scheme to get a fighting force into California, ready to act should war break out with Mexico. The groundwork for Frémont's role in the conquest of California was thus laid.

The expedition of 1845 was a microcosm of the westward march to the Pacific, a logical culmination of drives set in motion long before Lewis and Clark. It was a sincere effort to draft the precise paths of the continental crossing, to explore the routes and the mountains, the forests, the rivers, and the minerals of a land expected to be, but not quite yet, American. It was led by a young Galahad, the object of whose gallantry, too, was America, romanticizing its destiny. But Galahad was also a soldier, representing those imperialistic forces which would fight for expansion. Frémont and his men mirrored the kind of arrogance, confidence, vanity, and aggressiveness that cast shadows over the lives of explorer, trapper, and dreamer on the westward march to the Pacific.

Frémont's party at Lake Pyramid, Nevada, during the 1843–44 expedition. Frémont insisted on taking the howitzer because, he said, it would be needed to frighten off hostile Indians.

Although he found few routes himself, John Charles Frémont earned the name "the Pathfinder" for his expeditions in the Far West. He became a living symbol of the spirit of Manifest Destiny and awakened the westering instinct in many Americans. Inset: Jessie Frémont, who encouraged her husband's adventures. Her father, Thomas Hart Benton, was a leading exponent of western settlement.

Chapter 2

THE SPANISH PRESENCE

Life in the regions known today as California, Arizona, New Mexico, and Texas was markedly Spanish in character in the first half of the nineteenth century. Colonized by Spain a hundred years earlier, these settlements had been founded on the imported institutions of the mission, the presidio, and the pueblo. After the 1821 Mexican war of independence they came under new rulers who secularized the missions and took over their land. In Texas, however, the constant stream of immigrants from the north helped identify the area as an extension of the American South rather than a Mexican province. And in the 1830s the irksome rule of Mexico City was finally scorned as the Texans fought for independence.

Life Across the Border

In 1821 revolutionaries in Mexico City forced the viceroy to surrender, and the Spanish flag ceased to fly above the capital of what soon would style itself the Republic of Mexico. Word of this momentous event slowly filtered north to the provinces of Texas, New Mexico, and California. In most of this region, which one day would form the American Southwest, the eleven-year struggle for Mexican independence had meant little. Soldiers and civilians alike had waited to hear the outcome, but with little sense of excitement or drama. Their existence was tied more closely to the daily quest for food, companionship, enjoyment, and security.

In California the population of 3,720 "Europeans"— and a single drop of Spanish blood qualified one for this designation—and some 30,000 mission Indians were remote from the conflict. They were isolated by the tyranny—and blessing—of distance. Since the founding of the colony in 1769, California had been connected to Mexico only by a difficult sea route, for the Indians along the Colorado River had prevented the permanent opening of an overland road. The war in Mexico therefore meant only that additional months would pass between the arrival of ships bringing soldiers' salaries, new government officials, and legally approved import items.

California in 1821 was marginally Spanish in territory. Spaniards held only a thin fringe of land stretching south from San Francisco to San Diego and west from the Coastal Sierra to the Pacific. The interior, as always, was the domain of nomadic Indians whose level of civilization was so low that only occasionally did they attack the newcomers. This Spanish settlement, as in Arizona, New Mexico, and Texas, rested on the three colonial institutions which had developed in the New World: the mission, the presidio, and the pueblo.

Spaniards considered the mission of prime importance in colonizing the northern frontier, for it served both God and king. Missionaries of one order were awarded the right to work in a specified region. In California this right was given the Franciscans. For each mission the Crown gave a block of land, just as it paid the salaries of the

Three centuries of Spanish rule in Mexico come to an end. This painting depicts the entry of independence forces into Mexico City in September 1821. The governor was deposed without a shot being fired.

missionaries (for church and state were one). These soldiers of God then would go among the local Indians to preach their gospel message. Converts were gathered onto the mission lands. There they were put to work building a chapel, shops, and living quarters for themselves and their spiritual advisers, as well as tending flocks of animals and tilling the fields. As quickly as possible these missions were supposed to become self-supporting, for, according to theory, the natives would be civilized. This naturally involved converting them to Christianity and Spanish ways. The mission then would be secularized: the land would be divided among the Indians, as would the sheep and cattle. The mission chapel would become a parish church, and the individual residences grouped as in a typical Spanish village.

Through the mission system the natives therefore were to be converted from barbarism into tax-paying citizens of the Spanish empire with all the rights and obligations of other citizens. In California in 1821 there were twenty of these missions (another would be founded at Sonoma during the early Mexican years). And, in part, these were

Above: The mission of San Carlos Borromeo dates from 1770. Established in Monterey, it was moved to its present site at Carmel in 1771. After San Diego de Alcala, it is the oldest mission founded by the Spanish in California.

highly successful. They grew huge amounts of grain, they owned numerous cattle and sheep, and they served as the religious, educational, and cultural centers of the province. However, the missions ultimately failed in that they did not bring the natives to the level of Spanish civilization before secularization was ordered by the Mexican government.

When missionaries went into the wilderness to recruit converts, soldiers accompanied them to afford protection. Then, when the mission became operative, the soldiers would erect their presidio nearby. Usually located near good farming land and built on high ground, presidios were built of adobe in the form of a square or rectangle. The walls were at least ten feet high, with round bastions at two opposite corners to allow the soldiers stationed

Missionaries sent to Spanish possessions in North America were charged with transmitting Christianity and Spanish culture. In Upper California, Franciscan Father Junípero Serra founded the first mission in the region in 1769; by 1823 twenty-one had been established. San Luis Rey de Francia (above), near Oceanside, dates from 1798. The Spanish moved into Texas from New Mexico and strengthened their hold by missionary activity from 1690. The remains of San Francisco de la Espada at San Antonio are shown at left. Below: Cemetery at Taos Pueblo.

there to fire down the length of all four walls at any attackers. Inside these walls, buildings were constructed, the roofs of which were high enough to serve as parapets from which the men could fire. Among these buildings were storage facilities, a chapel, and rooms for the fifty officers and enlisted men. Four such presidios were established in California: at Monterey, Yerba Buena (later renamed San Francisco), Santa Barbara, and San Diego.

Outside these presidios, which were fortresses in name more than in reality, the families of the soldiers built their *jacales* (huts). Merchants came to sell them goods, and farmers and ranchers settled nearby for protection. The result was the growth of the pueblo. These four military towns were not planned cities, but two others were established in the ancient Spanish tradition: San Jose and Los Angeles. The colonists who agreed to move to these locations were granted, in each case, four square leagues of land (about 17,600 acres) on which to establish fields, build homes, and graze livestock. Finally, civilian towns grew near several missions in much the same way they did near the presidios: at San Juan Capistrano, San Luis Obispo, and San Juan Bautista.

Life was good for these Spanish and Mexican Californians, although the province never boasted any manufacturing. Food was easily had, for the mission fields produced wheat in abundance and cattle increased without check—and almost without work—in a region without natural predators to thin their numbers. Indeed, it was cattle, or rather part of them, that paid for imports from the outside world to make life even more enjoyable.

Spanish law forbade trade with any foreign nation. The intent was to increase trade with the mother country and to bring additional tax monies to the royal treasury. However, California was isolated, and Spanish ships arrived so irregularly that the *Californios* quickly developed smuggling to a high art. Government officials winked at this illegal trade so long as they were paid what the citizens laughingly referred to as the *mordido* (the bite). By the 1790s British and American ships were to be seen along the coast of the province. There they exchanged manufactured goods for the hides and tallow of cattle. For export purposes, cattle were killed solely for their hides, which could be turned into leather, and for the tallow, used to make candles, which was boiled from their carcasses in huge vats. The rest of the animal was thrown away to rot, in an age before refrigeration made possible the lengthy transport of meat.

This trade brought cloth, manufactured metal items, coffee, tobacco, sugar, spices, rum, even the fireworks used for celebrations. Spaniards and their Mexican heirs lived high during this era. Their Indian *vaqueros* (cowhands) performed the labor, leaving the wealthy time for lassoing bears, courting dark-eyed *señoritas*, dressing in elaborate, silver-encrusted costumes, and drinking *vino del pais* (local wine). Almost anyone with Spanish blood

A Texas ranchero, painted by a military draftsman employed by the Mexican government about 1828. The Mexican settlements bordering the United States depended for their livelihood on farming.

could secure large grants of land on which to run cattle, 40,000-acre holdings—and more—being granted. The province was so large and the number of residents so small that few *rancheros* bothered to survey their property. Yet many Californians were not satisfied. They wanted more land, specifically the mission lands. In 1834 they secured their wish.

Secularization of the missions was pushed by covetous Mexicans anxious to acquire title to the good acres on which the missions stood. They justified their desire by claiming they wanted only to separate church and state, a stand that became popular in Mexico in 1832 when a revolution swept a reform government into power. Lobbying in Mexico City by these Californians resulted in a congressional decree in 1834 ordering secularization. Governor José Figueroa opposed this, saying that the Indians were not yet sufficiently educated for citizenship. But he had to obey the decrees of the central government. On August 9, 1834, he issued a proclamation ordering ten of the missions to be secularized, half the property to go to the Indians and the other half to be administered by secular officials. In 1835–36 another ten missions were secularized (leaving only Santa Barbara in Franciscan hands thereafter).

The result was disastrous for the Indian converts. Former mission property rapidly found its way into the hands of the Californians. Most of the cattle were butchered in an orgy of Indian feasting, followed by starvation. And the natives, who had not yet learned the ways of civilization well enough to compete, were forced to take employment as ranch hands or to join wild tribes in the interior—or else live on the fringes of settlement in a state of degradation. Their numbers dwindled rapidly from 30,000 to 10,000—and by 1846 they were approaching extinction.

Southwestern Settlement

The Spanish settlement nearest to California was in the area now known as Arizona, where Jesuit missionaries had arrived in the late seventeenth century. In 1752 the first presidio was constructed at Tubac, but in 1776 it was moved north to Tucson and there a small pueblo grew. Yet Spanish Arizona was not a separate province; rather it was part of Sonora, and its population never numbered more than 600. After Mexican independence this northern part of Sonora failed to increase in population because of continued raids by Apaches. The few settlers around Tucson huddled near the shadow of the presidio, trying to farm a few acres, raise cattle, prospect in the hills during periods of peace, and see their children grow. Life for them was hard and bleak, for the Apaches and their cousins to the north, the Navajos, were the real masters of Arizona.

New Mexico proved a far more successful Spanish colony. In 1821 it had some 30,000 citizens, 6,000 of them in the capital city of Santa Fe. Life in New Mexico in the nineteenth century was largely dictated by the experiences of the previous hundred years. The province then had been divided into two districts which took their names from the Rio Grande: *Rio Arriba* (upriver) and *Rio Abajo* (downriver). The dividing line was La Bajada Hill between Santa Fe and Albuquerque. The upriver area was mountainous, demanding hardy—if poor—people. Most families lived on communal lands, each having a small parcel on which to raise its corn, chili, beans, pigs, chickens, and goats. These people generally were a mixture of Spanish and Indian, called *mestizos*. Yet they were subject to raids by Apaches and Navajos who came to steal their livestock and enslave their women and children.

Street scene in Santa Fe about 1800. The town was chosen as the capital of the Spanish province of New Mexico in the first decade of the seventeenth century.

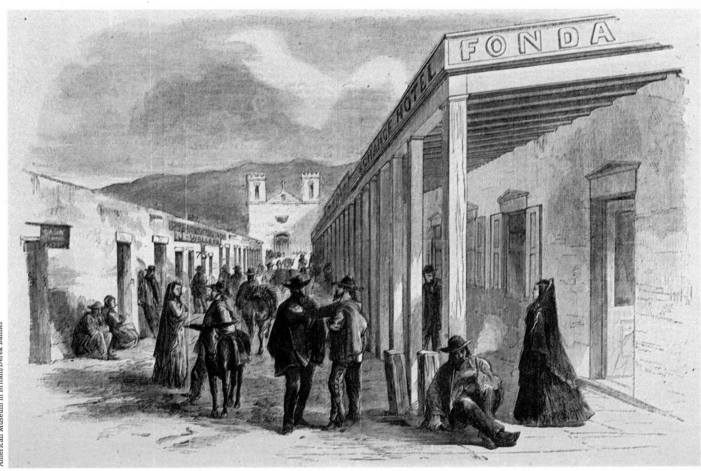

American Museum in Britain/Derek Balmer

The downriver district was the area of the *hacendados*, large landowners who built their homes like fortresses and thus were relatively free of Indian raids. Dozens, even hundreds, of employees might work on a single hacienda, the owner living like a medieval nobleman— and with many of the same privileges. These wealthy citizens, claiming to be of pure Spanish blood even when they were not, believed in the good life. They imported their furniture from Spain, along with their wine and their clothing. In return they exported the produce of their estates, generally wool and leather hides. Their manners were elaborate and their social code rigid.

If New Mexico had had a symbol during these years it should have been the sheep, for it was this animal that made possible any prosperity. Cattle never thrived there because of Indian raids, but the lowly sheep increased in such numbers as to supply the needs of both Spaniard and the Navajo intruders. Mutton became a basic food and woolen garments the most common apparel. Christian

Right: A hacienda-owner's elaborate residence. The great size of the haciendas was matched by the power of their owners. Below: The pack mule, the New Mexicans' favored method of transporting goods and produce.

Courtesy Southwest Museum, Los Angeles, California (detail)

Thomas Gilcrease Institute, Tulsa, Oklahoma

Indians were taught to be herders, and they learned to weave fine blankets. Some of the haciendas had more than a million head, while one governor claimed to own more than 2 million. Each spring about 2,000 sheep would be sent out to graze under the care of two herders. The sheep was ideally suited to the semi-arid country. These animals could go long distances without water.

The other source of income for New Mexico, especially in the Mexican period, was copper mined at Santa Rita del Cobre. Work began there in 1804, and from the crude smelter came a steady stream of the reddish-orange metal. This was used locally as well as exported south.

The Mexican war for independence had little effect in New Mexico except for the inconvenience it caused. No longer were the goods craved by the rich brought north by caravans of carts, for the revolution disrupted trade with Europe. For eleven long years the rich ones saved their money and waited. Then, with the coming of independence, the old Spanish restrictions on trade with foreigners fell along with the Spanish flag—and Americans quickly arrived to sell the items which New Mexicans wanted. In 1821 William Becknell arrived in Santa Fe with a pack train of trade goods and easily disposed of them at a profit of 600 per cent. The following year he returned, this time with three wagons driven

from Missouri. In the process of bringing this merchandise down what came to be known as "the Turquoise Trail," he opened the famous Santa Fe Trail. By 1824 Becknell had many competitors and the trade was flourishing. In return for the goods they desired—clothing, cotton cloth, lace, jewelry, furniture, china, musical instruments, tobacco, and spices—the New Mexicans exchanged gold, silver, horses, woolen goods, furs, cowhides, and mules.

Yet these traders who swarmed from Missouri to New Mexico every spring had to pay a price for doing business in the province. Government officials in New Mexico wanted a share of the profits which they exacted in the form of taxes and fees. And the form of government made acceptance of bribes a way of life for its bureaucrats.

Under the Mexican constitution of 1824 New Mexico was a territory until 1836, after which it was declared a department. The governor, more often than not, tried to use his office for personal gain. He and his underlings imposed the customs laws in an arbitrary and capricious

Mexican independence brought an end to restrictions on foreign trade. Below: American traders express their delight on arrival at Santa Fe. In 1843, twenty-one years after the trade had begun, 350 Americans took goods worth $430,000 to the city.

manner. The amount of taxes to be paid annually on each wagon depended more on the balance in the governor's personal account than in the provincial treasury. Those Americans who protested too violently found themselves in prison and their goods confiscated. They paid—and passed the cost along to those who bought from them.

Also coming down the Santa Fe Trail to New Mexico were bearded mountain men, fur trappers in quest of beaver pelts. A whim of fashion had made the beaver hat popular, and grizzled Americans fought icy streams, wild animals, and angry Indians to make eastern and European gentlemen happy. They came southwest from St Louis, the center of the fur trade, because the northern Rockies had been trapped almost clean. Arriving in New Mexico, they made their headquarters at Taos. There they married Mexican girls and adopted many of the manners and customs of the region, including the religion. Theirs was a quest for beaver, not an evangelical zeal to convert the local populace to the "American way of life." Many of them became Mexican citizens, even to the point of protesting to New Mexican officials about "Americans" who were trapping beaver. James Baird, formerly of Missouri, in 1826 asked the governor to exclude "foreigners" so that "we Mexicans may peacefully profit by the goods with which the merciful God has been pleased to enrich our soil." Most notable among these new citizens was Kit Carson, later to gain fame as a trapper, Indian fighter, guide, and soldier.

In their quest for beaver, these mountain men trapped northward along the headwaters of the Rio Grande into southern Colorado. Others went west along the banks of the Gila, the Salt, the Verde, the Santa Cruz, and the San Pedro. Some even pushed along the banks of the Colorado River northward into the Grand Canyon region. So strong was their desire to find beaver that these mountain men fought the Apaches, the Yumas, the Navajos, and the Mojaves, along with an inhospitable nature. They even reached far-off California by going overland from the Colorado River across the burning desert of the Imperial Valley to the coastal settlements.

The Enduring Spanish Influence

Despite this American intrusion, the regions once owned by Spain—with the exception of Texas—retained Spanish culture, food, architecture, music, and Indian policy. The social, economic, religious, and intellectual life of these remote provinces continued in the old ways. All the usual services were to be found in each of the settlements. A census taken in San Antonio, Texas, in 1795 listed such diverse work groups as servants, tailors, merchants, shoemakers, cart drivers, carpenters, burro drivers, fishermen, blacksmiths, a barber, a sewer cleaner, and a

host of government officials. Yet everywhere the chief occupations were farming and ranching. Cattle and sheep became the chief forms of wealth, as well as the major items of export.

Water was not of overriding importance to these Spanish ranchers, for the longhorn was a sturdy beast capable of walking sixty miles between drinks. For the farmer, however, water—or the shortage of it—was of major significance. Only along the California coast did rain fall in sufficient quantity to make farming a certainty. Elsewhere in the region the would-be farmer had to dig irrigation ditches. Every Spanish settlement, no matter how insignificant, was located alongside some stream or another: the San Antonio River in Texas, the Rio Grande in New Mexico, the Santa Cruz in Arizona. Usually the missionaries were first to dig ditches to bring water from the river to their fields. Later the civilians, using Indian labor where possible, extended these ditches or constructed new ones. Plows were then hitched to animals, fields were broken, and the precious seed was planted.

Corn was the agricultural staple everywhere in this region. A native American plant, it had become a major part of the Hispanic diet, so much so that its price was regulated by the government. When it had matured, the plant was allowed to dry in the fields, then was harvested to be shucked, shelled, and stored. The frontier housewife each morning had to grind enough corn for the day's meals. If she lived in a small settlement she did this by hand on a small mill known as a *metate*. If she lived in a large settlement, she took her corn to a water-driven mill where the owner made his living by keeping a small portion of all the meal he ground. Her corn ground, the housewife patted out tortillas (flat cakes of meal) which she fried. Wrapped around beef, chicken, or beans, these tortillas served as bread for sandwiches. If nothing else was available they were eaten alone.

These farmers also raised beans, chili, and a little sugar cane at each settlement. Other crops might include gourds, pumpkins, and melons, whatever the climate and soil allowed. The only means of preserving these vegetables and fruits from the orchards was by drying. Every autumn the harvest was spread on the ground for the sun to dry it for storage. When the crops were bountiful and the Indian raids not too severe, everyone ate well. Some years, however, drought limited the crops or else Indian raids came just at harvest season and the crops were not gathered. At such times the governors of the various provinces wrote piteous letters to their superiors in Mexico City asking that food be shipped north. Until this arrived, and some years it never came, the local residents —soldiers, civilians, missionaries, and Christian Indians alike—were reduced to eating mesquite beans, wild game, and assorted native plants.

The home life and living conditions of these pioneers varied little from province to province. Civilians huddled their homes as closely as possible to a presidio, or else in a village. Soldiers, most of whom were married, built their family quarters in the same area as the civilians. Generally these dwellings were of adobe with brush-and-mud ceilings laid over wooden poles. The floors were dirt, the walls unplastered. Only wealthy civilians and army officers could afford to import tile and wrought iron from the interior of Mexico to make their roofs, floors, and window casements more attractive.

There in a home that was little more than a hut, the soldier or civilian passed his days with his family. They slept on the floor rolled in blankets, as beds generally were not available. A small fireplace built into one corner served as cookstove and source of heat. Chairs and tables also were in short supply, so meals were served on the floor or on the ground outside the hut. Perhaps a trunk or chest held the family's few possessions, which seldom included more than a few pieces of clothing, cooking

utensils, and religious objects. Candles, when available, provided a source of light during the evening hours. But generally all retired shortly after sunset.

When supplies were brought up from the south, and when the individual had enough money to afford them, some luxuries could be obtained. The rich rancher or merchant ordered furniture, good clothes, and quality wine to make life more enjoyable. But for the ordinary citizen the height of luxury was chocolate. This was served hot in the morning and afternoon to supplement a diet largely composed of beans, ground corn, beef or mutton, and sometimes fruit. Another luxury was brown sugar. Where possible, this was made locally from sugar

Corn, the staple crop in Mexican lands, was the basic ingredient in tortillas. This 1840s painting shows a housewife in San Antonio, Texas, preparing a fresh batch.

cane or else brought up from the south.

These people found little relief from the hard work of their lives, even in moments of relaxation. Mescal, brewed locally from the juice of the agave plant or imported from the south, provided a liquor that drowned many insults and sorrows. In most villages there was a *fandango* every Saturday in the town plaza. These featured music and mescal, flirtations and fighting, dancing and romance. Other amusements included cock fights, horse races, and the observance of the local patron saint's day and various religious holidays. Another amusement was a gruesome sport known as *gallo*. This involved burying a chicken in the sand with only its head showing. The men in turn rode by on horseback at full gallop, leaned down, and tried to pull the chicken's head off. Finally, gambling was widespread, even a mania among the population. People who had so little, loved a chance to win some wealth. So they staked their savings on a favorite horse, a promising rooster at a cock fight, or anything where Lady Luck might favor a man.

Life for these Spanish pioneers was not all work or fighting Indians or even seeking amusement. It also involved raising families. Women were in short supply on the northern frontier, so the young man looking for a bride did not always find one of his own race. Instead,

Collection of the Oakland Museum

Courtesy of the E. B. Crocker Art Gallery, Sacramento, California (detail)

Life on the ranch was often slow-paced and the work tedious. But the high-spirited Californios and Mexicans had plenty of opportunity to give vent to their natural exuberance. Above: Two vaqueros race their horses to the line, cheered on by spectators. Left: A couple do the fandango, a traditional Spanish dance, while a vaquero and his girl set off for a ride on a palomino. Right: Parades and ceremonies were colorful occasions. Carved images such as this one were carried in Mexican religious processions.

37

*A Mexican market stall, painted about 1700, with an
array of tempting foods. Many aspects of Mexican
life had an exotic touch unique in North America.*

he often was forced to marry an Indian girl from the local mission. This happened with such frequency that children of pure Spanish blood became rare. By 1846 more than seven-eighths of the inhabitants of the Mexican provinces were classified as *mestizos*.

Colonizing Texas

Only in Texas was this ratio different, for there a large-scale immigration of Anglo-Americans had taken place. These sons of Virginia and Tennessee, of the Carolinas and Alabama, were descended from hardy pioneers who had steadily pushed west from the Atlantic Seaboard in search of new land to farm. Like their forefathers, they wanted a plot of ground on which to cut trees and build a log cabin, split logs and erect rail fences, clear fields and plant a crop, kill game to secure meat, and distill a little corn to make sipping whiskey.

As these independent men moved west to gain freedom from unwanted neighbors, freedom from a host of man-made laws, freedom from a plague of government officials and restrictions, they arrived at last at the edge of the Great Plains. To the west they saw a land that lacked trees, a land where the rainfall was below twenty inches a year and even drinking water was difficult to secure, a land where the crops they had raised so long, principally cotton and corn, would not grow. The Great Plains was a region where all the pioneering techniques that they and their ancestors had been perfecting for 200 years would not work. So these frontiersmen turned their eyes toward Texas.

And they liked what they saw. On the far side of the Sabine River were the same towering pines so familiar across Louisiana, Mississippi, Alabama, Georgia, and much of the Atlantic region. In East Texas the annual rainfall totaled forty inches or more. Even the soil was similar to that in the East. Moreover, it was a land thinly populated. Several thousand Indians and approximately 3,500 Spaniards called Texas home in 1820. Neither nationality disturbed the American frontiersman. He had long since decided that the Indian should either be driven westward or else exterminated. And the Spaniard he saw as contemptible, a member of a weak, barbarous race of timorous cowards unable to conquer and populate an extremely promising land. Henry Clay, thrice to be nominated for the presidency, declared in Congress that Texas in the hands of Spaniards was the "habitation of despotism and slaves, subject to the vile domination of the Inquisition and superstition." But, he said, if the United States acquired the province it would be peopled by "freemen, and the sons of freemen, carrying with them our language, our laws, and our liberties." Clay and like-minded Americans claimed the ordinary Spanish

citizen of Texas would welcome liberation from his tyrannical king and church.

No large-scale immigration into Spanish Texas occurred prior to 1820, however. Then on December 23, 1820, there strode down the dusty streets of the capital city of San Antonio a Connecticut-born Yankee named Moses Austin. Presenting himself to Governor Antonio María Martínez, Austin made a revolutionary proposal. He asked to be allowed to colonize 300 American families in Texas through a contract with the Spanish government. He would profit from the scheme by charging each family a small fee; they in turn would gain the land they coveted —but legally, by becoming citizens of the Spanish empire. Governor Martínez quickly dismissed the proposal.

Austin continued to plead his case, however. He was, he said, a former Spanish citizen through residence in Missouri when that had belonged to Spain. And he promised that the Americans he brought would be loyal to their country of adoption. Eventually Martínez relented, approving the request on January 17, 1821. Subsequently this royal contract for colonization was approved by Martínez's superiors to the south.

Before Austin could begin to fulfill the terms of this contract, however, he died of pneumonia, leaving the work to his son and heir, Stephen F. Austin. This twenty-seven-year-old chose to give up a journalistic career in New Orleans in order to pursue his father's dream. He even traveled to Mexico City to get the contract renewed and approved by the Mexican government after it achieved independence from Spain. Subsequently he helped write a colonization clause in the Mexican constitution of 1824, one that practically invited Americans to emigrate to Texas. And he was instrumental in the writing of the colonization law of the state of Coahuila-Texas (the two were joined as one state by the 1824

Moses Austin (left) drew up plans for organized American colonization of Texas. After his death his son Stephen (right) executed the scheme which settled thousands of Americans in Texas.

constitution). This provided that any rancher who emigrated to Texas would receive a square league of land (4,428 acres), while a farmer would get a *labor* (177). In return the immigrant had to become a Mexican citizen and a member of the Catholic church, and he had to pay fees amounting to $44 (one-fourth down and one-fourth a year for three years). Most American immigrants promptly declared themsleves to be both farmers *and* ranchers, thereby receiving more than 4,600 acres of land.

Austin not only filled his quota of 300 families under his first contract, but also took additional ones. Where he pioneered, others were quick to follow. Soon there were a number of *empresarios* (contract colonizers), even one from Ireland who established a town called San Patricio. By 1830 the population of Texas was approaching 30,000, 90 per cent of whom were American by birth. These new Texans were busy building farms, establishing schools, even defying the law by erecting Protestant churches, and in every way displaying the same restless ambition that had driven them westward. Meanwhile the Mexican population, centered chiefly around San Antonio, continued the leisurely way of life that had characterized their activities in the area for more than a century. A cultural conflict was brewing.

The Rift With Mexico

The first eruption came in East Texas where Hayden Edwards, an American *empresario*, had been authorized to settle colonists near Nacogdoches. Already in that area were Hispanic settlers, some of whom had been there for half a century or more, but who did not have a secure title to their acres. Edwards threatened to expel them if they did not pay him, which caused hatred to grow between the races. The issue came to a head in the election of an *alcalde* (an official combining the functions of mayor, sheriff, and justice of the peace) for Nacogdoches in 1826. The anti-Edwards candidate was elected and began validating all contested land titles. Edwards's brother complained to the governor who took offense at the tone of the letter and, on October 2, 1826, canceled the contract. The standard of revolt was raised. Edwards declared a Republic of Fredonia and called on all "Americans" to join his cause. However, most of the new Texans had nothing to do with this rebellion; even the Indians refused to join, and Austin sent his militia to help end the revolt. In January 1827 the insurgents fled across the border into Louisiana, ending the short-lived Fredonian Rebellion.

Yet the damage had been done, for it created alarm and doubts in the minds of many Mexicans about the loyalty of the colonists from the United States. Officials in Mexico City therefore sent General Manuel Mier y Terán to tour the province and to make recommendations. Arriving in the region in February 1828, Terán visited all parts of Texas and was alarmed. In his letters to the president and in his final report, he stressed that the Americans had a close knowledge of the constitution, more so than most Mexicans. And he was afraid of the newcomers, warning that "Texas could throw the whole nation into revolution." He recommended reform—and quickly: "Either the government occupies Texas *now*, or it is lost forever." In his opinion the solution was to send industrious, progressive Mexicans north to settle in Texas to counter the influence of the Americans.

The new Texan colonists were naturally concerned about Terán's report and the consequences it might have. Then in 1829, just as the report was being delivered, came even more upsetting news from Mexico City: the government had abolished slavery. Not many colonists in Texas owned slaves, for few could afford them. But there were some plantation owners with large numbers of slaves, men such as Jared Groce who owned an estimated ninety. Some estimates of the number of slaves brought into Texas were as high as one-third of the total population. They had been brought in despite a clause in the constitution of the state of Coahuila–Texas prohibiting their introduction (and declaring that children born of slave parents were free). Colonists had skirted this law by means of a decree in 1828 permitting lifetime work contracts.

In 1829 the newly installed Mexican president, Vicente Guerrero, decreed the abolition of all slavery in Mexico. The decree was never promulgated in Texas, however, and the province was considered exempt from it. Yet it angered Texans, even those who did not own slaves. Most colonists came from the southern United States and believed in the right of slavery. Moreover, they considered abolition to be an unconstitutional means of depriving a person of his property. They watched uneasily to see what the government would do, for they saw this issue as a means of slowing further American emigration to Texas—something they did not want. In 1830 the government forbade the further introduction of slaves, and in 1832 labor contracts were limited to ten years' duration. Yet Mexican officials never made a genuine attempt to interfere with slavery in Texas, and this was not an issue in the difficulties of the ensuing years.

Instead, the rift between Texans and Mexicans was widened because of the final result of Terán's report. In the spring of 1830, following yet another revolution in Mexico City that saw the Centralist faction installed, the Congress passed what became known as the Law of April 6, 1830. This act stipulated that more soldiers be sent to Texas, that the customs laws be enforced to discourage trade with the United States, and that trade between Mexico and Texas be encouraged. More important to the

Texans, however, was Article 11 which said that no more Americans could settle in Texas. Within two years this act precipitated a crisis. Late in the spring of 1832 the Texans rose in revolt to drive all Mexican soldiers and tax collectors from the province, an act of open rebellion. Fortunately for them, however, yet another revolution was occurring in Mexico City at the time.

The Centralist-Federalist struggle over the direction of the Mexican government now allowed General Antonio López de Santa Anna to rise to power as the strong man of his nation. In the summer of 1832, posing as the leader of the Federalist faction, he installed a puppet government and then himself was elected president in elections in January 1833. The Texans who revolted in 1832 claimed that they were supporters of Santa Anna, not revolutionaries trying to overthrow the republic. As participants on the winning side of the revolution, they decided to send delegates to see Santa Anna in the hope of bringing changes, especially repeal of the Law of April 6, 1830, and statehood for Texas separate from Coahuila.

Two conventions were necessary before this petition was ready for forwarding to Mexico City. In the summer of 1833 it was taken to the Mexican capital by Stephen F. Austin. The great colonizer met Santa Anna and received a promise for repeal of the unpopular law and even a pledge of separate statehood. Before that measure could pass the Mexican Congress, however, a cholera epidemic sent the delegates scurrying from the capital. In a fit of impatience, Austin wrote to the city council at San Antonio urging a state government to begin functioning in Texas anyway. Then, after bidding goodbye to President Santa Anna, Austin departed for home—only to be arrested, returned to Mexico City, and imprisoned for eleven months without trial. The letter he had imprudently sent to San Antonio officials had been returned to Mexico City where it was interpreted as a threat against the government. Not until Christmas Day 1834 was he released from prison, and then he was not allowed to leave the capital city. Finally in July 1835 he was unconditionally freed by Santa Anna, who granted an amnesty to political prisoners when he abolished the constitution and established himself as dictator.

Fighting For Democracy

Seven Mexican states revolted against the pretensions and usurpations of this dictator, Texas among them. Fighting began in Gonzales, Texas, on October 2, 1835, when soldiers attempted to enforce one of Santa Anna's decrees to have all firearms turned in to the government. In rapid order these Texan rebels marched on San Antonio, conquered it, and drove all Mexican soldiers from their province. The fighting had begun, but it was for liberty and democracy, not for independence. A "consultation" of Texan leaders meeting in November voted on the aims of the rebellion, and by a vote of 33 to 15 they stated that they were fighting for the constitution of 1824.

During the winter of 1834–35 the Texans quarreled among themselves about the proper way to achieve their goals. Some wanted to hold firmly in Texas, others to invade Mexico. During this debate, all thought themselves safe from invasion by a Mexican army, at least until the following summer, because of their distance from Mexico City. However, President-General Santa Anna used his time to good advantage. Where possible, as in California, he ended the revolt against his dictatorship by naming the local strong man as governor. Elsewhere he used the large army he had raised to quell opposition. Then he marched north, arriving at San Antonio on February 23, 1836.

There he was opposed by a small army of Texans inside the Alamo. The death of these defenders was soon matched by more deaths at Goliad where a Mexican army captured Colonel James W. Fannin and approximately 450 volunteers. And on March 27, Palm Sunday—at the explicit orders of Santa Anna—they were marched out in small groups and executed.

The men at the Alamo had not died in vain, however, for their struggle delayed the advance of the Mexican army while delegates were meeting at Washington-on-the-Brazos to debate the future of the province. Gathering on March 1, 1836, it took these men only one day to vote a declaration of independence. Then, in rapid order, they elected Sam Houston commander in chief of their army, wrote a constitution for the republic, and named an interim government to serve until elections could be held. Then they fled before the approach of Santa Anna's army. The Mexican dictator thought that his victories at San Antonio and Goliad had signaled the end of armed resistance. He had rashly divided his army and now led one part in a determined attempt to capture the rebel government.

While Santa Anna was marching, Houston, a former congressman and governor of Tennessee, was organizing his army. Strengthened by volunteers from the United States, he pursued tactics of delay and evasion to gain time to train his force. Then he set out to intercept the Mexicans. The two armies came together at San Jacinto Bayou on April 20 to decide the future of Texas. The following day at 3:00 PM, Houston had his 783 men parade in battle formation. Then, to the tune "Will You Come to the Bower I have Shaded for You," played by an improvised band, the Texans charged. Eighteen minutes later the battle was over, but the pursuit and slaughter of Mexicans lasted for two days. A final count showed 630 Mexicans dead and 730 captured, among them President Santa Anna. Eight Texans were killed and seventeen wounded.

Remember the Alamo!

On the evening of March 5, 1836, twenty-six-year-old Lieutenant Colonel William B. Travis realized that his garrison and fort were doomed. He had now to inform his men of their fate. He paraded them in single file before him, and drew a line on the ground with his sword. He then challenged them: "I now call upon every man who is determined to stay here and die with me, to come across this line. Who will be first? March!" All but one did.

A few months before, in December 1835, a group of Texans led by Travis had captured and occupied the Alamo mission-fortress near San Antonio. This had been the Mexicans' military headquarters in Texas when the revolution broke out against the dictatorship of General Santa Anna.

Toward the end of January, news reached Travis and his men of an imminent attack on the fort by Santa Anna. General Sam Houston, head of the Texan armed forces, therefore ordered that the Alamo should be abandoned and destroyed. He sent Colonel James Bowie (of bowie knife fame) back to carry out the orders. When Bowie arrived, morale was low and the condition of supplies, men, and weapons was extremely bad. Yet Bowie hesitated. He felt determined not to give up, and decided to disregard the general's orders and defend the mission. The Texans were quickly infected by his enthusiasm, and the fort became well organized. But Travis gloomily noted that there were not enough soldiers, and "volunteers can no longer be relied upon."

On February 8, Colonel David Crockett arrived with a group of amiable companions. Everyone flocked to the main plaza to greet the great man. But a few days later there was despondency in the fort again as Colonel Neill, the officer then in command, went on "twenty days' leave."

Travis was now left in control. Bowie was annoyed and resented Travis. But finally the two men agreed to a joint command of the garrison. Travis reported that Bowie was quarrelsome and "roaring drunk all the time." But soon after, Bowie fell ill, and the young colonel was left in sole command.

In late February, Santa Anna arrived in San Antonio with a force of about 6,000 men. The general ordered the Texans to surrender, but Travis would not. Instead, as he reported in a message to Houston, "I answered them with a cannon shot." Travis had only about 150 men, so he sent out desperate messages for help. Meanwhile the siege continued, with minor skirmishes around the fort wall. It seemed that very shortly General Santa Anna would make his final assault.

During those last gray days, Texan morale was very low. Bowie, desperately ill, did what he could to encourage the men. Crockett and John McGregor staged a musical duel with an old fiddle and bagpipes, each trying to play the loudest. But this kind of joviality could not keep up their spirits for long, and there seemed no chance of further reinforcements. New arrivals had increased the total fighting force to only 184.

A few days before the final battle began, in his last defiant message for help, Travis wrote: "I have sustained a continued bombardment for twenty-four hours and have not lost a man. . . . *I shall never surrender or retreat.* The enemy are receiving reinforcements daily . . . I am determined to . . . die like a soldier. . . . *Victory or death!*"

So, on the night of March 5, all those who had crossed the line knew what awaited them. The only man who refused to stay was Louis Rose. Bowie and Crockett tried to dissuade him from an almost impossible escape, but he scrambled across the wall and fled.

The siege had lasted nearly two weeks and at dawn on March 6, the Mexicans prepared for the assault on the Alamo. They moved forward to the threatening strains of the *deguello*, a tune which promised that none of the enemy would be spared. Santa Anna took his station at a battery north of the Alamo. Two columns were to attack from northern directions; two others were to assault the large gate and the chapel from the south. They arranged to be at the foot of the walls by daybreak.

The guns from the fort opened fire as the northern columns of invaders arrived at the walls. The Texan riflemen and the heavy guns proved an early obstacle for the Mexicans, who appeared to be in serious trouble. But there were just too many Mexicans for the Texans to handle. They broke through the wall and the northern postern was opened. Even the gunners facing south could not hold out: a group of Mexicans seized the prized 18-pound cannon and swarmed into the plaza. But Crockett's Tennesseans, forced back near the palisade, battled on with mad fury.

William Travis had been killed early

The Bettmann Archive

in the fighting when the outer wall had been captured. At his death, Adjutant John Baugh took over command and signaled to the Texans to retreat and hold the barracks. They bravely defended themselves in their barraged rooms as the Mexicans stormed the buildings. For a while deadly gunfire poured out from the doorways, and Mexicans scattered for cover. Meanwhile Crockett had taken refuge in a small room in the low barrack. Alone, he gallantly fought on, and it was probably there that he was killed.

Santa Anna's men were in control of the fighting, now at the stage of hand-to-hand combat. All that remained in Texan hands was the chapel. Here only eleven men were left, and they were quickly wiped out by the invaders' cannon. Colonel Bowie was shot in his bed as he fired his last rounds at the Mexicans. The last Texan to die was Jacob Walker, a gunner. By 6:30 AM the firing had ended. Over a thousand Mexicans were killed as well as the 183 Texans. The Mexicans had achieved their objective, but it was a Pyrrhic victory.

As General Santa Anna greeted Captain Fernando Urizza at the fallen Alamo he said: "It was but a small affair." Little did he realize that the Alamo incident had made a deep and lasting impression on the American people. And at San Jacinto, when Houston had his revenge on the Mexican general, his men went into battle with the cry: "Remember the Alamo!"

Left: The Alamo at San Antonio, preserved as a national monument. The former mission fortress, now a museum, is known as the ''cradle of Texas liberty.'' Far left: Frontiersman and former congressman David Crockett headed a band of Tennessee reinforcements who came to aid the Texans. Their arrival helped boost flagging morale. Below: The battle lasted less than a day. Though the defenders fought well, they could not hold out against vastly superior numbers.

The Texans won their independence with a stunning victory at San Jacinto. This Mexican flag (above) was captured during the battle. Left: Sam Houston, the Texans' commander and first president.

The Battle of San Jacinto established Texas in effect, if not legally, as an independent nation. In return for his freedom, Santa Anna negotiated treaties with the temporary government recognizing the independence of Texas. But these were repudiated in Mexico where yet another revolution had deposed the dictator. In the fall of 1836 the Texans held an election which ratified the new constitution and elected Houston as president. During the two years of his first term, Houston contended with an unruly army, an empty treasury, Indian raids, and Mexican determination to reconquer the lost province. He placated the Indians, reduced his army in size, held the public debt to $2 million, and maintained a watchful policy toward events in Mexico.

However, the major thrust of Houston's first term was toward securing annexation to the United States. In the election of 1836, Texans had voted on a referendum about annexation; overwhelmingly they expressed this desire. Before Houston could secure this, however, he had to gain recognition of Texas's independence. To his surprise, his old friend Andrew Jackson, president of the United States, moved slowly. Jackson's reticence was motivated by financial negotiations with Mexico which he feared would be endangered if he recognized Texas, and by the election of 1836. He did not want to anger New England abolitionists by recognizing Texas and thereby losing the election for his chosen successor, Martin Van Buren. Finally on March 3, 1837, just before going out of office, Jackson appointed a chargé d'affaires for Texas, thereby recognizing the independence of the new nation.

Recognition secured, Houston moved to gain annexation, but on this score he was thwarted. New England abolitionists asserted that the Texas Revolution was a conspiracy on the part of southern slaveowners to gain yet more territory for the United States where their "peculiar institution" might be practiced. Their strength in Congress was such that no bill of annexation could be passed. Houston reluctantly was forced to conclude that annexation was impossible. Therefore he tried to secure recognition of Texas's independence in Europe. James Pinckney Henderson, formerly of North Carolina and of aristocratic bearing, was sent to England as minister. He was warmly received, but found that abolitionist sentiment blocked recognition. Finally in France on September 25, 1839, he secured a treaty of recognition. Then, through the work of James Hamilton, a former governor of South Carolina, Texas was recognized in September 1840 by Holland, by England in November and by Belgium the following year.

The formal recognition of Texas as an independent member of the community of nations did not mean that Mexico accepted this fact. Though governments rose and fell there, both political factions persisted in claiming Texas as part of Mexico. Long after it was evident that the Lone Star Republic was lost forever to Mexico, politicians there still found it popular with the people to speak for reconquest and against Yankee imperialism. Eventually the issue would have to be settled on the battlefield, a conflict that came inexorably closer as the 1840s unfolded.

Chapter 3

THE SPIRIT OF EXPANSION

In their drive for expanded national boundaries in the 1840s, Americans reflected a growing sense of confidence, an increasing awareness that their destiny involved the settlement and ownership of territory from the Atlantic Seaboard to the Pacific Coast. This mood of expansion was most clearly expressed over Texas and Oregon. Settlement in Texas was accomplished with relative ease, but the long trek to the sparsely inhabited Northwest was a much more hazardous journey. Furthermore, British interests were well entrenched in Oregon. How valid, therefore, were American claims to the region, and how influential was the lobby that pressed for a boundary line at "fifty-four forty"?

"Fifty-four Forty or Fight"

For the American people in the early 1840s Oregon was more than a distant frontier touching the shores of the Pacific. It was an essential element in the nation's awakening sense of destiny which encompassed a future of political and territorial grandeur. As the more immediate objective of American expansion, Texas exerted far greater influence on American thought and emotions before 1845 than did Oregon. But long before Texas entered the Union the regions beyond the Rockies had beckoned the attention of editors and politicians as well as many of the nation's more imaginative and hardy citizens. During the election of 1844 Oregon no less than Texas emerged as a household word. If the campaign focused primarily on Texas, it was because that question was on the point of being solved. Oregon, less pressing, could wait another year.

Clearly the Americans of the 1840s were in an

expansive mood. Their belief in a special national destiny was not new. But in the 1840s it had a special quality. It was created in part by an unprecedented conviction of superior energy and power, in part by the specific issues of the times—Texas, Oregon, and California—that stimulated dreams of empire. In large measure the nation's mood reflected overpowering advantage. From New England and Pennsylvania, stretching on into the Ohio Valley and the Great Lakes region, an industrial revolution was multiplying the productive resources of the country. Steamboats transformed the Ohio and Mississippi rivers with their numerous tributaries into a mighty system of human and commercial traffic. Railroads were creeping from the Atlantic Seaboard toward the burgeoning cities of the Middle West, binding distinct

To the empty vastness of the Far West—often breathtaking in its beauty—emigrants were drawn in search of a better life. This view of the Oregon Trail is by Albert Bierstadt.

regions into one national economy. Augmented by Europe's ceaseless outpouring of humanity, the population of the United States had quadrupled in less than fifty years. The visible evidence of the country's expanding power contrasted markedly with the rest of the New World. It assured the Republic that one day it would surpass in wealth and power even the great states of Europe. As one British traveler warned his countrymen in the late 1840s:

> We cannot conceal from ourselves that in many of the most important points of national capabilities they beat us; they are more energetic, more enterprising, less embarrassed with class interests, less burthened by the legacy of debt. This country, as a field for increase of power, is in every respect so infinitely beyond ours that comparison would be absurd. . . . They only wait for material power, to apply the incendiary torch of Republicanism to the nations of Europe.

Manifest Destiny, as an expression of American nationalism, required more than an appreciation of power and energy. It required also a sense of mission—a conviction that the people of the United States held the future of republican government in their hands. Andrew Jackson asserted in his Farewell Address that Providence had selected the American people to be "the guardians of freedom to preserve it for the benefit of the human race." This mission had long been part of the American creed. But the generation of the 1840s was the first to attach it to territorial expansion. The addition of new states from the Louisiana Purchase without subverting the federal system dispelled earlier fears that expansion would disperse political authority too widely. Viewing the country's growth with deep satisfaction, Stephen A. Douglas of Illinois declared in January 1845 that "our federal system is admirably adapted to the whole continent." Thus Manifest Destiny, in essence, decreed that the American people were destined to extend their democratic principles over the North American continent. And the greater its territorial limits, the better the United States might serve as a refuge for Europe's oppressed millions.

For Americans in the 1840s a sense of destiny came easily. Never were a people better placed to transform their whims into reality. The logic of geography and claims to superior right effectively rationalized each territorial demand. Confronted neither with problems of conscience nor with extensive opposition, Americans could pursue as a natural right boundaries which seemed to satisfy the needs of security and commerce. Expanding as they did into a vast continental vacuum, they could ignore the elements of power and conclude that they were merely fulfilling the dictates of Manifest Destiny.

Whatever its limited costs, continental expansion still required the formulation and successful execution of national policy. The reason is clear. Those regions into which the nation threatened to expand belonged to other governments. None was there for the taking. Every boundary change required negotiation. Thus the final delineation of expanded boundaries demanded precisely defined territorial objectives as well as adequate means to carry them out. But the initial impulse which widened the country's horizons clouded such long-term considerations, for it sprang from the pioneering movement.

Expansion Into Spanish Territory

That heavy migration into the lower Mississippi Valley which brought Mississippi and Alabama into the Union in 1817 and 1819 also sent a flood of settlers into Louisiana, where they worked their clearings up the Red River toward Spanish Texas. Colonization schemes followed so that by 1825 the American colony in Texas numbered 1,800 including over 400 slaves.

To encourage further immigration the government of Coahuila-Texas in March 1825 established the *empresario* system. Under this scheme an *empresario* undertook to establish within six years an agreed-upon number of families on the land. If he fulfilled his contract the *empresario* would receive over 22,000 acres. Eventually fifteen individuals or companies signed contracts. Not one was able to import the required number of families. Settlers who drifted into Texas generally preferred Stephen Austin's colonies which, by 1832, had a population of 5,660.

Mexico's colonization scheme proved to be ill advised. One British diplomat in Mexico City warned as early as 1825 that the American settlers were bold and hardy but were "likely to prove bad subjects, and most inconvenient neighbors." And despite the laws against the importation of slaves, the American community in Texas became merely an extension of the American South.

After independence had been achieved, Texas faced numerous if limited reprisals from Mexico. Otherwise the Texan experiment in self-government seemed promising enough, especially after France and Britain recognized the Republic and adopted policies designed to assure its continued independence. The vast majority of Texans probably favored admission to the United States. What sustained independence, however, was the opposition to annexation within the United States. Anti-slavery forces and the Whig party suspected correctly that annexation would lodge two additional southern Democratic votes in the Senate where the balance of power on such issues as the tariff, internal improvements, and the Independent Treasury (granting the federal government control of its own funds) was very precarious. But in 1844 Democratic politicians

*Americans who settled in Texas preferred Stephen
Austin's colonies to those promoted by the
Mexicans. The lithograph above shows the Texas
capital in 1840. Right: President John Tyler,
who paved the way for the annexation of Texas.*

seized the Texas issue, convinced that they could exploit
the country's latent expansionist mood to serve both the
nation's interests and their own political ambitions.

President John Tyler developed a special affinity for
Texas as early as 1843. He hoped that such a major issue
would mend his political fences within the Whig party
and enable him to win another nomination. In April 1844
he urged annexation on broad national grounds. No region
of the United States, he said, would fail to benefit. Soon
Secretary of State John C. Calhoun, a South Carolina
Democrat in a Whig administration, began to promote
annexation as a sectional issue, one that would secure
the interests of the South and its slave system. Calhoun
hoped, moreover, that Texas might overthrow Martin
Van Buren's dominance of the Democratic party and
perhaps gain him the Democratic nomination in 1844.
As it happened, the Tennessee expansionist James K. Polk
secured the nomination.

Democratic expansionists sought to turn the election
into a referendum on Texas. Henry Clay, the Whig
candidate, had rejected the issue. He believed annexation

to be unconstitutional and a sure guarantee of war with Mexico. Under the compulsion of the campaign, Democratic oratory and newspaper editorials fused Texas with all the elements of Manifest Destiny to carry American expansionism to the highest pitch of the decade. Dixon H. Lewis of Alabama noted the impact of the Texas question on American emotions. "It is the greatest question of the *age*," he wrote, "& I predict will agitate the country more than all the other public questions ever have. Public opinion will boil and effervesce . . . more like a volcano than a cider barrel—but at last it will settle down with *unanimity* for annexation in the South & West & a large majority in the North." Texas had upset the Whig calculations. Polk's victory was narrow, the issues which produced it unclear.

Texas was the catalyst which combined all the elements of Manifest Destiny into one national movement. Yet throughout the campaign of 1844 it was the Democratic

Unlike his Whig opponent, James Polk rode the issue of Texas annexation to the utmost in the 1844 election and won a narrow victory. The lithograph at right appeared during the campaign. Below: A cartoon critical of Henry Clay's stand against annexation.

party that monopolized the appeals to destiny. The election returns revealed that the doctrines of Manifest Destiny had limited influence on the electorate. When in December 1844 President Tyler submitted the annexation question to Congress, Texas remained a partisan, not a national, issue. In its crucial vote of approval the Senate divided 27 to 25, largely along party lines. But however limited the impact of the Texas agitation on American emotions, it still mattered.

Already expansionism encompassed regions far beyond Texas. If pioneers could invade Texas in large numbers, they could reach the Pacific as well. "[The] Alleghenies may be piled upon the Rocky mountains," boasted Senator David R. Atchison of Missouri in 1844, "and our people will scale them. The march of empire is westward; nothing will, nothing can check it." Factors geographic and diplomatic had decreed that Oregon would emerge one day as an object of major American concern.

British and American Claims to Oregon

Thomas Jefferson's purchase of Louisiana in 1803 first brought American claims to the Pacific shores. The Spanish treaty of 1819, which defined the trans-continental boundary with Spanish Mexico, granted the United States all Spanish rights north of the 42nd parallel and west of the Rockies. In 1818 the United States and Britain had agreed to the 49th parallel from the Lake of the Woods to the Rocky Mountains as the northern boundary of Louisiana. But beyond the mountains the United States found itself in conflict with the Hudson's Bay Company then pushing southward into Oregon from western Canada. In the convention of 1818 the United States and Britain, in lieu of a settlement, agreed to leave the region west of the Rockies freely accessible for ten years to the vessels and citizens of each country. Whatever the Russian claims to the Oregon coast, they ended abruptly in 1824 and 1825 when London compelled Czar Alexander I to sign treaties with Britain and the United States which ceded all Russian rights south of latitude 54°40'. The British-American negotiations of 1826–27, which again failed to produce a permanent boundary settlement, extended the principle of joint occupancy indefinitely. Each nation could end the arrangement upon twelve months' notice. As late as the 1840s diplomatic deadlock kept Oregon in a state of equilibrium while both powers struggled to establish the primacy of their interests in the region.

In these early negotiations London and Washington put forth their historic claims to Oregon. For the United States this involved establishing the country's rights at least as far north as the traditional line of the 49th parallel (the present-day border with Canada). American officials

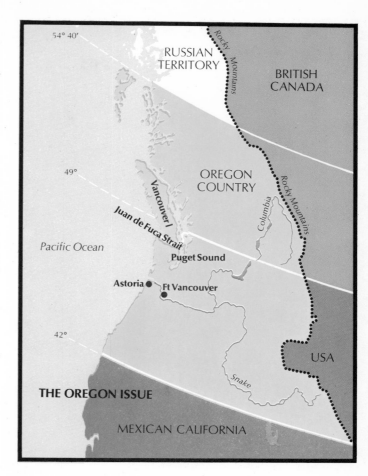

Map showing the disputed Oregon area as it appeared to American and British negotiators in 1840. Despite the claims of expansionists, an agreement was finally reached in 1846 which settled on the 49th parallel as the boundary line between the United States and Canada.

noted that Captain Robert Gray had discovered the Columbia River, and that the Lewis and Clark expedition first explored its course. The waters of Juan de Fuca Strait and Puget Sound, they agreed, had been explored gradually by Spanish, British, and American navigators. But even here American diplomats claimed the Spanish rights and those accruing from the fur trade. Through the American fur trading post of Astoria at the mouth of the Columbia the United States laid claim to prior settlement. Lastly, the Americans insisted that the extension of the 49th parallel to the Pacific was the natural continuation of the line east of the mountains on which the two countries had agreed as early as 1818.

London likewise based its claims to Oregon on discovery and occupation. Captain James Cook, the famed British navigator, explored the North American coast from the 44th parallel northward to Alaska in 1778, trading for sea otter fur among the coastal natives. The easy profits

Fort Vancouver on the Columbia River was the Pacific headquarters of the Hudson's Bay Company. Built in 1825, it buttressed British claims to the Oregon country north of the Columbia.

from fur in Chinese markets brought a stream of British traders into Oregon waters. Then in 1792 a British seaman, Captain George Vancouver, mapped the entire coast from San Diego to Alaska, circling the island that bears his name. Alexander Mackenzie, an agent for the North West Company, the Montreal-based rival of the Hudson's Bay Company, had reached the Pacific overland long before Lewis and Clark crossed the continent. He explored both the Mackenzie and Fraser rivers of western Canada although he wrongly identified the latter as the Columbia. Claims based on such exploration were impressive enough. But increasingly the British based their claims on actual occupation. By such argument they had clear title to the regions above the Columbia, for as late as 1845 that entire area remained the private preserve of the Hudson's Bay Company. Oregon south of the Columbia the British had always been ready to concede. This concession would have given the United States a beautiful, rugged coast of 300 miles between the

Columbia and the 42nd parallel, but one without a single port accessible even to small ocean-going vessels. For that reason no American negotiator, beginning with John Quincy Adams in 1818, would accept a settlement at the Columbia River line.

What mattered for early American officials was the acquisition of adequate ports on the Pacific to enable the United States to exploit the commercial resources of that great ocean. Early travelers spelled out the terrors of the sand bar at the mouth of the Columbia. During the winter months violent storms rendered the entrance almost impassable. "Mere description," wrote the noted American sea captain, Charles Wilkes, "can give little idea of the terrors of the bar of the Columbia: all who have seen it have spoken of the wildness of the scene, and the incessant roar of the waters, representing it as one of the most fearful sights that can possibly meet the eye of the sailor." Ship captains often stood off for weeks awaiting a favorable opportunity to run the bar.

In sharp contrast was the uniform praise with which early travelers viewed Fuca Strait and the inlets to the east of it. "No part of the world," wrote Thomas J. Farnham, the American traveler and author, "affords finer inland sounds or a greater number of harbours than can be found here." Wilkes's description was equally impressive: "Nothing can exceed the beauty of these waters, and their safety: not a shoal exists within the Straits of Juan de Fuca, Admiralty Inlet, Puget Sound, or Hood's Canal, that can in any way interrupt their navigation by a seventy-four gun ship. I venture nothing in saying, there is no country in the world that possesses waters equal to these."

In his early negotiations with the British, John Quincy Adams had based his demands for the 49th parallel on maritime considerations. British Foreign Minister George Canning attempted unsuccessfully to quiet this demand during the Oregon negotiations of 1826–27 by offering the United States a frontage of isolated territory on Fuca Strait. As late as the 1840s Adams's successors refused to depart from his judgment that American interests in the Far Northwest required full landed access to the regions of Puget Sound and Fuca Strait.

In 1826–27 Britain's foreign minister, George Canning (below), offered to cede an isolated stretch of coast on Fuca Strait. But America wanted nothing less than access by land to navigable harbors on the Pacific.

The Lure of the Northwest

Early diplomats and observers had seen correctly that permanent American settlements in Oregon would be the only way to dislodge the Hudson's Bay Company from its monopoly of trade and occupation. With remarkable foresight Albert Gallatin had favored the postponement of a settlement in 1827 "until the citizens of the United States shall have acquired a respectable footing in the country." Scarcely a dozen intrepid leaders, supported by numerous followers, responded to the challenge. If the number was small, it was enough to transform that distant wilderness into a promising outpost of American civilization and thereby pull the region into the mainstream of American consciousness.

As early as December 1820, Dr John Floyd, a Virginia congressman closely identified with members of the Lewis and Clark expedition, urged Congress to "inquire into the situation of the settlements upon the Pacific Ocean and the expediency of occupying the Columbia River." Floyd's repeated efforts throughout the decade failed to enlist congressional support for an American commonwealth in Oregon. Meanwhile the enthusiasm of an independent Yankee promoter, Hall Jackson Kelley, promised greater success. Convinced of Oregon's importance, Kelley directed his great energy and limited knowledge at the people of Boston through speeches, pamphlets, and letters to local newspapers. By 1831 he had incorporated an emigrant society determined to build a New England village in Oregon. He could generate a following, but he lacked both the skill and the knowledge to lead an expedition.

Kelley's campaign to advertise the opportunities for merchants, farmers, and missionaries in distant Oregon was not lost on Nathaniel J. Wyeth, a young Cambridge businessman. Wyeth recruited a company in Boston prepared to make the long journey to the Pacific. After several weeks of camp and drill on an island in Boston Harbor, Wyeth's party in March 1832 proceeded by sea to Baltimore and thence overland to St Louis. With them they brought an "amphibious machine"—part boat, part wagon—but decided to abandon the craft before they continued up the Missouri to Independence. At Independence the inexperienced Wyeth attached his party to the annual caravan of the Rocky Mountain Fur Company, preparing to leave under the leadership of the famed mountain man, William L. Sublette. At Pierre's Hole, the end of the trail for Sublette, several of Wyeth's men voted to return to the Missouri. But Wyeth and eleven of his party, guided through the Blackfoot country by Milton G. Sublette and aided thereafter by employees of the Hudson's Bay Company, reached Fort Vancouver on the Columbia. Earlier, Wyeth had sent a ship from

Boston to prepare for a rendezvous with his party at the mouth of the Columbia. At Fort Vancouver he learned that his ship and cargo had been lost. The following year Wyeth retraced his journey to organize another venture.

In Boston Wyeth formed the Columbia River Fishing and Trading Company to exploit the salmon fisheries of the Northwest. Again he sent a ship to the Columbia and in 1834 set out on his second overland trip to Oregon, travelling with Jason and Daniel Lee, vanguard of the new missionary movement into the Columbia country. Wyeth built Fort Hall on the Snake River to store his excess merchandise. Continuing on to the Columbia he joined his ship at Fort Vancouver. Despite his efforts he could not establish a profitable fishing enterprise against the competition of the Hudson's Bay Company. Eventually he sold his entire interest, including Fort Hall, to the giant British monopoly. Wyeth, like Kelley, had succeeded in advertising Oregon. Beyond that he had opened no avenue to easy riches.

But where Wyeth failed, others, building more slowly, succeeded. Jason and Daniel Lee, the Methodist mission-

Nathaniel Wyeth tried unsuccessfully to exploit the Northwest's fishing resources during the 1830s. He made two overland trips to Oregon and built Fort Hall (below) on the Snake River as a storage depot.

aries who had accompanied Wyeth in 1834, received a warm welcome at Fort Vancouver. Guided by men of the Hudson's Bay Company, they explored the Willamette Valley. There, sixty miles up the valley from Fort Vancouver, they established a tiny but permanent American settlement. This community became the mecca for American settlers in the region. Meanwhile the American Board of Foreign Missions, at the request of the Flathead Indians, sent Dr Marcus Whitman, a Presbyterian, along with the Reverend Samuel Parker to the Indians of eastern Oregon in 1835. From the rendezvous on Green River, where the two missionaries met delegations of Snake, Flathead, Nez Percé, and Ute Indians, Whitman returned to the East for additional help. Parker continued on to the Flathead country. In 1836 Whitman, accompanied by his young bride, reached Oregon after a long, hard journey and immediately established missions among the Indians. In time he became the most noted of all Oregon missionaries. The apparent success of the Protestants encouraged the Catholic church to enter the field. Father Pierre-Jean de Smet of the Catholic University in St Louis reached the Oregon country where, in 1841, he established the mission of Sacré Coeur.

For their sponsors the Oregon missions proved disappointing. The effort produced few converts. Indian apathy gradually turned to hostility. Even Whitman soon

Oregon Historical Society

All pictures: Oregon Historical Society

From left: Oregon missionaries Jason Lee,
Marcus Whitman, and Elijah White. Lee founded
a permanent settlement in the Willamette Valley
in 1834. Whitman followed soon after and had
early success among the Indians. White was
appointed Indian agent in Oregon in 1842.

questioned the future of the effort. But the missionaries had established permanent agricultural settlements which exposed the charm of the Columbia River country. Missionary descriptions of the land and climate prompted friends and relatives alike to join the annual caravans to Oregon.

The Oregon Trail

Events in 1842 transformed the slow drift of population into a great migration later in the decade. Having decided to appoint an Indian agent for Oregon, the government selected Dr Elijah White, three years an associate of Jason Lee who had returned to the East in 1840. By 1842 the Midwest, awakening at last from its long depression, was ready to move. The renewed pioneering trek scarcely centered on regions beyond the Rockies, for the heavy traffic of the 1840s flowed into Illinois, Wisconsin, Iowa, Missouri, and even portions of Michigan. But the flood of Oregon propaganda, the accounts of traders, trappers, missionaries, and travelers as well as the volume of personal letters from earlier emigrants—all circulated freely in the press—created an Oregon fever even among those who chose to forgo the long journey. Through speaking engagements and interviews with prospective

emigrants, White managed to assemble a party of 120–30 men with eighteen wagons. His successful crossing of the plains and mountains established the Oregon Trail, the most famous wagon route across the continent.

Wagon trains and horsemen headed for the Rockies and beyond generally followed the Sante Fe Trail from Independence to the divide between the Osage and Wakarusa rivers. They then moved northwest across the rolling prairies toward the head of Grand Island on the Platte. Between this route and the line of the Platte, other trails crossed the Missouri from Iowa and converged at Grand Island. During May the heavy-flowing streams rendered every route difficult. From Grand Island to the forks of the Platte near Julesburg, Colorado, the routes along both sides of the river were generally trouble-free.

Beyond Julesburg the Oregon Trail followed the Platte's north fork into a region of high hills and magnificent vistas. At the head of the Sweetwater branch of the North Platte the trail entered South Pass, a broad rolling plain a thousand miles from Independence, which cut through the Rockies at an elevation of 7,500 feet. Beyond South Pass the streams flowed westward into the Colorado and Columbia.

Whatever the hazards, the trail from Independence to the great divide of the Rockies was infinitely more negotiable than the thousand miles which followed. The crossings of the various tributaries of the Green River en route to the Snake began to test the endurance of migrants and stock alike. Already in 1842 the trail was marked by the graves of emigrants, the bones of oxen, discarded household goods, and broken wagons. At Fort Hall on the Snake River, some 1,300 miles from Independence, the California Trail branched off to the southwest. The Oregon Trail continued on to

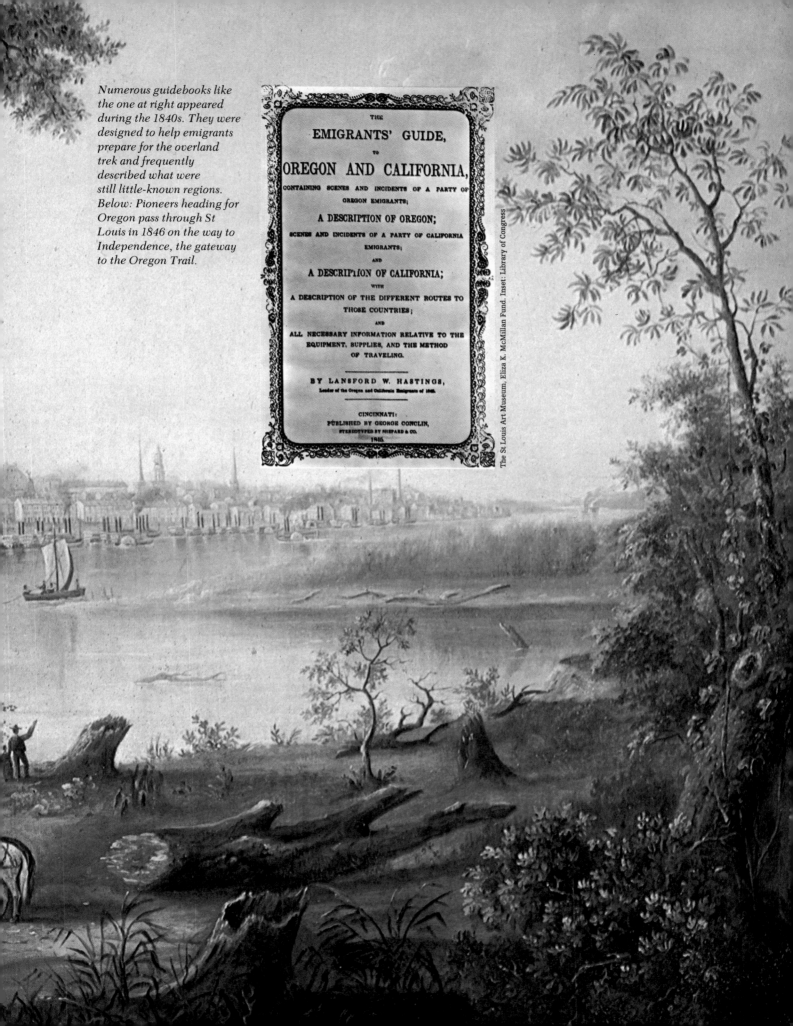

Numerous guidebooks like the one at right appeared during the 1840s. They were designed to help emigrants prepare for the overland trek and frequently described what were still little-known regions. Below: Pioneers heading for Oregon pass through St Louis in 1846 on the way to Independence, the gateway to the Oregon Trail.

THE
EMIGRANTS' GUIDE,
TO
OREGON AND CALIFORNIA,
CONTAINING SCENES AND INCIDENTS OF A PARTY OF
OREGON EMIGRANTS;

A DESCRIPTION OF OREGON;
SCENES AND INCIDENTS OF A PARTY OF CALIFORNIA
EMIGRANTS;
AND
A DESCRIPTION OF CALIFORNIA;
WITH
A DESCRIPTION OF THE DIFFERENT ROUTES TO
THOSE COUNTRIES;
AND
ALL NECESSARY INFORMATION RELATIVE TO THE
EQUIPMENT, SUPPLIES, AND THE METHOD
OF TRAVELING.

BY LANSFORD W. HASTINGS,
Leader of the Oregon and California Emigrants of 1842.

CINCINNATI:
PUBLISHED BY GEORGE CONCLIN,
STEREOTYPED BY SHEPARD & CO.
1845.

Fort Boise, a Hudson's Bay Company post on the Snake, and on to Grand Ronde east of the Blue Mountain barrier. Beyond the Blue the trail followed the Umatilla River to the Columbia and finally to Fort Vancouver, a full 2,000 miles from the Missouri River crossings.

Those who converged on Independence in the spring of 1843 gave the Oregon Trail a new significance. That migration also left a noted description of life on the trail in Jesse Applegate's *A Day with the Cow Column.* Peter H. Burnett, recently settled in Platte County, Missouri, assumed command of the thousand men, women, and children who had drifted in from Missouri, Ohio, Indiana, Illinois, Kentucky, and Tennessee. In the entourage were some 500 head of oxen and cattle. When those without cattle refused to take any responsibility for the herds, the emigrants split into two groups of about sixty wagons each. The unburdened column moved ahead while the "cow column," under the leadership of Applegate, followed at a supporting distance as far as Independence Rock on the Sweetwater. Having traversed the dangerous Indian country, the emigrants separated into small parties to better negotiate the narrow passages beyond South Pass.

Crossing the plains, Applegate's cow column followed the classic routine of a disciplined wagon train. Aroused by discharging rifles at 4:00 AM, the herders rode to the outer edge of the surrounding herds of horses and cattle, rounded up the strays, and began to move the well-trained animals toward the camp as smoke drifted upward from the morning fires. Teamsters selected their oxen—preferable to horses and less desired by the Indians—and drove them inside the corral for yoking. "The corral," wrote Applegate, "is a circle one hundred yards deep, formed with wagons connected strongly with each other, the wagon in the rear being connected with the wagon in front by its tongue and oxchains. It is a strong barrier that the most vicious ox cannot break, and in case of an attack of the Sioux would be no contemptible entrenchment."

Between six and seven o'clock the travelers ate breakfast, struck their tents, loaded their wagons, and hitched the teams as they prepared to move into line at the signal to march. Applegate recalled the ensuing scene: "It is on the stroke of seven; the rushing to and fro, the cracking of the whips, the loud command to oxen, and what seems to be the inextricable confusion of the last ten minutes has ceased. . . . The clear notes of the trumpet sound in the front; the pilot and his guards mount their horses, the leading division of wagons moves out of the encampment and takes up the line of march, the rest fall into their places with the precision of clockwork, until the spot so lately full of life sinks back into that solitude that seems to reign over the broad plain and rushing river."

Moving across the plains, Applegate divided the sixty wagons into fifteen platoons of four wagons each. The company's band of horses followed the wagons closely and willingly. Not so the cattle which brought up the rear. They moved only at the crack of the whips.

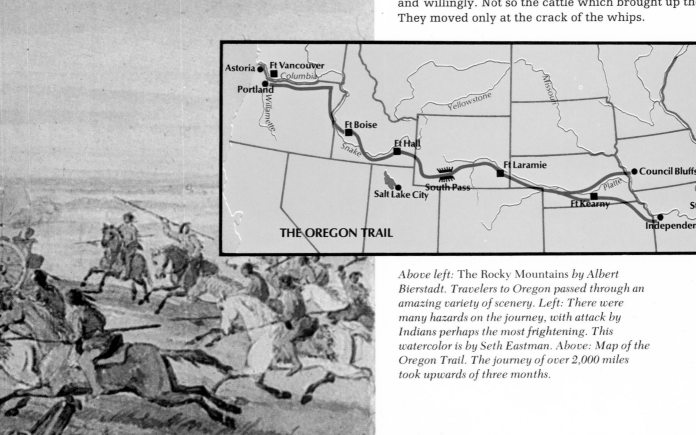

THE OREGON TRAIL

Above left: The Rocky Mountains *by Albert Bierstadt. Travelers to Oregon passed through an amazing variety of scenery. Left: There were many hazards on the journey, with attack by Indians perhaps the most frightening. This watercolor is by Seth Eastman. Above: Map of the Oregon Trail. The journey of over 2,000 miles took upwards of three months.*

Noting carefully the speed of the wagons, the pilot and his frontiersmen moved ahead of the column to select and prepare the nooning place which, hopefully, the wagons would reach after a five-hour march. At noon the wagons drew up in columns four abreast with the lead wagon of each platoon at the left. This procedure brought friends together at noon as well as at night. At one o'clock a bugle blast sent the caravan again on its westward journey. Gradually, weariness overcame men and beast alike. By evening the noisy bustle of the morning had given way to softer commands and slowly creeping oxen. As the day dragged to its close, the pilot conducted the train into a circle, precisely measured and marked, to form the corral for the night. So accurate was the practice that the rear wagon closed the gateway precisely. Minutes after the leading wagon had halted, the oxen had gone to pasture and the corral was again alive with fires and preparations for the night.

The Westward Push Goes On

Such experiences showed that the Oregon emigrant needed to be hardy but not insane—as Horace Greeley once insisted—to complete the journey. The migration of 1844 continued the trend, although heavy rains delayed the departure and compelled a late and dispirited arrival in the region of the Willamette. But the 3,000 emigrants who crossed in 1845 almost doubled the population of the Oregon frontier. Never had the pioneering enthusiasm exceeded that which pervaded Independence that spring. The local *Expositor* of May 3, 1845, described the scene:

> Even while we write, we see a long train of wagons coming through our busy streets; they are hailed with shouts of welcome by their fellow voyagers. . . . On looking out at the passing train, we see among the foremost a very comfortably covered wagon, one of the sheets drawn aside, and an extremely nice looking lady seated inside very quietly sewing. . . . That fine manly fellow riding along by the side of the wagon, and looking in so pleasantly, is doubtless the lady's husband; we almost envy him. But they are past, and now comes team after team, each drawn by six or eight stout oxen, and such drivers! positively sons of Anak! not one of them less than six feet two in his stockings. Whoo ha! Go it boys! We're in a perfect *Oregon fever*. Now comes on a stock of every description; children, niggers, horses, mules, cows, oxen; and there seems to be no end of them. From present evidences, we suppose that not less than two or three thousand people are congregating at this point previous to their start upon the broad prairie.

That migration sealed the fate of Oregon. Yet as late as 1845 American settlers had not ventured north of the Columbia where the Hudson's Bay Company still held sway. Most were still concentrated in the Willamette Valley which opened southward from Fort Vancouver on the Columbia. Oregon City, at the falls of the Willamette, was the chief center of American occupation, with a population in 1845 of about 600 white inhabitants.

Even as pioneers crossed the great silent wilderness to Oregon, other frontiersmen—trappers, adventurers, and settlers—pushed into Mexican California. Some followed the Old Spanish Trail from Sante Fe on the Rio Grande across the desert to Los Angeles. But the key

Right: A corral formation at Independence Rock on the Sweetwater in Wyoming. The massive landmark was a popular stopping place for Oregon travelers and hundreds scratched their names on its surface. Below: Oregon City as sketched by Henry Warre in 1845. By this time the town had about 600 white settlers. From 1849 to 1852 it was the capital of Oregon Territory.

Fort Laramie, a Wyoming trading post on the Oregon Trail, was bought by the government in 1849 and fortified. This interior view is by A. J. Miller.

routes to California lay to the north.

In 1833 Joseph Walker and his party threaded their way through the Sierras into the San Joaquin Valley. In 1841 a caravan followed the familiar Platte route to Fort Hall. From there the party made its own trail across the alkaline plains to the Humboldt River, which it then followed to the Humboldt's "sink." The party then crossed the Sierras to San Francisco Bay. Not until 1844 did Elisha Stevens blaze the Truckee Route into the Sacramento Valley. This discovery brought new significance to John Sutter's post, located on the Sacramento River a few miles above its confluence with the American. On the direct route from Truckee Pass to the Bay of San Francisco, Sutter's post became a rendezvous for American travelers. By the mid-1840s California emigrants generally followed the Oregon Trail to Fort Hall, and from there traveled southwest along the established Humboldt-Truckee route into the lower Sacramento Valley. Beyond South Pass the California pioneers had choices. The famed Donner Party of 1846 did not proceed to Fort Hall, but followed the Hastings Cutoff to the south of Great Salt Lake into the Great Basin country.

Led by George Donner, an elderly farmer, the eighty-seven settlers had left Illinois in April 1846. Badly equipped and with little experience among them, they managed to survive the rigors of the Nevada desert, but internal dissension resulted in murder. Upon reaching the eastern Sierra Nevada the twenty-wagon party was caught by early snowfalls. While a group set out for help, the rest sheltered as best they could. But food ran out and cattle died. In order to keep alive some members had to resort to cannibalism, for many of their number had already died from exposure, starvation, and exhaustion. Rescue parties brought out the survivors from January through April. In all, forty had perished.

Not until 1846 did Congress instruct the War Department to secure the Oregon Trail by establishing military posts along the route. The first—Fort Kearny—stood near the head of Grand Island on the Platte, over 300 miles from Fort Leavenworth on the Missouri. At the mouth of Laramie Creek, 337 miles west of Fort Kearny, the army established Fort Laramie, thereafter the center of official United States relations with the powerful Sioux. Beyond South Pass were the private posts of Fort Bridger, Fort Hall, and Fort Boise.

A Settlement in Sight

As early as 1843 the Oregon settlers met at Champoeg and organized a provisional government. By raising the issue of permanent government they pushed the Oregon controversy into Congress. Now Democratic politicians of the Old Northwest began to demand an immediate territorial settlement. For them the answer lay in ending joint occupation by giving Britain the necessary twelve-month notice.

What action would follow was never clear, for the rapid strengthening of the American position in Oregon produced a determination to challenge the British claim, even to territory north of the 49th parallel. Senator Lewis F. Linn's unsuccessful fight in Congress for the creation of a United States territorial government in Oregon led to public meetings from Ohio to Illinois. One convention at Cincinnati in July 1843 firmly declared the rights of the United States along the Pacific from California to Alaska. In his December 1843 message to Congress, President Tyler repeated this growing demand for the whole of Oregon. "After the most rigid, and, as far as practicable, unbiased examination of the subject," he argued, "the United States have always contended that their rights appertain to the entire region of country lying on the Pacific, and embraced within 42° and 54°40′ of north latitude."

Such claims to the whole of Oregon unleashed a new burst of nationalism. At the Baltimore convention of 1844, the Democratic party adopted a resolution which affirmed "that our title to the whole of Oregon is clear and unquestionable; that no portion of the same shall be added to England or to any other power." But the Democratic slogan of "Fifty-four forty or fight" was as untenable diplomatically as it was divisive politically. For A. F. Pollard, the British historian, the phrase was "possibly the crudest as well as the crispest expression of international relations to which democracy ever gave utterance." Many leading Democrats, joined by the overwhelming majority of Whigs, condemned the claim to all of Oregon as unnecessarily dangerous to the peace. For them a settlement at the 49th parallel would satisfy all United States interests along the Pacific shores and, hopefully, without war.

Whatever their power to stir American emotions and ambitions, neither the Oregon pioneers, the rhetoric of expansion, nor the pressures of congressional Democrats could resolve the question. British claims remained strong above the Columbia and incontestable north of the 49th parallel. Still British-American diplomacy on Oregon appeared increasingly promising.

Secretary of State Daniel Webster's negotiations of 1842 with British Minister Lord Ashburton, which produced the Webster-Ashburton Treaty, touched all major issues in United States-British relations except Oregon. Ashburton's instructions demanded that any northwestern boundary settlement follow the Columbia River to the Snake and thence a line due east to the Rockies. Britain, moreover, refused to renew the special offer of 1827. Webster was not opposed to the Columbia River line provided that the negotiations included a cession of Mexican California above the 36th parallel.

The Webster-Ashburton Treaty of 1842 settled many outstanding issues between America and Britain—except Oregon. Lord Ashburton (above) held fast to British claims to the area above the Columbia. From 1844, however, Britain no longer insisted on the Columbia River as a boundary line in Oregon. Lord Aberdeen (right) recommended instead a settlement with America further north at the 49th parallel.

This would bring San Francisco Bay into the United States.

Webster resigned in May 1843. Abel P. Upshur, his successor, reasserted American rights to land north of the Columbia. Claims based on discovery, he reminded US Minister Edward Everett in London late in 1843, were too exclusive to permit a settlement of the issue. For Upshur it was a matter of right. And the right of the United States to all territory as far north as 54°40', he asserted, was "now susceptible of very satisfactory proof." Because Britain might refuse to settle the question on the basis of mere right, continued Upshur, the president, in the interest of preserving harmony between the two countries, would accept a settlement along the 49th parallel, granting England the right of free navigation along the Columbia.

During 1844 Britain decided to retreat from the Columbia, encouraged by the growth of American power south of the river. In September Calhoun, the new secretary of state, reminded British Minister Richard Pakenham: "Our well-founded claim, grounded on continuity, has greatly strengthened . . . by . . . the greatly increased facility of passing to the territory by more accessible routes, and the far stronger and rapidly-swelling tide of population that has recently commenced flowing into it."

As early as March 1844, Lord Aberdeen, the British foreign minister, recommended a settlement which would include the 49th parallel to the sea. The British would retain Vancouver Island, there would be free ports south of the parallel, and free navigation of the Columbia. In a letter to Prime Minister Sir Robert Peel on September 25 Aberdeen wrote that such a settlement would be "most advantageous."

For the prime minister the offer was too generous. For Aberdeen it was realistic and satisfied Britain's essential interests. That the British were withdrawing diplomatically to the 49th parallel became even more apparent in 1845. That year the Hudson's Bay Company, less concerned with the fur trade than with the general development of commerce in the Pacific, moved its chief depot from Fort Vancouver on the Columbia to the southern coast of Vancouver Island. This symbolic surrender of the Columbia became the key to the Oregon settlement. British interests in Oregon, like those of the United States, centered ultimately on Fuca Strait. Clearly Washington and London had reached negotiable positions before the end of 1844. The secretary of state, John Calhoun, refused to sign a treaty, however, without the approval of the Senate. But the Senate, resounding with loud appeals to destiny and the whole of Oregon, was scarcely reassuring.

Polk's Political Dilemma

Unmindful of the limits of diplomacy, the Democratic party in 1844 had made a public commitment to total victory in Oregon which the new president, James K. Polk, could not escape. Indeed, Polk soon discovered that his party had destroyed his freedom of action. To insist on 54°40′ meant either a continuing stalemate or war with Britain. To retreat from the party platform meant conflict with the western Democrats. Polk shrank from both. As president, he accepted without question the judgment of his predecessors that the United States could obtain all that it desired by way of ocean frontage with a settlement at the 49th parallel. Juan de Fuca Strait and the sea arms east of it, he agreed, comprised one of the best harbors in the world. During July 1845, Polk offered Britain a settlement at the 49th parallel, for, he explained, "the entrance of the Straits of Fuca, Admiralty Inlet, and Puget's Sound, with their fine harbors and rich surrounding soil, are all south of this parallel." He believed the country north of 49° unfit for agriculture and incapable of sustaining anything but the fur trade. With his advisers, Polk doubted "whether the judgment of the civilized world would be in our favor in a war waged for a comparatively worthless territory north of 49°, which his predecessors had over and over again offered to surrender to Great Britain, provided she would yield her pretensions to the country south of that latitude."

In Washington, the British minister balked at the details—such as the extension of the boundary line across Vancouver Island—and rejected the proposal without instructions from London. Out of deference to his fellow Democrats, Polk withdrew the offer and assured his cabinet that he would not repeat it. Following a conversation with Secretary of State James Buchanan in the late fall of 1845, the president confided in his diary: "I told him that if that proposition had been accepted by the British Minister my course would have met with great opposition, and in my opinion would have gone far to overthrow the administration; that, had it been accepted, as we came in on Texas the probability was we would have gone out on Oregon." In keeping with his promise to settle the controversy on American terms, he asked Congress in December 1845 to extend the required year's notice to terminate joint occupancy in Oregon.

When Congress met that December there was little indication that within six months the disturbing Oregon question would be settled peacefully. The proponents of "fifty-four forty" had apparently captured control of public sentiment. Calhoun, entering the Senate, reported from Washington that it was dangerous even to whisper "forty-nine." Polk's message to Congress, reasserting full American rights to Oregon, seemed to promise the

Despite the bellicose cry of "fifty-four forty" calmer voices could still be heard. Richard Rush (left) urged moderation while Thurlow Weed said aggressive expansionism would provoke British anger.

Democratic extremists that he would not weaken again. It did not matter that the American title to territory north of the Columbia remained questionable, and its right to lands north of the 49th parallel practically nonexistent. It had become, wrote John L. O'Sullivan of the *New York Morning News,* "our manifest destiny to occupy and to possess the whole of the Continent which Providence has given us." That seemed sufficient to settle the issue.

Backed by a variety of "higher law" claims to Oregon, Polk was prepared to exert pressure on Britain. But what pressure and to what end? In December Richard Rush, who knew the British ministry well, warned the noted expansionist, Lewis Cass of Michigan, that Aberdeen would never concede all of Oregon. The alternative to compromise was war. With the choices clear, what purpose was the requested notice to serve? Fearful of antagonizing congressional extremists and moderates alike, Polk simply refused to say what course of action he intended. With American policy apparently adrift, moderates feared that the impending Oregon debate would further endanger the cause of peace. Congressional rhetoric, warned New York's conservative Thurlow Weed, would provoke angry replies in the British press and Parliament. This, in turn, would merely reinforce demands for the whole of Oregon. Weed wondered how the noisy appeals to patriotism, the daily references to the American eagle, the endless recriminations against those who "would yield an inch," and the charges that a compromise at the 49th parallel was a sellout of American rights would permit any favorable settlement.

Such fears overestimated the power of rhetoric. The nation's expanding outlook was doomed from the beginning, for the arguments favoring compromise were overwhelming. Demanding a settlement at the 49th parallel, Robert Winthrop of Massachusetts reminded congressmen of New England's objectives. "We need

ULTIMATUM ON THE OREGON QUESTION.

This 1846 cartoon illustrates the international attitudes toward the Oregon claims. By this time, the moderates in Congress had exposed "fifty-four forty" as an inflated and untenable claim.

ports on the Pacific," he cried. "As to land, we have millions of acres of better land still unoccupied on this side of the mountains." With such phrases not even Polk could quarrel. If no American leader would concede to Britain more than the 49th parallel, none—not even the most belligerent—would willingly fight for more. Throughout the East, writers and political spokesmen condemned the extremists for engaging in war talk merely to advance their political fortunes. They accused Democratic expansionists of clinging to a fraudulent issue, not to obtain the whole of Oregon but to sustain their political power. Whatever their motives, Democratic proponents of 54°40' had broken Polk's initiative to promote a reasonable settlement with Britain.

Long before 1846 Polk had ended all negotiation. Louis McLane, the American minister in London, reminded Calhoun that the two countries were approaching a crisis.

Compromise would come from leadership in the British government and the United States Senate, or it would not occur. "Now we must wait for your action," wrote McLane. "When we hear what that is, we will get on; and then you will have the real struggle in the Senate." Already two powerful Democratic factions were leading the movement toward compromise in the Senate: the old Van Buren group under Thomas Hart Benton of Missouri and John A. Dix of New York, and the southern conservative bloc led by Calhoun. Supporting them was the entire Whig party in Congress. By the early spring of 1846 it was clear that any British proposal to give up their claims south of the 49th parallel would secure the overwhelming approval of the Senate. For the eventual settlement, the powerful compromise movement in the Senate was as crucial as the earlier British retreat from the Columbia. Together they reduced Polk's final diplomatic role on the question to that of a willing messenger between London and the Senate. That role, thrust upon him by his opponents, permitted him and the nation to escape his self-imposed dilemma of promising a triumph in Oregon which he could not achieve.

Chapter 4

A CLASH OF REPUBLICS

The war against Mexico resulted in large measure from the mood of expansion that prevailed in the United States in the mid-1840s. On the other side, aspiring politicians in Mexico incited their people with dreams of the recapture of Texas. President Polk's decision to send troops into Texas was answered swiftly by the Mexicans, and the two republics went to war in April 1846. At each successive victory the majority of Americans basked in a glow of satisfaction at the triumph of the nation's might. But the Mexican War was the first American conflict which met with significant opposition at home. The cost in human lives was great, and the conflict renewed sectional suspicions and fueled the fires of debate over the extension of slavery.

The Mexican War

On March 3, 1845, President John Tyler signed the joint resolution of Congress inviting Texas to join the United States as the twenty-eighth state in the Union. The Mexican ambassador in Washington, Juan N. Almonte, exploded that this was an act of aggression against his nation. He demanded his passport, and stormed out of the country. Almonte maintained that the joint resolution was tantamount to a declaration of war.

But it was not the Texas question alone which started the war between the United States and Mexico, although this was the immediate and superficial cause. There were many other points of friction between the two republics: debts owed to Americans by the government of Mexico, the American desire for California, and a cultural conflict that saw epithets such as "gringo" and "greaser" shouted at members of the opposing race. Finally, perhaps even most important, there was the chaotic and unstable political situation within Mexico. Politicians in Mexico City were ready to exploit any issue that promised to bring them to high office. And the quarrel with the United States over Texas seemed a likely cause.

Relations between the two nations had begun warmly when the United States promptly recognized its southern neighbor's declaration of independence. The first note of discord was sounded in 1829 when the American minister opened discussion of the claims question—the payment of debts owed to American citizens by the Mexican government. Nothing came of this effort. Then in 1837, just before going out of office, President Andrew Jackson again made an attempt to collect these debts, but he too was unsuccessful. After a French invasion and a British show of force had brought payment of their claims, the Mexican government in 1839 agreed to arbitration of the American claims by the King of Prussia. Mexico delayed eighteen months before coming to the conference table, argued four months over procedure, and settled less than one-third of the cases before the arbitration process broke down. President Santa Anna, back in power in the early 1840s, refused to pay even the $2 million agreed upon. Finally in June 1843, Mexico made the first payment of this settlement, but refused the following April to pay the second installment. There the matter rested until Texas entered the Union and diplomatic relations were severed.

California was not a cause of the Mexican War, although American politicians definitely did hope to acquire it. This desire was made most apparent in 1842

The issue of Texas annexation aroused wild support in some quarters of America. This 1845 engraving shows a demonstration in Jersey City, New Jersey, supporting the movement.

when Thomas ap Catesby Jones, commodore of the American Pacific Squadron, mistakenly assumed that war had begun between his country and Mexico. Sailing into Monterey, California, he occupied the port without opposition—only to learn that no war had been declared. He withdrew with an apology that did little to mollify Mexican honor. But by 1846 all impartial observers agreed that California already was lost to Mexico. The only question to be resolved was who would get it: England, the United States, or (possibly) France?

In the spring of 1846 California had no schools or newspapers, no postal system, almost no police or court system, few books, and little protection from Indian raids from the interior. Even communication with Mexico was rare. Many Californians openly voiced their desire to be annexed to the United States. Others favored English sovereignty. And there was virtually a civil war going on in the province, as Governor Pío Pico contended with Colonel José Castro for domination. Polk was well aware of these currents of intrigue and naturally tried to offset British and French influence in the region. Thus he had the Pacific Squadron of the United States Navy standing by to intervene, just as he had sent Captain Frémont and a detachment of American soldiers to California waiting for the right moment to advance American interests. But in addition to Texas and California, Polk had one other area of difficulty with which to contend—Oregon.

British officials realized that the United States could not fight both Britain and Mexico. They wanted to get the most favorable settlement to the Oregon dispute, and the American quarrel with Mexico placed them in a good position to bargain. Furthermore, Polk's Oregon policy had severe critics, especially among southerners. Unknown to Polk, the British had decided to settle for the 49th parallel as the Oregon boundary. This decision, made in 1844, arrived in Washington in the form of a compromise proposal in June 1846. It settled on the 49th parallel as the northern boundary and allowed both countries to have free navigation of Juan de Fuca Strait and the Columbia River. The Senate immediately accepted it (for war had been declared against Mexico a month before). Ratification of the Oregon Treaty averted any possibility of war with Britain—and freed the United States to give its undivided attention to Mexico.

A year before this, however, Polk and his administration were busy negotiating with Mexico in the vain hope of avoiding war. Polk was an expansionist, but he sought peaceful means that would avoid conflict. Yet the political situation in Mexico was such that no peaceful settlement was possible. The Mexican ambassador's claim that the congressional resolution was tantamount to a declaration of war was very popular in Mexico. It was a rallying cry for the Centralist faction just deposed in December 1844 by the Federalists led by José de Herrera, whose desire to avoid war proved his undoing.

Political Maneuvers Over Texas

Late in the spring of 1845 Herrera indicated through Richard Pakenham, British minister to Mexico, that he was willing to negotiate a treaty of recognition for Texas. As his foreign minister explained it, Texas was not worth a war and Mexico would be wise to recognize the province as lost. In October the Mexican Congress met in secret session. It approved Herrera's decision to receive a representative from the United States, one with authority to negotiate a settlement of the "present dispute."

This was communicated to Polk by Pakenham, who had been transferred to Washington. Polk and his secretary of state, James Buchanan, interpreted the term "present dispute" to mean all issues between the two nations. Congressman John Slidell was appointed to negotiate with the Herrera government. The instructions given to Slidell in November 1845 included the purchase of California, as well as recognition of Texas's annexation to the United States. On the issue of the Texan boundary, his instructions were firm. The United States would accept the Nueces River as the southern boundary if Mexico paid the claims promptly. But if Mexico agreed to the Rio Grande as the southern boundary then America would pay the claims. The United States would pay an additional $5 million if New Mexico became American. Slidell could offer $5 million more for American title to northern California, and as much as $25 million for all of California.

These instructions were responsible for one of the lingering misunderstandings about the Mexican War. What was the southern boundary of Texas? Was it the Nueces River or the Rio Grande? This boundary had been inexact since the days of Spanish ownership, for few people lived in the area between the two rivers. During the Texas Revolution Mexico in effect, if not officially, had agreed to the Rio Grande as the boundary. Mexican troops had retreated south of that river during the war, and in December 1836 the Congress of the Republic of Texas had asserted that the Rio Grande was the boundary. Moreover, Texas forces twice chased Mexican troops south of this river in 1842. Yet no official of any Mexican government ever asserted that the Nueces River was the proper boundary of Texas. No evidence exists to show that any of them even privately made such an assertion. The official Mexican position was that their nation owned all of Texas clear to the Sabine River (the present boundary of Texas and Louisiana). Thus in reality there was no dispute over the Nueces, for Mexico never claimed it as the boundary of anything.

In November 1845 it little mattered what instructions Polk gave Slidell or what boundary he was to strive for, as Herrera's overthrow was imminent. It even mattered little if Polk wanted California or not, for Centralist

White House Historical Association (detail)

Paredes.

Library of Congress

President James K. Polk followed an ambivalent policy over Texas. While encouraging negotiations with Mexico, he ordered troops into the region before it had been finally annexed.

When Mariano Paredes came to power in Mexico he vigorously denounced American policy in Texas. He mobilized the army and vowed that Mexico would go to war to recover its former province.

politicians in Mexico were using the quarrel as a vehicle to power. In December, when Slidell arrived at Veracruz to begin negotiations, he was informed that Herrera would receive no minister from the United States until Texas was returned to Mexico. This impotent and foolish gesture was designed to save face for Herrera—and it did make Slidell leave the country. But already Herrera's cause was lost. On December 29, 1845, the same day that Polk signed the Texas Admission Act and proclaimed Texas part of the Union, Mariano Paredes entered Mexico City and assumed the presidency without firing a shot. The Centralists had assumed power and strengthened their position largely by vehement denunciation of the United States and their announced intention of recapturing Texas. Paredes and his junta named Juan N. Almonte secretary of war and declared their intent to make war on the United States to recover Texas. Immediately President-General Paredes mobilized his troops, reorganized the army, and bombarded the Mexican public with anti-American propaganda.

In this ambitious drive toward war, the Centralists were emboldened by their belief that Mexican arms could win a contest with the Yankee imperialists. Most foreign observers, especially the French and British, rated the Mexican army as one of the strongest in the world, noting that it was well armed, disciplined, and very experienced. The Spanish minister to the United States said bluntly that there were no better troops in the world than the Mexicans, while Pakenham believed it impossible that American arms could defeat the Mexicans on their own territory. The London *Times* correspondent in Mexico was positive that Mexican soldiers were superior to American soldiers, while another British newspaper stated that American troops were contemptible and "fit for nothing but to fight Indians."

In 1846 the Mexican regular army was four times larger than the American regular army. The United States would have to rely, in the event of war, on volunteers and citizen-soldiers to fight against professionals—and most observers of that day had no faith in volunteers. One commentator wrote of American volunteers: "They are not amenable to discipline, they plunder the peasantry, they are without steadiness under reverses, they cannot march on foot." The Centralist leaders accepted such statements and totally believed in the superiority of Mexican arms.

Two other factors seemed to be to Mexico's advantage:

In 1845–46 President Polk had boundary problems in Oregon and Texas. This cartoon portrays an aggressive Polk baiting Britain with "fifty-four forty" and kicking Mexicans out of Texas.

geography and political divisiveness in the United States. The war obviously would begin in Texas, which was far from the population center of the United States. Paredes and his advisers believed the Mexican army could sweep through Texas easily, possibly capturing New Orleans and Mobile. To them it seemed inconceivable that logistical support could be given to an American army in Texas—and the more volunteers the greater the problem of supply. Thus it seemed that any war would be one of offense by Mexico, with the United States on the defensive. Yet if Americans should invade Mexico, they would come through Texas into northern Mexico—a region of deserts and barren mountains—to face a scant population, guerrilla warfare, and local resistance. And, just as important, the Americans were divided politically. Almonte assured Paredes that the North, represented by abolitionists in Congress, would not vote to support the war. Internal conflict would destroy morale, while those convinced that a war with Mexico was unjust might revolt against the government. Finally, the Indians surely would join with an invading Mexican army to fight the Americans. And slaves in the South would revolt against their masters and welcome Mexican forces as liberators.

Polk meanwhile was doing his best to avoid war. Simultaneously, however, he was making prudent preparations. Just as he sent Frémont to California and a naval squadron to the Pacific, so also he ordered General Zachary Taylor, commander of the Department of the Southwest, to occupy Texas and prepare to defend it from attack. This order of July 4, 1845, came before Texas had been annexed and stipulated that Taylor was to move to a point "on or near the mouth of the Rio Grande." However, Taylor decided to encamp at the mouth of the Nueces River because the land between it and the Rio Grande was unsettled and offered no logistical support. When Slidell was rejected as a diplomatic envoy, Polk ordered Taylor to take up a position on the northern bank of the Rio Grande. Even then Polk sent instructions to Slidell to try to negotiate with Paredes. But the Mexican president rejected this last effort in rude and abusive language meant for public consumption.

71

Zachary Taylor Enters Texas

Taylor arrived at the mouth of the Rio Grande on March 23, 1846, with 4,000 troops. He occupied Point Isabel near the coast and began construction of a post that would become known as Fort Brown, opposite the Mexican town of Matamoros. President Paredes angrily sent orders north for General Francisco Mejía, who commanded the Mexican troops amassed at Matamoros, to attack Taylor. Mejía chose to ignore this order of April 4, although he did enter into a heated correspondence with Taylor. Paredes, angry that an attack had not taken place, replaced Mejía with General Pedro de Ampudia, who ordered Taylor to withdraw northward and told American citizens at Matamoros to leave because a state of war existed between the United States and Mexico. Taylor responded by blockading the mouth of the Rio Grande with chains.

President Paredes anxiously awaited news of war from the north. On April 18, he wrote to General Ampudia: "At the present time I suppose you to be at the head of our valiant army, either fighting already or preparing for the operations of the campaign. . . . It is indispensable that hostilities be commenced, yourself taking the initiative against the enemy." When no word came of war along the Rio Grande, Paredes on April 23 issued a proclamation declaring a "defensive" war against the United States: "I solemnly announce that I do not declare war on the United States. . . . From this day commences a defensive war."

The following day, some time before this declaration could be communicated as far north as the Rio Grande—but undoubtedly by prearrangement—Ampudia was superseded by Mariano Arista. He immediately ordered 1,600 cavalry across the Rio Grande and notified Taylor that "hostilities have commenced." Indeed they had, for that afternoon the Mexican cavalry came upon Captain William Thornton and some sixty American dragoons. After intensive skirmishing in which some Americans were killed and others wounded, Thornton surrendered. Taylor, when notified of this, immediately sent a dispatch informing President Polk of the new turn of events.

Taylor's dispatch arrived in Washington on May 9, a Saturday evening, about six o'clock. The next day Polk drafted his famous war message, and on Monday, May 11, he presented it to Congress. The statement closed with his famous words: "American blood has been shed on American soil." The opposition, mostly New England abolitionists, sneered in return: "American blood has been shed in a Mexican corn field." Abraham Lincoln, then serving in the House of Representatives, spoke bitterly against the occupation of "disputed" territory, implying that the Nueces was the boundary of Texas. Another abolitionist declared during the debate, "The river Nueces is the true western boundary of Texas. . . . It is our own President who began the war." Yet another asserted: "It is grievous to know that when we pray 'God defend the right' our prayers are not for our own country." And John C. Calhoun said that war could not exist until Congress declared it.

Here Calhoun was referring to Polk's war message, a masterpiece of evasion. Polk began by saying a state of hostilities existed. He asked for a war bill approving a call for 50,000 volunteers and appropriating $10 million for conduct of the war. Calhoun's objection caused the administration to add a preamble to the bill which served in place of a declaration of war. This was carried in the House by 123 to 67. The war measure itself passed by a vote of 174 to 14. On Tuesday, May 12, the measure

"Old Rough and Ready" Zachary Taylor was sixty-two when war began with Mexico. Short and stocky, he had a common touch which made him popular with troops. Taylor ran for president after the war and won, but he died sixteen months after taking office. Above: A daguerreotype of Taylor in the 1840s. Right: This printed handkerchief incorporates scenes of Taylor's victories in Mexico.

Courtesy Chicago Historical Society

passed the Senate by 40 to 2, with three abstaining (including Calhoun).

At the mouth of the Rio Grande, Brigadier General Zachary Taylor needed no declaration of war by Congress to convince him that hostilities had commenced. Muscular and stocky, rarely in full uniform, the sixty-two-year-old soldier had been dubbed "Old Rough and Ready" by his troops. Although he had no formal military training—in fact, his education as a youth had been poor—Taylor was a man of long military service. Commissioned a lieutenant in 1808, he had fought with distinction in the War of 1812 and the Black Hawk War. He had contended with the Seminoles in Florida in 1837, and since 1840 had commanded the Department of the Southwest. Opposing him across the river was General Mariano Arista, born in San Luis Potosí in 1802. Joining a provincial regiment at the age of fifteen, Arista rose from captain to lieutenant colonel in six months in 1821. Then he successfully rode out the years of revolution and counterrevolution—except for one brief period of exile in Cincinnati, Ohio. He came to Matamoros in 1846 a proud, red-haired, fiery Mexican patriot intending to conquer all the way to Washington.

The two armies came together on the afternoon of May 8 at a pond on the north side of the Rio Grande known as Palo Alto. Taylor arrived on the scene at one o'clock, his army mainly a peacetime one but officered at the junior level by men trained at West Point. The Mexican army already was arrayed in battle formation, its numbers vastly superior to the Americans. Both sides prepared to fight in their characteristic ways. Arista rode along his

line shouting "*Viva la República*" and making speeches almost drowned out by the noise of bands playing in the rear. Taylor slumped sidesaddle on his horse, chewing tobacco, spitting, and talking to anyone who wandered by. Finally the Mexicans charged with lances, banners fluttering from their tips. The American frontiersmen-militia calmly waited until they were within fifty yards, then fired with telling effect. Then the American artillery, which was regular army not volunteer, opened fire with grape shot. Arista sent troops forward to silence the guns, but they were destroyed by them. When darkness came, the armies encamped. A count showed five Americans dead and forty-three wounded. Arista later reported 250 dead or wounded. Little did Taylor realize that night the devastating blow to Mexican morale his cannon had wrought. The next morning he knew, however, for the light of day revealed that Arista had retreated.

The American general ordered an advance toward Fort Brown—only to confront Arista and the Mexicans once again, this time in an ancient channel of the Rio Grande known as Resaca de la Palma. Again an artillery barrage opened the way to victory for Taylor and his men,

although it took a charge by infantry to secure it. Arista was so demoralized by this reverse that he fled, not only south of the river but all the way to Linares. His route was littered by dead animals, abandoned equipment, and Mexican soldiers who had died of exhaustion and even of suicide. When he reached Linares his Army of the North had dwindled from 7,000 to a little over 2,500.

Taylor followed up these two victories by demanding—and receiving—the surrender of Matamoros. On May 18, his soldiers crossed the bridge and raised the Stars and Stripes as they sang "Yankee Doodle." In the United States the reaction to Taylor's victories was a soaring confidence in the army and in the volunteers. Taylor was the hero of the hour. He was breveted a major general and named commander of the Army of the Rio Grande.

The Battle of Palo Alto, fought north of the Rio Grande, was the first major clash of the war. Though outnumbered, Taylor's army made effective use of their cannon to smash the Mexicans' advance; Taylor lost only five soldiers in the battle. Below: The Americans' cannon open fire.

UNITED STATES

● Sonoma

● Monterey

Los Angeles
JAN 10, 1847 ✗
✗ San Pasqual
DEC 6, 1846
San Diego ●

Santa Fe
AUG 18, 1846 ✗

El Brazito
DEC 25, 1846 ✗

Nueces

Rio Grande

MEXICO

Pacific Ocean

Palo Alto
MAY 8, 1846 ✗
Matamoros ●

Monterrey
SEPT 24, 1846 ✗
✗
Buena Vista
FEB 23, 1847

THE MEXICAN WAR

Veracruz
MAR 29, 1847
✗

Mexico City
SEPT 14, 1847
✗

‒ ‒ ‒ ‒ ‒ ‒ ‒ 1848 Boundary
▬ ▬ ▬ ▬ ▬ 1819 Boundary

Map showing battle sites in the war with Mexico. The two areas of conflict were northern and central Mexico and California. Taylor and then Scott commanded the American troops in Mexico while Kearny led the invasion of California. By the terms of the treaty which ended the war, more than 500,000 square miles of territory were ceded to the United States. It increased the size of the country by about 17 per cent.

Congress voted him two gold medals, and several Whig politicians began to explore the possibility of running him for the presidency.

Yet at Fort Brown and Matamoros there was no happiness among the troops. The climate at the mouth of the Rio Grande was so hostile that Taylor was forced to move his soldiers upriver to the little town of Camargo. But that proved even more unhealthy. In fact, it was a place of death for 1,500 Americans due to heat and mud and the various diseases brought from Matamoros. So many died during the move itself that, according to legend, the Texas mockingbirds learned to sing the death march from listening to the band. At Camargo the troops pitched their tents too near the camp supply of water, which was used for drinking, disposal of wastes, and bathing. Because of the blistering heat and the primitive sanitary conditions, sickness spread among them and many died. Yet recruits poured into Taylor's camp, swelling his army to 20,000 and more. Texans came especially. They regarded this war as a chance for revenge against their enemies from the Alamo. Even the governor of Texas, J. Pinckney Henderson, took a leave of absence to rush to the colors.

The Conquest of Northern Mexico

Taylor at last was forced to order his men into Mexico toward the nearest large city, Monterrey, as much to get away from the suffering along the Rio Grande as to make progress in the war effort. He found a new military commander awaiting him. Arista's defeats had shocked Mexico City. Centralist leaders had been predicting victory, especially President Paredes who believed that the nation would rally behind him in victory and proclaim him king. Arista was therefore replaced by General Francisco Mejía. Just twenty-four years old, the new commander was a political appointee filled with bombast and self-importance. But he lasted only a few months before being succeeded by Pedro de Ampudia, a competent general but one noted for his cruel and barbarous treatment of prisoners and for his intense hatred of Texans. Ampudia heavily fortified Monterrey, placed cannon on the nearby hills, stockpiled ammunition, and waited, confident of victory.

Taylor advanced along a path scouted by Texas

San Jacinto Museum of History Association

Rangers, arriving on September 20, 1846, to survey the town and plan strategy. The next day the battle commenced. For three days it raged as Texas Rangers, assisted by infantrymen, stormed the hills and captured Ampudia's cannon. These were turned on the city and used to assist the American troops entering the town to begin house-to-house fighting. Late in the afternoon of September 23 Ampudia sent word that he wished to discuss terms. Artillery shells were falling near the cathedral of the central plaza inside which Ampudia and his staff were quartered—along with the munitions. Terms were arranged, and on September 25 Ampudia and the Mexicans were allowed to withdraw from the town. They were permitted to retain their sidearms and accouterments, along with six pieces of artillery. The Americans agreed not to pursue them for eight weeks. Taylor had taken the ''impregnable'' city in just three days of fighting. But his losses—800 killed or wounded—were heavier than those suffered by the Mexicans.

News of this conquest caused wild celebrations throughout the United States. But in Washington, where the Whigs were talking more strongly of running Taylor for the presidency, Polk's Democratic administration was

The Texas Rangers were originally formed to protect American settlers in Texas from the Indians. During the war, they served with distinction under Taylor and Scott.

openly critical. ''In agreeing to this armistice,'' said the president, ''Genl. Taylor violated his express orders & I regret that I cannot approve his course.'' On January 26, 1847, he ordered Taylor to remain near Monterrey. Four-fifths of Taylor's troops were to be sent to General Winfield Scott to aid in the invasion of Mexico at Veracruz. Taylor was left with only 6,000 soldiers, mainly volunteers, to stay on the defensive.

He chose to defy the president's orders, however. His soldiers advanced to capture Saltillo on November 16, and by mid-January he had a line some 400 miles in length stretching from Monterrey to the Gulf of Mexico. But Taylor's moves and the strength of his army was known in Mexico, for American couriers carrying information about his army had been captured. The new commander of the Mexican army (now restyled the Army of Liberation) believed he could win a stunning victory over Taylor's volunteers. This new commander was General

Ringed by hills and fortified
by cannon, Monterrey
presented a daunting
challenge to the Americans.
Only after three days'
fighting did the "impregnable"
city fall to Taylor's men.
But losses were heavy.
Below: Panorama of the battle
scene. Left: Troops storm
the bishop's palace inside
the town.

Antonio López de Santa Anna, the villain of so many Mexican disasters and a veteran of long military background. Twice president and twice dictator of Mexico, he still was the best general in the republic. When he returned from exile in 1846 he was immediately voted to the presidency and command of the army. He rushed north with 20,000 hastily recruited troops in the hope of achieving a resounding victory.

The two armies came together on February 22, 1847, at the hacienda of Buena Vista. There they fought a two-day battle. Twice the Mexicans seemingly had victory within their grasp, but twice they were routed by American artillery fire and the fighting ability of volunteer troops. Moreover, the Mexicans were without food, almost exhausted, and demoralized. Their ammunition was largely expended. On the night of February 23, Santa Anna ordered a retreat. He left his wounded men behind while he rushed south ahead of his army to proclaim a "victory." During the night Taylor conferred with his staff, who wanted to retreat. But Taylor held firm, and the

Outnumbered four to one, the Americans came close to defeat by the new Mexican commander General Santa Anna (right) at the Battle of Buena Vista (below). But after two days' fighting the Mexicans withdrew and Taylor had won his greatest victory.

sunrise of February 24 revealed that he had won. Taylor and his second in command hugged each other with relief. To his brother Old Rough and Ready wrote: "The great loss on both sides . . . has deprived me of anything like pleasure." For the remainder of the war he would remain in northern Mexico. The war had ended for him, and he knew it. The Battle of Buena Vista brought him another official vote of thanks from Congress, along with another gold medal—and criticism from the president. Late in 1847 Taylor would return to the United States to campaign for the presidency.

Kearny Sweeps West

While Taylor was winning his stunning victories in northern Mexico, a second major offensive was begun in the American Southwest. At Fort Leavenworth, Kansas, Colonel (later General) Stephen Watts Kearny assembled a rag-tag army at the orders of the president in June 1846.

Designated the Army of the West, it numbered some 2,700 men, most of whom were mounted. It included a battalion of 500 Mormons, enlisted at the request of Brigham Young who needed their salaries to help finance the sect's move westward to the Great Salt Lake. The major portion of Kearny's army marched toward Santa Fe on June 26, 1846. After a hot, thirsty march of 565 miles, the Army of the West reached Bent's Fort on the upper Arkansas River. There it rested while Kearny and his staff pondered reports that 3,000 Mexicans had marched north from Chihuahua to defend New Mexico against the gringo invaders.

In Santa Fe, Governor Manuel Armijo was aware of the approach of the Americans—and no doubt wishing that his 3,000 men were seasoned veterans instead of chiefly raw recruits of little value and with no inclination to fight. He had at his command only 200 regulars, mostly ill equipped and poorly trained. Still, he might have won a contest of arms with the Americans had he made full use of his geographical advantage. A short distance east of Santa Fe was Apache Canyon, a narrow pass in the

Taylor's military successes made him a national hero and provided an irresistible stepping stone to the White House. This cartoon comments savagely on his "qualifications" for the job.

Stephen Watts Kearny commanded the Army of the West which marched from Fort Leavenworth to New Mexico. After capturing Santa Fe, Kearny led a small force on to California.

mountains through which the Americans had to come. A handful of loyal Mexicans of stout heart could have held off Kearny's army there until heat, hunger, and thirst forced their retreat or surrender. But Armijo made no stand, thanks to the persuasions of James W. Magoffin, a Santa Fe trader accompanying Kearny with orders from President Polk.

Magoffin went ahead of the army while it waited at Bent's Fort. Accompanied by twenty men he made his way to Armijo's headquarters. There Magoffin, an old friend of the New Mexican governor, persuaded Armijo that resistance was useless. According to rumor the persuasion was a satchel of gold passed under the table. But one Mexican officer wanted to fight. To him Magoffin held out the promise of governing the area west of the Rio Grande, either deliberately misleading him or not

knowing that Kearny had orders to continue to California and to annex all territory from the Rio Grande to the Pacific. As a result, the American army encountered no resistance when it passed through Apache Canyon on August 17, for Armijo had fled south. Santa Fe fell into American hands the following afternoon without a single shot being fired.

At ceremonies in the capital city of the province on August 19, General Kearny tried to settle all doubts in the minds of the New Mexicans. He guaranteed them freedom of religion, recognition of their land titles, and full rights of American citizenship. Most local officials were left in office once they took the oath of allegiance to the United States. Kearny organized a territorial government with Charles Bent as governor and Preston Blair, Jr as attorney general. Once the principal chiefs of the leading

Left: a group of men eagerly gather round to learn the latest news from the battle front. Although some critics loudly opposed "Jimmy Polk's war," the majority of Americans supported the nation's involvement. The broadside at right calls in rousing language for New Hampshire recruits to join the American fighting force in Mexico. The conflict was most popular in Texas and the Mississippi Valley. These districts contributed almost 50,000 volunteers, the original thirteen states only a quarter that number. Far right: This earlier poster spelled out extracts from the terms of service. Cavalry volunteers were to receive a clothing allowance of $3.50 a month.

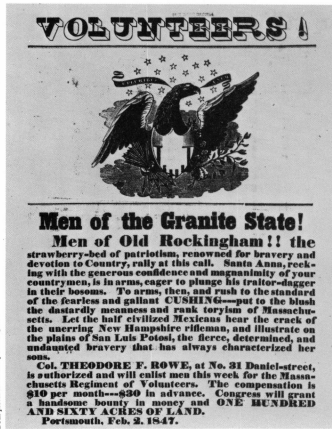

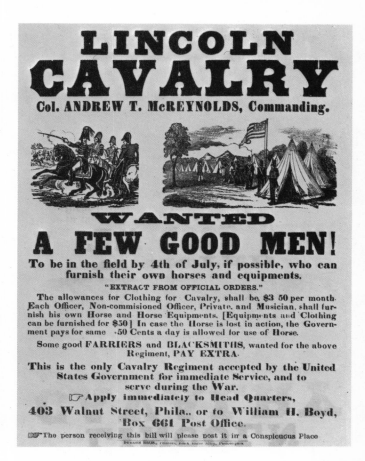

pueblos came to Santa Fe and took the oath of allegiance to the United States, Kearny finalized his future plans.

He divided his army into sections. Part would remain in New Mexico as an army of occupation under the command of Colonel Sterling Price. A second portion, the Missouri Mounted Volunteers, went south under Colonel Alexander W. Doniphan. They were to meet briefly with the Navajos to draft a peace treaty, then proceed south down the Rio Grande to El Paso, cross the desert to Chihuahua City, and then move eastward to link up with Taylor in northern Mexico. This Doniphan did, winning the Battle of El Brazito just north of El Paso and the Battle of Sacramento near Chihuahua City. He finally linked with Taylor's command on May 21. In all, the Missouri Mounted Volunteers marched 6,000 miles, won two major battles against superior forces, promoted commerce with the United States in Chihuahua, and inflicted heavy casualties on the Mexicans. All this was achieved without government uniforms, supplies, a commissary, or a paymaster. The third part of the Army of the West Kearny led personally to California.

Some elements of Kearny's army had more excitement than they wanted. Philip St George Cooke, breveted a lieutenant colonel, led the Mormon Battalion from Santa Fe to San Diego between October 1846 and January 1847. In his final report of January 29, 1847, he said: "March

ing half-naked and half-fed, and living upon wild animals, we have discovered and made a road of great value to our country." Colonel Sterling Price, left behind in New Mexico with an army of occupation, had to fight Mexican patriots who rose in rebellion at Taos. Price gathered an army of 500, marched north in the face of wintry cold, and defeated the rebels at La Cañada on January 24 and again five days later. Then his troops scaled the walls of Taos Pueblo, captured the insurgents, and hanged fifteen of the ringleaders after a makeshift trial. The victory at Taos marked the close of fighting in the southwest.

Winfield Scott Takes Mexico City

While the army was winning victories in the southwest, the United States Navy was active off the coast of California and northwestern Mexico. Most of the major ports of Baja California and Sonora, including the important cities of La Paz and Guaymas, were captured by elements of the Pacific Squadron, and these were held until May 1848. The navy used the Mexican customs revenue to pay the expenses of its exploits. And in the Gulf of Mexico the Home Squadron was performing equally well, enforcing a total blockade of the east coast of Mexico and capturing

Winfield Scott (below) was general in chief of the US Army when President Polk chose him to lead the invasion of central Mexico. His 1847 successes enhanced an already impressive military reputation. Scott's first encounter with the Mexicans came at Veracruz in March. He laid siege to the city and after a two-day bombardment (left) the Mexicans surrendered (above).

the ports of Tampico and Antón Lizardo (near Veracruz). These activities made possible the invasion by General Winfield Scott.

He was chosen to lead the invasion of central Mexico by President Polk who feared the growing popularity of Zachary Taylor. For a time the president toyed with the idea of appointing Democratic Senator Thomas Hart Benton. But his better judgment prevailed and he appointed Scott, although he, like Taylor, also was a Whig.

Scott was picked because he was easily the greatest American military mind of his age. Born in Virginia in 1786, he was admitted to the bar in 1806 but two years later accepted a commission as a captain in the army. The War of 1812 saw him first display his genius. He rose to brevet major general, was voted the thanks of Congress and a gold medal, and was offered (but declined) the post of secretary of war in the Madison administration. After the war ended, he studied military tactics, conducted military institutes for his officers, and worked to professionalize the army. He led troops against the Seminoles in Florida, but he was a great peacemaker at the same time. He negotiated settlements with the British in 1837 to bring peace to the Niagara region, persuaded the Cherokees to remove peacefully to the Indian Territory in 1838,

and in 1839 brought about peace over the disputed boundary between Maine and New Brunswick. For these services he was named general in chief of the army in 1841, a position he held for the next twenty years.

The orders given to him by the president on November 18, 1846, were vague: "To repair to Mexico, to take the command of the forces there assembled, and particularly to organize and set on foot an expedition to operate on the Gulf Coast, if, on arriving at the theater of action, you shall deem it practicable." Scott sailed to New Orleans, then moved to Brazos Santiago at the mouth of the Rio Grande. There he assembled a force that eventually would number about 12,000 troops. With these men he embarked aboard a motley fleet of ships to Tampico and then to Antón Lizardo where he prepared to assault Veracruz, a heavily fortified city. His general staff argued for a frontal assault (that would have resulted in heavy loss of life). But Scott chose to send his men ashore in whale boats some three miles downshore from Veracruz. (This landing on March 9, 1847, was America's first amphibious landing.) The Mexicans, when confronted with an American army coming toward Veracruz from the landward side where there were few fortifications, chose to surrender after a few days' bombardment. Scott's

Cerro Gordo and Chapultepec were two of the battles fought by the Americans on their march toward Mexico City. At hilly Cerro Gordo (left) the Americans encircled the Mexicans. The engraving below depicts Santa Anna and one of his officers scurrying from the encounter. Above: The Americans scale the walls of Chapultepec castle which guarded the entrance to Mexico City.

brilliant victory had cost him nineteen killed and sixty-three wounded.

Leaving a token force behind to hold the city, Scott moved inland with 8,500 men to meet General Santa Anna and the Mexican army entrenched on the heights of Cerro Gordo, a narrow defile guarding the road to Mexico City. Again Scott's general staff advised a frontal assault, but again he outflanked the Mexicans. Captain Robert E. Lee and Lieutenant George H. Derby scouted trails that enabled the Americans to encircle the Mexicans, and American artillery produced panicky flight even among seasoned Mexican troops. Further victories followed until Scott stood at the walls of Mexico City by August 1847. He received scant support from Washington as he fought his way inland. President Polk gave almost no help other than to send Captain Jack Hays and a detachment of Texas Rangers to Veracruz with orders to keep Scott's inland supply road open. The Texans took few prisoners, shot quickly, and fought so ruthlessly that soon Mexicans were crying *"Los Diablos Tejanos"* ("The Devil Texans") at their appearance. They fought Mexican irregulars and bandits and kept Scott's route to the sea open.

Despite the meager help from Washington, Scott continued inland, supplying his army by buying goods from

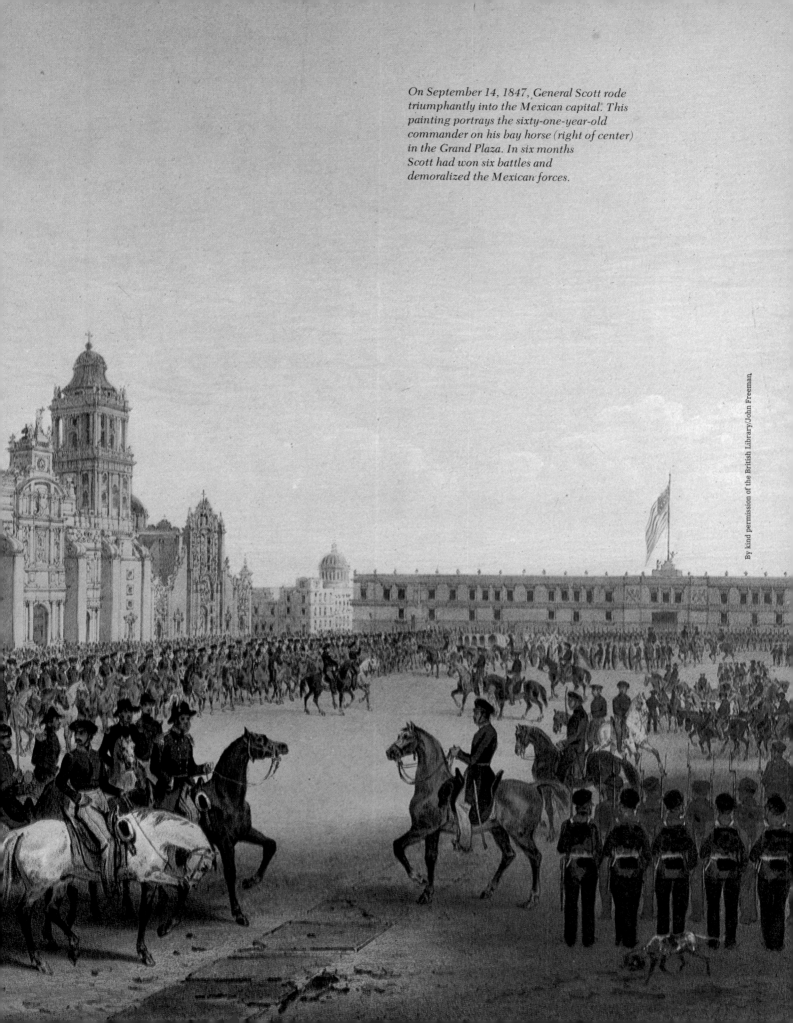

On September 14, 1847, General Scott rode triumphantly into the Mexican capital. This painting portrays the sixty-one-year-old commander on his bay horse (right of center) in the Grand Plaza. In six months Scott had won six battles and demoralized the Mexican forces.

friendly Mexican merchants. Without this aid, he would have been forced to surrender. But increasingly the Mexicans chose to do business with Scott, even to aid the Americans, because of their dislike of the mismanagement, the exactions, and the forced loans of Santa Anna and his government. They preferred an occupation by Scott and his troops to that of their own government. Scott treated them fairly, taxed them equitably, and kept his soldiers from looting.

The battle for Mexico City began on August 20 with fighting at Contreras, followed by an engagement at Churubusco. Both ended in American victories. Scott then granted a Mexican request for an armistice in order to negotiate. The Mexicans interpreted this as an act of

This publication was one of many accounts published after the war. The illustration refers to an incident at Fort Texas (later Fort Brown) which the Mexicans bombarded in April 1846.

weakness and used the time to reinforce their positions. No peaceful settlement could be reached, however, and fighting resumed on September 8 at Molino del Rey and Chapultepec. The Americans won both encounters. This time Scott did not hesitate. He hurried his troops across the causeway and into Mexico City itself. Santa Anna tried desperately to rally his men one last time. When he could not, he abandoned the city. On the morning of September 14 Scott rode into the central plaza of Mexico City to see his men raise the Stars and Stripes. In far-off London one of Britain's greatest generals, the Duke of Wellington, who had been following the campaign avidly, declared that Scott's feat in Mexico was "unsurpassed in military annals." He urged his junior officers to study this march to victory, referring to Scott as "the greatest living soldier."

Once headquartered at the *palacio nacional*, Scott set his troops to ending the banditry that plagued the countryside and many towns. So effective was he that a delegation of leading Mexican citizens asked him to become dictator of Mexico. He refused. Unfortunately for Scott, however, his own country was not grateful—at least not its leaders. The Polk administration did not want another military hero from the Whig party. When petty charges were filed against Scott by quarrelsome generals on his staff, the administration chose to accept them. "Old Fuss and Feathers" (as the troops referred to the six-foot-four-inch, 250-pound Scott) was forced to submit to a court of inquiry. But Polk realized that he could not discredit him and withdrew the charges, especially after Congress had again voted Scott its thanks and yet another of its gold medals.

Disruptive Effects of the War

Paredes and his Centralist advisers were disillusioned to discover that their dreams of British support and French aid were nothing but delusions. Then, following Taylor's victories, they were even more alarmed by the threat of several north Mexican states to secede. Some cities sent representatives to Taylor seeking support. But he refused for he was authorized only to give them protection during the war. Had the United States guaranteed the independence of this incipient "Republic of the Rio Grande," the history of the war would have been far different. The state of Yucatán did rebel against the Centralist government. It had done so in 1839 and had maintained its independence since that time. Thus at the outbreak of the war Mexico was faced with a hostile government to its south. However, in November 1846 the Mexican government offered such concessions that Yucatán voted to rejoin the republic. Thereupon American naval forces occupied several key ports, a rebellion broke out, and in

January 1847 these victorious insurgents sent an emissary to Washington asking for recognition of Yucatán's neutrality. There even was talk of annexation, but Secretary of State Buchanan refused.

The Mexican government was thrown into virtual chaos by the war. Revolution followed revolution with such frequency that most Mexican states cut off all aid and refused all requests for help. Seventeen times the presidency changed hands until Centralists and Federalists finally gave way to the dictatorship of Santa Anna. After the final American victory at Mexico City, Santa Anna retreated to Guadalupe Hidalgo—only to resign on September 22 when he saw all support melt away. Manuel de la Peña y Peña, the reasonable and moderate chief justice, assumed the presidency. Establishing himself first at Toluca outside Mexico City, he moved his capital to Querétaro in October. But on November 11 Congress named Pedro María Anaya acting president. Peña y Peña became foreign minister. At last a government of sorts had come into existence, one capable of negotiating a peace settlement with the United States.

The United States suffered no such political chaos, but there was significant opposition to the war—and political maneuvering within both parties to gain from the conflict. At first the opposition came mainly from abolitionists and, strangely, from southerners. Abolitionists thought it was being fought to add slave territory to the Union. Southerners, such as Calhoun, feared that additional territory might bring about intensified sectional rivalries. For the majority of Americans, however, the war was popular. In North and South, volunteers rushed to the colors. A public demonstration at city hall in New York City was attended by 50,000 enthusiastic supporters. Many members of the Catholic clergy saw the conflict as a means of adding Mexican Catholics to their fold, while many Protestant ministers wanted to annex Mexican territory as a means of converting Papists.

Yet as the war progressed, the Whigs, who had opposed it from the start and who continued to hate it, saw the conflict as a means to political power. Both Taylor and Scott were members of their party, and both had backers pushing their nomination for the presidency. The Whig party had tasted victory only once and that only briefly when William Henry Harrison had been elected in 1840. But he died less than a month later and was succeeded by John Tyler, a Democrat in everything but name. Whigs therefore began referring to the conflict as "Jimmy Polk's War," but were happy to rally behind Taylor.

Abolitionists never lost their zest for opposing the war. In this, at least, they were constant. And they found their hero in David Wilmot. In August 1846 this Pennsylvania Democrat introduced an amendment to a war appropriation bill. Called the Wilmot Proviso, it provided that no form of involuntary servitude, specifically slavery, should ever exist in any territory acquired as a result of the war.

The proviso indicated that even opponents of the conflict expected that territory would be annexed, and it polarized Congress into two camps. (It also forced Wilmot from the Democratic party; later he would be a founder of the Republican party.) The measure did not win approval, but it did provoke explosive and bitter debate, and it delayed a much-needed war appropriation for six months. Moreover, it was introduced again and again. Lincoln later stated that he believed he had voted for it at least forty times. The Wilmot Proviso never passed, but it did heat up the sectional controversy—and in the off-year election of 1846 the Whigs won control of the House.

Certain religious denominations—Quakers, Unitarians, and Congregationalists—also offered opposition to the war. New England Congregationalists did so on moral and antislavery grounds, while Unitarians and Quakers hated all war. On the other hand, a Presbyterian newspaper summed up a common Protestant prowar attitude: God "had his own purpose to accomplish upon the wicked treacherous and idolatrous people of Mexico and He is making the United States . . . the rod of his anger."

Opposition was never widespread, but it was vocal. Yet the Whigs had their eyes so firmly fixed on the presidency in 1848 that they never brought all this dissent together to halt the conflict. About all they did was to vex President Polk. They repeatedly held up appropriation bills and slowed the passage of acts to raise money for the treasury. But by mid-1847 a surprising prosperity existed in the United States. In addition, Scott's army was collecting the customs in Mexico, as was the navy on the west coast, thereby helping to finance hostilities. Thus the war was fought for fewer dollars than originally predicted.

Negotiating Peace Terms

Despite what the Whigs thought of the president, Polk eagerly sought a means to peace. He did this in part because the antiwar forces were so outspoken. But he did it also because he personally—from religious conviction—was against the war. In addition the conflict was strengthening the Whig party and creating military heroes who might aspire to the presidency. As a firm believer in civil supremacy over the military, the president wanted no generals sweeping into power. His first effort at peace came in May 1846 when he discussed with Bishop John Hughes of New York the possibility of Hughes influencing the Catholic hierarchy in Mexico to open peace talks. Next Polk sought British mediation. But that was spurned by the Paredes government. And in July 1846 Secretary of State Buchanan sent dispatches to Mexico suggesting negotiations for peace which would ignore the causes of the war. They were rejected. Finally the president gave Moses Yale Beach authority to negotiate at any suitable moment. Editor of the New York *Sun* and a prominent Catholic layman, Beach was in Mexico during much of the war on British passports, but eventually had to flee for his life.

Polk eventually got his peace treaty through the efforts of Nicholas P. Trist, chief clerk of the State Department. With an eye on the election of 1848, Polk chose Trist as his commissioner to Mexico because he was unlikely to make political capital out of the mission. Born in Virginia in 1800, proficient in Spanish, married into the Jefferson family, and a staunch Democrat, Trist seemed ideal from every standpoint. On April 15, 1847, he was given his instructions. He was authorized to offer up to $30 million if Mexico would cede Upper and Lower California and New Mexico, along with the right of transit across the Isthmus of Tehuántepec. He could offer less for a smaller amount of territory, but as an absolute minimum he was to get Upper California and New Mexico. Even as Trist slipped out of the country, news of his mission leaked to the newspapers. This news was so detailed that only someone high in the government could have done it. The suspicion lingers that Trist himself was the culprit, for he was a man of vanity.

After arriving at Veracruz on May 6, 1847, Trist immediately fell to quarreling with General Scott. Soon both were bombarding each other and Washington with indignant letters. But by the end of July the two had become fast friends. Following the victory at Churubusco on August 20, they agreed to an armistice to allow negotiations to begin. This truce, arranged through the mediation of the British and Spanish ambassadors, proved disastrous. Trist opened negotiations with Mexican commissioners who had no instructions from their government and who were inferior to him in diplomatic rank. The Mexicans arrogantly stated that no peace could be considered until the American army withdrew from Mexico and the United States paid an indemnification for the entire cost of the war. Trist continued to negotiate, but in the end neither side would accept the result. "Mr. Trist has managed the negotiations very bunglingly," said Polk, and on October 6 he issued orders recalling the State Department clerk. The order was repeated on October 21.

In the United States the attitude toward peace was changing. Polk had decided that before new negotiations could begin, Mexico must sue for peace. Moreover, he was leaning toward the "all-of-Mexico" movement that was growing rapidly. This view had been expressed at the outbreak of the war only by a few expansionists. Nothing came of it until Moses Beach published an editorial in the New York *Sun* in May 1847 arguing that Mexican lands would never support slavery and that the Wilmot Proviso was thus unnecessary. Beach asserted that "Mexico will be occupied and eventually annexed." By September many northerners had convinced them-

selves that Mexico indeed would not support slavery, and they began to think in terms of annexation. Northern ministers liked the idea, for it would bring an opportunity to convert Papists to Protestantism. Businessmen saw new markets opening, while those intellectuals who disliked Europe argued that annexation was necessary to prevent Mexico from falling into the hands of a European power. "Penny press" newspapers called loudly for annexation. Patriots said that Mexican silver could be used to "pay every expense of the war." Those who dreamed of a canal linking the Atlantic and Pacific saw the Isthmus of Tehuántepec as a feasible route and urged American acquisition.

Representatives of the midwestern states joined the all-Mexico movement. Senators Lewis Cass and Stephen A. Douglas were active supporters. Illinois was the only state to have both its senators vote against the eventual treaty ending the war, on the grounds that it did not annex sufficient Mexican territory. By the fall of 1847 even Polk was openly flirting with the idea. Only among diehard New England abolitionists and, curiously, southerners was there strong opposition to the movement. John Calhoun and his cohorts saw the entry of states from such territory as non-slave and thus a threat to the South. Moreover, they considered the Mexican population inferior and did not want them in the Union.

The all-Mexico movement hardened the stance of the Polk administration and made it less enthusiastic to secure peace at any price. However, Nicholas Trist frustrated the scheme by negotiating a settlement. He did so without authority and contrary to his recall order. But in the process he saved Mexico as a republic. Even as Polk and others were warming to the all-Mexico concept, a firm government was emerging with Pedro María Anaya's appointment as president in November. He at once informed Trist that peace commissioners would be named shortly. But on November 16 Trist received Polk's recall order. He was thus faced with a dilemma. He could negotiate a treaty although he had no authority to do so, or he could go home—in which case the war might continue indefinitely, for if the Mexican government did not secure peace there surely would be uprisings, revolution, and anarchy. Trist reached his decision on December 4. He would negotiate. To his wife he wrote: "I will make a treaty, if it can be done on the basis of up the Bravo [Rio Grande] and across by the 32°. . . ." Two days later he sent a sixty-one-page letter to Secretary of State Buchanan stating his intentions, haughtily concluding that neither Buchanan nor Polk knew "what was going on in Mexico."

Sixty days of negotiations followed in which Trist secured most of what Polk wanted: Upper California, New Mexico, the Rio Grande as the boundary of Texas, and the right of American citizens to cross the Isthmus of Tehuántepec. But he did not get an outlet on the Gulf of

California. He agreed to pay Mexico $15 million for the ceded territory, along with American assumption of the Mexican claims owed American citizens in return for recognition of the Rio Grande as the boundary of Texas.

The Legacy of the War

This, the Treaty of Guadalupe Hidalgo, was signed on February 2, 1848. It arrived in Washington on February 19 and caused a sensation. It was an agreement between a discredited clerk and a government of little influence and questionable legality. With surprising logic, Polk ignored the question of Trist's legal status and sent the treaty to the Senate, for it gave the United States what the president wanted. On March 10 the Senate ratified the document by a vote of 38 to 14. One week later in Mexico, Trist was arrested and escorted out of the country, but he was never put on trial. He lost his job in the State Department and went into private law practice. When this proved unsuccessful, he became a railway paymaster. Not until 1871 did the government pay him $14,599 for back pay and expenses in connection with his treaty mission. Despite his suffering, he had negotiated a treaty that had remade the map of North America and changed the destinies of thousands of people.

An exchange of ratifications of this treaty took place on May 30 at Querétaro, and soon the American army began withdrawing from Mexico. President Polk proclaimed the treaty in effect on July 4, 1848. At last the war had ended, the costliest conflict in American history in terms of deaths per thousand of participants. Of 100,182 soldiers, sailors, and marines who took part in the Mexican War, 1,548 were killed in action and 10,970 died from disease and exposure.

What then did the war between the United States and Mexico accomplish? For Mexico it meant a reduction in national territory of about one-half. And it did not produce a stable constitutional government. Within five years Antonio López de Santa Anna again would be president and dictator through revolution. Thousands more would die, millions of pesos would be spent, foreign aggressors battled, and tyranny endured before liberty, equality, and justice were achieved.

For the United States the peace treaty settled the Texas question, the claims were paid (albeit by the American taxpayer), and the possibility of British annexation of California was ended. Moreover, a vast amount of territory had been added to the Union, and from it would come mineral riches in the next three decades to finance the industrial revolution. (Even today a majority of American oil, sulphur, copper, and several other minerals come from Texas, the Mexican Cession, and the 1854 Gadsden Purchase areas.)

Library of Congress

Nicholas P. Trist handled the peace negotiations with Mexico. Despite Polk's disapproval of his methods, and ignoring recall orders, Trist went ahead and successfully completed the task.

But the war was not an undivided blessing. Because of the territory added, the country suffered renewed political bitterness over the issue of slavery in the territories which culminated in the most bloody and tragic of all conflicts, the Civil War. The Mexican War trained most of the leaders of that future conflict, giving them combat and leadership experience that would prolong the war between brothers. Even today, the American mind appears burdened by a lingering sense of guilt over the war with Mexico. And just as there is controversy about the causes of the war, so also might there be doubts over who was the real victor.

Chapter 5

THE MORMON TREK TO UTAH

The murder of Joseph Smith and continued harassment by non-Mormons in Nauvoo brought the fortunes of the Mormon church to rock bottom. The survival and growth of the religion, its leaders realized, would depend on establishing a remote settlement far removed from outside interference. An exploratory party decided that Salt Lake Valley, desolate and forbidding, would suit their purpose well. Then the great trek west began. From abroad, too, thousands upon thousands of converts came to join the gathering in the valley. The early years were difficult, but by the 1860s the Mormons had laid the foundations for a movement that, one day, would span the world.

"This is the Place"

In February 1846 the Mississippi was icebound from its eastern bank in Illinois to its western bank in Iowa. As he viewed the scene Brigham Young, the Mormon leader, must have been grateful that nature had provided an auspicious beginning for his followers' trek to the West.

Intense anti-Mormon feeling had led to the murder two years earlier of Joseph Smith, founder of the movement. And continued persecution now made them tear up recently established roots in Illinois and seek a new place to settle. Bearing the first of more than 16,000 Saints (as the Mormons called themselves), the wagons creaked down the banks of the river and moved onto the broad expanse of firm ice. The fate of thousands would depend upon the wisdom and courage of Young's leadership. The Saints had begun their great migration to the Far West.

In the fall of 1838 the Mormons had been driven from Missouri, their leaders jailed, and much of their property confiscated by mobs of angry settlers. They crossed the Missouri River to Illinois, acquired a large tract of land

Right: Joseph Smith, the founder of the Mormon church. His murder in 1844 convinced church leaders of the need to shift from Nauvoo and find a new home. Below: The Mormon temple at Nauvoo.

around the village of Commerce, and established a city called Nauvoo (The Beautiful). They built a large temple and university, and opened shops and factories. The arrival of several thousand English converts contributed greatly to the growth of the city. As in Missouri, however, their cohesiveness in political affairs, their strong penchant for settling their own problems outside regular legal processes, and their continual growth caused fear and resentment. Mobs began to pillage and burn Mormon homes and attack individual members in 1843. The following year Joseph Smith was killed by a mob while he was being held in a Carthage jail. For several months he had been planning a migration to a large territory of land where the Mormons could have sovereignty and autonomy. He had sent envoys to Texas, had made feelers to Britain over settling Vancouver Island, and had made overtures to the United States for Oregon or California.

Brigham Young further developed these plans. Eventually the Mormons made preparations to leave Nauvoo in the summer or fall of 1845 for a secret destination. Other settlers kept pressing them to leave. Finally, fearful of a protracted fight with local mobs, the Mormons began to abandon the city on February 4. By the summer of 1846, all but a small group had left.

In heading west, seeking a new life in a region known to them only by a mark upon a worn map, the Mormons found themselves in a similar situation to the thousands of European immigrants who had been settling the vast reaches of the continent since the early seventeenth century. Young and other leaders had decided that their new home would be in the arid basin bounded by the Rocky Mountains on the east and the Cascade Range and the Sierra Nevada on the west. The brackish and mineral-laden Great Salt Lake was its most distinctive feature. Something of the reputation of the area is suggested in lines of an old trail song, "Sweet Betsy from Pike," in which a hapless emigrant party

> . . . came to the desert and salt water lakes,
> The ground it was teemin' varmits and snakes,
> Beset by wild Indians Comanche and Sioux,
> 'Tis a glorious tale how they ever got through!

This dismal reputation of the Great Basin region appealed to the Mormons. Once there, they would be content to let other emigrants pass through en route to fruitful coastal areas, leaving them free to build their own religious, economic, and social order with a minimum of outside interference. Though they planned to settle in Mexican territory, it was likely that the region would one day become part of the United States.

From the first the Mormon church attracted controversy, and as it grew in strength, friction led to violence. These two Mormon illustrations portray (at top) the persecution and expulsion from Nauvoo, and (below) the organized exodus from the city.

If the Mormons had a general knowledge of the problems they would encounter in building a settlement amidst deserts and mountains, they could hardly have known what that effort would cost in terms of human labor and sacrifice. Before crops could be harvested, dams and canals would be needed to bring mountain water to the dry valley lands. It would be necessary to build sawmills before permanent homes and other buildings could be erected. Some means of acquiring an independent supply of essential commodities such as sugar, iron, cotton cloth, and glass must be devised. Such supplies could be brought from the East only by oxcart and at great cost. In the spring and summer of 1846, the rolling grasslands of Iowa afforded little in the way of experience to help the Mormons fully understand the magnitude of the task awaiting them in the Great Basin.

The Mormon Exodus

Nine miles into Iowa the "Camp of Israel," as the emigrants called their assemblage, stopped to organize themselves for the first leg of their journey. Following a pattern initiated by Smith, Brigham Young organized the families into groups of 100. These were further divided into companies of fifty and then of ten, each division headed by a captain appointed by church leaders. Other officers, including commissary agents, historians, clerks, and guards of the camp were appointed as needed. All wagons and teams were inspected by a camp committee. Families were urged to make up their loads with an eye to the needs of a colonizing expedition. Fruit trees, seeds, plows, and farm implements were to be transported wherever possible. Rules were established governing the rising hour, 5:00 AM, prayers, treatment of animals, punishment for moral offenses, and other matters.

Thus organized, the companies set out. They formed first a trickle and then a stream of wagons stretching nearly 300 miles across southern Iowa to a settlement called Kanesville (later Council Bluffs). Advance parties moved out ahead of the main camp to set up temporary communities as resting places for those to follow. At the principal camps, Garden Grove and Mount Pisgah, hundreds of acres were plowed, planted, and fenced. These were to be harvested by later companies. Houses and bridges were built and wells dug. At each location a fully organized station was established to service and equip the trains of wagons moving westward across the state.

As the emigrants reached the Missouri River in the summer and fall of 1846, they were settled into communities already laid out in the typical Mormon grid pattern. Some were temporarily settled in Council Bluffs, on the east bank of the Missouri. Others were settled in Winter

Quarters (now called Florence, a suburb of Omaha, Nebraska) where provision was made for the welfare of 3,200 families. During the fall and winter the community built wagons and made other preparations for the final leg of their journey. When they moved west of the river they would enter unsettled territory, pushing and hauling their possessions over a lonely, formidable terrain. Their trek would take them 500 miles across flat and treeless Indian territories (now Nebraska), up into the desolate rugged Rocky Mountain plateaus of the present Wyoming, over South Pass, and finally down through narrow mountain canyons to the valley of the Great Salt Lake. Across the thousand-mile route there would be but two major stopping places—Fort Kearny in Nebraska and Fort Bridger in southern Wyoming. They would break their own trail over much of the route to minimize contact with infectious diseases. Compared with the crossing of Iowa, this final push westward would tax their skills and resources to the limit. Before the railroad put a final end to wagon emigration in the late 1860s, the long trail from Council Bluffs to Salt Lake City would be dotted with the graves of the unfortunate and ill prepared.

Left: Brigham Young, who became leader of the church after Smith's death and organized the westward trek. Below: Winter Quarters, Nebraska, was a temporary Mormon home after the departure from Nauvoo.

Brigham Young himself led out with a pioneer company of 148 in April 1847. The journey was accomplished with relatively little difficulty. Herds of bison and occasional catches of fish provided fresh food for the emigrants. The burning of grasses needed for grazing and the occasional theft of horses and draft animals was kept to a minimum by offering gifts to the various Indian tribes encountered. An illness of unknown origin hit many of the company. It caused, at times, shortages of hands needed to wrestle the obstinate beasts and wagons across streams and through ravines and canyons. Young himself became ill with mountain fever as the party neared Salt Lake. So an associate led a scouting group into the valley to prepare for the arrival of the company.

On July 23 Young's wagon rounded a promontory from which a splendid view of the broad valley and the lake could be gained. Here and there small clumps of cottonwood trees crowded the banks of small streams. Sunflowers and lush grasses dotted the more fruitful meadows. But sagebrush, salt flats, and alkali deserts dominated the scene. As he looked out across the drab, lonely landscape, Young is reported to have stated simply: "It is enough. This is the right place. Drive on!"

Entering the valley the next morning, the party began preparations for the arrival of a much larger company which had set out from Iowa in July. This company reached the new settlement in September and October, bringing the numbers to nearly 1,700. The optimism engendered by the timely freezing of the Mississippi in February 1846 seemed justified in the fall of 1847. An epic journey had been completed with remarkably little loss of life. Though the first winter in Salt Lake Valley would bring its share of troubles, a home for thousands of future emigrants had been established. Brigham Young's first great challenge had been successfully accomplished. He now faced the equally demanding task of planning and supervising the taming of the wilderness into which he had brought his people.

Founding the Settlement

It must have taken considerable vision in 1847 to imagine that Salt Lake Valley possessed sufficient resources to provide a livelihood for the many thousands of Mormons still waiting in the Midwest. Timber and game were scarce. There was an abundance of large black crickets and a considerable number of rattlesnakes. Ninety-five per cent of the region was either desert or mountainous. Not least, the low annual rainfall—from eight to fifteen inches—presented a special challenge. But mountain streams held an adequate supply of potential irrigating water and ample grazing land existed. Spring grasses grew well in the valleys. But the region was isolated. To those used to more heavily settled regions a feeling of "empty immensity" prevailed. It was likely that the land would be "coveted by no other people."

The first weeks in the valley continued the pattern of cooperative work and central planning established during the exodus—a pattern destined to characterize Mormon colonizing activity throughout the region. The Saints divided into committees for work. Some set about laying out a city of 135 ten-acre blocks, each of which was further divided into eight home lots apportioned by lottery. Others sought timber, began the building of a fort and log cabins, and planted and irrigated a plot of thirty-five acres of land. Sermons preached in the Bowery —a roofed-over, open-sided meeting place—encouraged selflessness and commitment to a common cause. Within a few days most of the community were rebaptized in a solemn renewal of covenants and a sacred rededication.

On August 26, 1847, Young, Heber C. Kimball, and a majority of the top-ranking church leaders, known as the Council of the Twelve, left with most of the men to return to Winter Quarters and direct preparations for the migration of the bulk of the 16,000 members still located there. By October, the main body of the 1847 emigrants arrived in the valley. The first "stake" (an ecclesiastical division comprising several congregations) was organized with "Father John Smith," uncle of Joseph Smith, as president. The three-member Salt Lake Stake presidency and their twelve-member high council constituted "the municipal council" blending church and secular authority. Regulations controlling the use of wood, prices, and a voluntary rationing system were adopted.

Despite these measures a food shortage developed by spring. It arose from the large numbers permitted to join the second contingent from Winter Quarters, combined with frosts which damaged much of the winter wheat. In late spring, hordes of crickets—"Black Philistines"—descended, threatening to destroy what crops remained. The situation deteriorated rapidly. It was thought that some Mormons were considering leaving the valley. Almost simultaneously, however, seagulls appeared and devoured the crickets. Nevertheless, drought, mismanagement, and frost destroyed large amounts of potential food in the fields. But the settlers, with their strict rationing policies, were able to survive until summer brought new food sources.

While wintering in Kanesville, Brigham Young initiated two important moves. The Council of Twelve issued a General Epistle reaffirming the loyalty of the Saints to the United States and, more significantly, urging all who were abroad to join "the gathering." And the First Presidency of the Church was reorganized with Young as president, Kimball as first councillor, and Willard Richards as second councillor. About 2,400 Saints accompanied the new governing body to Salt Lake Valley, arriving in September 1848.

When Brigham Young sighted Salt Lake Valley he knew it would suit the Mormons' purpose. Right: Young's party on the shores of Great Salt Lake. The lake (below) covers an area of 940 square miles. When the Mormons arrived there it had been known to white Americans for less than five years.

Barnaby's. Inset: The Bettmann Archive

It was essential to a successful colonizing venture that institutions of government should be quickly established. Early government in the valley was basically theocratic. Membership of the First Presidency and the Council of Twelve, the Salt Lake High Council, and the Council of Fifty largely overlapped. The latter body was composed of "leading citizens" who would discuss and agree upon policies and procedures and then carry them out.

These civic and ecclesiastical bodies issued and administered policy and regulations. They exercised a degree of central planning and control of social and economic affairs that was unusual in America. Their regulations were designed to control the use of natural resources, the distribution of land, the construction of public works, and to prevent hunger. The main principles underlying each followed a similar pattern. Natural resources, whether water, timber, or minerals, were subject to public rather than private ownership. Land was distributed on the basis of equality—"equal according to circumstances, wants and needs"—and productive use. Land holdings were invariably small, permitting fair distribution of both land and water, cooperative fencing, and social compactness. Public works, whether buildings, canals, roads, or bridges, were erected primarily by informal cooperation. The large influx of immigrants, combined with a poor harvest and severe winter in 1848–49, resulted in much hunger. Community leaders therefore introduced voluntary rationing and a community storehouse whereby any surpluses were distributed to the poor. The pattern thus involved considerable planning and central direction, sharing burdens, and combining efforts.

The discovery of gold in California in the summer of 1848 and the subsequent rush overland greatly complicated the pattern of development in Salt Lake Valley, bringing both benefits and problems. The great majority of Mormons, on the advice of church leaders, chose not to search actively for gold. Members of the Mormon Battalion, which had left Winter Quarters in 1846 to participate in the Mexican War, were mustered out of military service in California in the summer of 1847. Some were working in the Sacramento Valley when the initial discovery of gold was made there. The way was open for Mormons to exploit their geographical proximity and acquire a large share of the resulting wealth. But Young responded firmly: "We are gathered here not to scatter around and go off to the mines, or any other place, but to build up the Kingdom of God."

However, some members of the Mormon Battalion took advantage of the opportunity to prospect for the church in a "gold mission," which ultimately proved of no consequence. Mormon earnings in California during 1848–51 contributed almost $60,000 to the church. It is likely that at least a comparable amount reached Salt Lake Valley on private account.

Much more important was the impact of the great migration of gold seekers. In 1849 and 1850 an estimated 30,000 passed through the valley. This influx led to inflated prices for the scarce commodities desired by prospectors—horses, mules, flour, and vegetables—and to lower prices for less-essential goods. Not only did trading exchanges benefit the Mormons, but servicing the gold seekers provided employment for blacksmiths, teamsters, millers, and others. An additional source of revenue came

Miracle of the Seagulls, a Mormon painting which depicts the occasion in 1847 when the timely appearance of seagulls saved the meager crops from being devoured by hordes of crickets.

from wintering emigrants stranded in the valley late in the year. Finally, the Saints profited from the windfall of goods abandoned by prospectors along the westward route. As a result the Mormons could now undertake ambitious immigration, colonization, and missionary efforts.

A Massive Program of Immigration

At the time of the gold-rush windfall 10,000 Mormons remained in the Missouri Valley and 30,000 new converts professed the faith in England. Gathering new converts continued unabated. But Mormon planning was complicated by the fact that they saw themselves building a spiritual as well as a secular kingdom. It would not be possible to slow immigration, for example, if readily arable lands became overcrowded. For the conversion of new members was little affected by the ability of the Salt Lake Saints to provide for them. Even while thousands of Mormons waited to move west, able-bodied men were called from the pressing tasks of building a settlement to go to Europe on proselytizing missions. Their remarkable successes added to the problem of transporting new settlers to Salt Lake.

The initial attempt to resolve this problem led to the establishment of a Perpetual Emigrating Fund in 1849. The fund was "to promote, facilitate, and accomplish the Emigration of the Poor." It was designed to maintain itself since those who received assistance were to reimburse it at a later date. In 1851 and 1852 the Perpetual Emi-

grating Company assisted some 12,500 from Missouri to Salt Lake Valley. Only a remnant now remained in the Missouri camps.

Subsequent emigration to the Great Basin largely came from abroad. In 1849 missionary work had been opened or expanded in the British Isles, France, Germany, Italy, Switzerland, Scandinavia, Malta, Spain, the South Pacific, and Australia. By 1853 Mormon missionaries had penetrated South America, China, Japan, India, and South Africa. European Protestants, mainly in Britain and Scandinavia, responded most quickly.

Three kinds of "companies," based on the ability to pay, were organized under the Perpetual Emigrating Fund. They were invariably large. Almost without exception an entire vessel was chartered for the ocean passage. The massive immigration program, one of the

Salt Lake City as it appeared in 1853, six years after the first Mormons arrived. The early years were difficult ones, and the steady influx of settlers at times strained the town's resources.

great achievements of the Mormons, provided not only safe and reasonably comfortable passage over great distances—it was supplemented by a scheme which assimilated the emigrants into a new environment.

The drive to bring as many as possible into the faith meant it was not possible to choose recruits with an eye to the skills they might bring to the new community. This was not the case, however, after conversion. It became a primary objective of the immigration effort to provide manpower, skills, and expertise for a self-sufficient economy in the Great Basin. Occupational skills were

second only to "integrity and moral worth" in determining the order of emigration. Missionaries were repeatedly told to seek out members trained in the manufacture of textiles, pottery, and metals and urge them "to emigrate immediately . . . in preference to anyone else." In Great Britain at midcentury, churchmen were instructed to promote the emigration of artisans and skilled workers. Such a policy would provide, through the accelerated growth of the Mormon center, the most rapid means of bringing in all who wanted to come.

On each ship church services were held twice daily, weather permitting. Schools, concerts, and other "productive" activities occupied the hours during the month-long voyage from Britain. Above all, discipline was the hallmark of Mormon emigrant ships. And life on board was characterized by cleanliness, order, and industry. The organization and efficiency of these vessels so impressed novelist Charles Dickens that he devoted a chapter to it in *The Uncommercial Traveller*.

For the average emigrant the long journey from Liverpool to Salt Lake normally took upwards of eight months. Before 1854, emigrant ships from England landed at New Orleans. From there passengers took a steamer up the Mississippi to St Louis and then traveled to Kanesville or

Mormons board an emigrant ship in England (above) and arrive in New Orleans (below). The drive for converts in Europe and their transportation to Utah were two of the Mormons' greatest achievements.

some other outfitting post to prepare for the westward trek. One family of seven from Bath, England, witnessed the death from cholera of the father, mother, and two of five children, before the three orphans were landed at Winter Quarters. The common occurrence of such disasters on the river journey caused the emigrant ships to switch in 1854 to New York and other eastern ports for landing. Passengers then traveled by rail to St Louis and the outfitting centers before beginning the approximately eighty-day journey across the plains to the Salt Lake Valley. As early as 1847 the practice began of sending supply trains from Salt Lake to assist the caravans during the final leg of the journey.

In their effort to provide a practical means of helping the needy make their way west, church leaders recommended in the mid-1850s the building of small carts which could contain the essential provisions of a family and be pulled by hand. The first of these handcart companies left Iowa City in June 1856. Many Saints successfully brought themselves and their meager possessions to Salt Lake in this manner between 1856 and 1859. But others, ill prepared or caught in Wyoming by storms, suffered incredible hardship. For some parties death was an everyday occurrence. The sadness of burial under rocks where the frozen ground would not yield to spade or pick was common.

Once in the valley, immigrants were warmly received. A typical welcoming address to a company of emigrants, delivered by Young, emphasized the values and priorities observed in the settlement:

> With regard to your obtaining habitations to shelter you in the coming winter—all of you will be able to obtain work, and by your industry, you can make yourselves tolerably comfortable in this respect, before the winter sets in. All the improvements that you see around you, have been made in the short space of four years. . . . All this that you now see, has been accomplished by the industry of the people. . . .
>
> Again, with regard to labour—don't imagine unto yourselves that you are going to get rich, at once, by it. As for the poor, there are none here, neither are there any who may be called rich, but all obtain the essential comforts of life.

The primary unit of assimilation was the local church congregation or "ward." Each bishop, the presiding authority in a ward, accepted responsibility for helping to find and generate employment, food, and shelter for newly arrived immigrants. Church officials kept careful records of each immigrant's skill and occupation. Ultimately, most newcomers found work in established communities in the territory or were "called" to colonize a new area.

Contributions by church members provided the major source of revenue for the Perpetual Emigrating Fund. In

This Mormon painting shows handcart pioneers caught by a snowstorm en route to Utah. A large number of church members hauled their possessions overland in the rickety wagons.

theory, those who benefited from the fund were to be the primary source of revenue through their repayments. In practice, though, repayments were few. This was a continuing irritation, and not infrequently tithing revenues were used to keep the fund solvent. Whatever the financial struggle, it succeeded in its task. In the years 1849–55 more than 15,000 immigrants were transported from Europe. By the end of the 1860s over 51,000 Saints had journeyed to Salt Lake Valley. The original settlement of 1,700 persons, huddled in 1847 at the foot of the Wasatch Mountains, was growing into a far-flung empire which would shortly extend from Canada to Mexico and from Wyoming to California.

The need to settle the incoming tide of immigrants, coupled with economic and military considerations, resulted in the formation of satellite colonies throughout the Far West. Like the missionary and immigration efforts, this ambitious program received initial impetus from the gold-rush windfall. The establishment of an inner ring of settlements in the valleys adjacent to Salt Lake Valley was the first stage. The second concentrated on setting up colonies at strategic points—Carson Valley, San Bernardino, Las Vegas, Fort Bridger, and Fort Supply. These formed an outer ring embracing nearly one-sixth of the area of the continental United States. In addition, church leaders began a string of settlements, known as the Mormon Corridor, stretching south from Salt Lake City and designed to reach San Diego and the Pacific Coast. By 1855, twenty-seven communities had been established along the route.

During the first decade in the Great Basin, the Mormons founded about ninety-six communities. By the end of the century, at least 500 had been established. The pattern of colonization was always orderly, systematic, and ecclesiastically directed. The concept of "group steward-ship" prevailed. Not only were water, timber, and metal resources community property, forts, roads to timber lands, and public works of all kinds were constructed on a cooperative basis. Land assignments were drawn by lot, and, as in Salt Lake City, there was no land speculation.

Lithograph of surveyors at work near Salt Lake Valley. Apart from the main township, almost a hundred settlements throughout Utah were established by the Mormons in the first decade.

Economic Progress and Setback

A persistent theme in the economic development of the Mormons was the goal of self-sufficiency. Brigham Young spelled out the concept in his 1852 message to the territorial legislature:

> Produce what you consume; draw from the native element the necessities of life; permit no vitiated taste to lead you into the indulgence of expensive luxuries, which can only be obtained by involving yourself in debt; let home industry produce every article of home consumption.

The arguments supporting the ideal sprang from both theological belief and economic pragmatism. Joseph Smith's counsel that Latter-day Saints should wear only home-produced garments was buttressed by doubt about relying on a world filled with wars and instability. And now the influx of thousands of skilled artisans and mechanics, the overall employment needs, and the expense and drain on scarce cash resources of importing goods from the East combined to provide a reasonable and justifiable case.

During the 1850s the church took an active part in industrial enterprises and economic ventures. The Office

of Public Works rapidly became the largest employer and purchaser in the territory, employing an average of between 200 and 500 men throughout the period. Construction projects including important church buildings comprised the bulk of public works in the early 1850s. Tithing resources also supported numerous ventures to establish infant industries.

No prospective undertaking daunted what has been called the Mormons' "spirit of daring enterprise." Ultimately, sugar, wool, pottery, paper, lead, and iron ventures all failed or stagnated during the 1850s. Mechanical problems, insufficient understanding of chemical processes, and financial difficulties repeatedly beset new projects. So did natural disasters such as bitter winters, long summer droughts, and grasshopper invasions. Smaller enterprises received less attention and effort. Agricultural improvements, in particular, lagged in the competition for scarce resources.

A series of natural disasters from the summer of 1855 threatened to reduce life in the territory to a subsistence level. Hordes of grasshoppers descended on Salt Lake

Right: The Tithing Office, one of the first church buildings erected after the Mormons arrived in Utah. Below: Designed by William Folsom, the Tabernacle was built in the 1860s.

Valley "like snow flakes in a storm." In many places crops were almost entirely destroyed. And a late summer drought added to the distress. The total harvest was estimated to be between one-third and two-thirds the normal size. The bitter winter which followed destroyed the better part of the cattle herds, killing upwards of 80 per cent of the livestock in some areas.

Two important movements followed. In order to help prevent starvation, fast-day offerings were introduced. Each member of the church was requested to abstain from food on the first Thursday of each month. The food saved was to be distributed amongst the needy. Voluntary rationing also operated for a time.

A spiritual reformation movement, only indirectly related, followed in the wake of the disasters. It began in

Designed by Brigham Young and Truman O. Angell, the Mormon Temple at Salt Lake City was a massive construction project. Begun in 1853, it took forty years to complete. Blocks of granite had to be hauled by oxen from a quarry twenty miles away. Right: Quarry workmen are dwarfed by the huge granite slabs. Below: The temple as it looked during construction.

National Archives

Mansell Collection

the autumn of 1856. Church leaders urged, in conferences and meetings throughout the territory, the virtues of unity, cleanliness, selflessness, purity, and renewal of spiritual commitments. Strict observance of the Sabbath, prayerfulness, and the rooting out of moral laxity received special attention. The impetus for the movement was provided by the influx of non-Mormons, the natural disasters which were interpreted by some as a sign of divine displeasure, and accusations of licentiousness.

Friction with Government Officials

Ecclesiastical government prevailed in the Great Basin until the adoption of the constitution of the Provisional State of Deseret in March 1849. There was a broad-based enthusiasm for statehood in the Union, however, and soon Senator Stephen A. Douglas introduced Deseret's petition. Anti-Mormons and former members of the church opposed it. But the decisive issue was the slavery question. The application coincided with the Compromise of 1850 which admitted California as a free state and assigned territorial status to New Mexico and Utah (an Indian name more acceptable to Congress than Deseret).

Their petition for statehood denied, Mormons accepted the creation of the territory. But their own legislative assembly continued to function until the summer of 1851. President Millard Fillmore meanwhile appointed a mixture of resident Mormons and non-Mormon "foreign" appointees to executive and judicial offices in Utah. Young was governor.

The arrival of the federal appointees in the summer of 1851 was soon followed by the first confrontation. In early September a special conference of the church, to which Young invited the newly arrived officials, provided the occasion. Judge Perry Brocchus openly referred to a lack of virtue among Mormon women, drawing a heated reply from Young and other church officials. Friction persisted in a series of letters exchanged by Young and Judge Brocchus culminating in the departure within the month of Judges Brandebury and Brocchus, Secretary Harris, and Henry Day, an Indian agent. The so-called "run-away officials" charged the Mormon leaders with sedition and lawlessness. Secretary of State Daniel Webster ordered the appointees either to return to Utah or resign. All chose to resign. No action was taken against Governor Young or other territorial officials. But the public attention given the incident and the accusations leveled at the Mormon leaders damaged the image of the new territory. Friction between Mormon officialdom and the United States government was to be a recurring theme throughout the remainder of the century.

The attitude and viewpoint of Mormons to federal government combined resentment and loyalty with a strong attachment to local self-government and an abiding commitment to church leadership. This ambivalent attitude resulted from their persecution in Missouri and Illinois. They believed that local matters should be handled locally. This, in part the outgrowth of their largely Puritan New England origins, was strengthened by the mediocre ability of many of the first federal appointees. Several quickly won the praise and admiration of Mormons. But many did not.

A central issue of the 1850s in the United States was whether national supremacy or states rights and sectional interests should be dominant. Assertions of regional autonomy met stiff resistance. Public announcement of the Mormon doctrine of plural marriage provided additional friction at a time when tolerance of unusual practices was low. Not only was polygamy directly opposed to the marriage traditions of the nation—in many minds it was associated with less civilized parts of the world.

When the doctrine was publicly announced in 1852 it was thought that plural marriage would be protected under the first amendment of the Constitution guaranteeing freedom of religion. But Congress interpreted these rights quite differently and from 1862 passed a series of antibigamy laws. Prosecutions began in the 1870s, and the Supreme Court upheld the validity of the laws in 1879. This led eventually to disfranchisement of Mormons practicing polygamy, confiscation of church property, and the forced exile of church leaders.

Polygamy was an important factor in a confrontation which culminated in the "Utah War" of 1857. It was precipitated when three government officials notified President Buchanan that federal laws were openly violated in Utah, that federal records had been seized and burned by Mormon officials, and that the territory was in a state of rebellion. Buchanan responded by ordering troops to the territory. He later admitted that he had not taken the time to investigate the validity of the charges.

Political motivations played a part in his decision. The Mormon question had entered the party political struggle in 1856 when Republican candidate John C. Frémont, an ardent opponent of plural marriage, promised that Republicans would stamp out polygamy and slavery, the "twin relics of barbarism." Reports of a rebellion in Utah gave Buchanan an ideal opportunity to prove that Democrats could be as zealous in this as Republicans. In addition, dealing decisively with the Mormons allowed the administration to show how any future states'-rights rebellion would be met.

Economic motivations also played a role. Some complainants feared competition from an overland express company being organized by the Mormons. And non-Mormon businessmen in Salt Lake City looked forward to the large potential market an occupying army would offer. Cultural and social motivations also played a part.

Above all, plural marriage was an abnormal practice, out of harmony with the rest of the nation. Likewise, the Mormons' cooperative institutions were contrary to the national emphasis on a free market, private property, and unfettered enterprise. The Mormon community represented an enclave in which business was, in effect, subordinated to religion. The 1857 expedition represented, in part, the beginning of a long hard struggle to impose and entrench national institutions and customs in Utah.

Governor Brigham Young received no official word that federal troops were on their way, so considered them a hostile force. Mobilization in the face of the approaching army was swift. In September 1857 Young declared martial law, mobilized the territorial militia under Daniel H. Wells, and prohibited armed troops from entering the territory. Small companies were sent from Salt Lake to scout the approaching army, identify possible points for interception, and harass the supply trains. A "scorched earth" policy was applied to Mormon outposts on the route. The intense apprehension felt by the Saints is revealed by the decision to draw in their boundaries, abandon flourishing settlements at San Bernardino, Carson Valley, and elsewhere, and recall missionaries scattered throughout the world.

While federal troops approached Utah in the summer of 1857, emigrants continued to pass through the territory bound for California. One such group was composed of people from Arkansas and Missouri. The Arkansas

The Mountain Meadows massacre horrified the nation. Mormon settlers aided by Indians killed about 140 emigrants, including women and children. This engraving depicts the aftermath of the incident.

members were peaceful but the Missourians were rough and arrogant. Their passage was uneventful until they reached Cork Creek. There it was reported that some of the party had "poisoned the springs and the body of an ox which had died." The carcass was subsequently eaten by Indians, ten of whom died from poisoning.

As the emigrants continued through southern Utah the Missouri contingent made known their participation in the expulsion of the Mormons from Missouri. They boasted of their intention to return later to Utah and aid the federal troops. Aroused Indians surrounded the emigrant camp at Mountain Meadows, some 320 miles southwest of Salt Lake. Nearby Mormons were resentful too. Some openly declared that the travelers should be killed. Nevertheless, a messenger was sent to Salt Lake to seek the advice of Brigham Young. He said that the party should be allowed to go "free and unmolested." But by by the time the messenger returned with the news, events had gone too far.

Indians had initially attacked the emigrants, inflicting casualties. Two of the travelers then went to seek assistance from the local settlers. One was killed by three whites. Then, aided by Indians, the Mormons massacred all adult members of the 140-strong party.

Marriage and the Mormons

Brigham Young publicly announced the doctrine of plural marriage for the first time to Mormons at Salt Lake City on August 29, 1852. Plural marriage had been approved in a revelation to Joseph Smith in 1843. But the practice began with him about ten years earlier. By 1843 he already had thirteen wives, several quite young. His first wife, Emma, strongly opposed these additions to the household, and the revelation has been interpreted by some as an attempt by Smith to justify his ways. For in 1838 he had said that "a community of wives" was "an abomination in the sight of God." And when some inquirers asked about the young women in his house he claimed they were his nieces. Before 1852, plural marriages were confined to members of the church hierarchy.

Under the doctrine, men could take any number of partners, but women could have only two at most. Two types of marriage were now recognized. One united a couple on earth ("for .time") until a partner died; the other, performed in a temple, "sealed" them for eternity. This last promised Mormons a god-like existence as rulers of a heavenly world. A man could take a wife for time, for eternity, or both. In all cases an immediate aim was to produce offspring, to provide earthly bodies for the gifted spirits that church leaders said were awaiting entry into the world. The head of the church had to approve all plural marriages.

The church claimed support for plural marriage in the Bible. It simply restored an institution practiced in earliest Hebrew times. One leading churchman claimed that Jesus had three wives.

Like many others raised on traditional Christian belief, Brigham Young found acceptance difficult at first. But he soon took several women and later expanded the practice into official church policy. He may well have seen it as a means of boosting Mormon numbers and increasing the strength of the church, even as he believed in the divine nature of the practice. Young took wives with seeming casualness. "I never refuse to marry any respectable woman who asks me," he was reported as saying, "and it is often the case that I separate from a woman at the marriage altar, never to meet her again to know her." He denied lustful intentions. Yet a Swiss convert said that once when a man appeared before Young to take a third wife "greatly to his astonishment that worthy changed the programme slightly, and married the lady to himself."

Young probably had more wives than the twenty-eight officially credited to Smith. During his life, estimates ranged from seventeen to a hundred. But such huge families were rare. Few men could afford to house and keep numerous wives and children. The vast majority of Mormons who took more than one wife had two or three. And only between 10 and 20 per cent of all members endorsed plural marriage. Moral revulsion and political hostility forced the church to end the practice in 1890. And only after it did so could Utah enter the Union.

Below: An engraving of a polygamous family. The years during which polygamy was practiced damaged the church. Dissidents formed breakaway sects and Mormons were jailed under federal antibigamy laws.

Settlement of the Dispute

Meanwhile, the harassment raids and scorched earth policy of the Mormons, accompanied by an early winter, halted the advance of the federal troops at Camp Scott, near the burned Fort Bridger. The willingness of the Saints to sacrifice a decade of effort was revealed at a conference held on September 13, 1857. One speaker challenged the congregation: "All you that are willing to set fire to your property and lay it in ashes, rather than submit to their military rule and oppression, manifest it by raising your hands." Agreement was unanimous.

In Washington, President Buchanan was heavily criticized for his hasty dispatch of troops. He thus accepted Thomas L. Kane's offer to act as mediator in seeking a compromise. A long-time friend of the Mormons, Kane met first with Young and other church leaders in Salt Lake City. Later at Camp Scott he met General Albert Sidney Johnston and Alfred Cumming, who had been selected in June to replace Young as governor. Kane secured an agreement whereby Cumming would travel to Salt Lake City and assume the governorship. After his arrival on April 12, Cumming satisfied himself that the charges against the Mormons were misrepresentations. He ordered the federal troops to pass through, but not encamp in, Salt Lake Valley. Buchanan later granted an amnesty to the Mormons. But church leaders had a lingering suspicion of federal intentions. So they decided on a massive movement southward.

It was conducted in characteristically orderly fashion. Surplus food, church records, and light machinery were moved first. They were followed by thousands of Saints over two months beginning in mid-March 1858. Concerned over possible desecration by marauders, the stones cut for the Salt Lake Temple were hidden. And the foundations were buried and covered over so as to appear as a plowed field.

An account left by a member of the expedition which marched through Salt Lake City on June 26 gives an engaging glimpse of it.

> The city is beyond my power of description. It is beautiful—even magnificent. Every street is bordered by large trees beneath which and on either side run murmuring brooks with pebbly bottoms. Not a sign of dirt of any kind to be seen. The houses are surrounded by large gardens now green with summer foliage. All the houses are built of adobe nicely washed with some brown earth, the public buildings large and handsomely ornamented surrounded by walls of stone. . . .
>
> But oh how beautiful is this city, not unlike the foliage of plants nourished by corruption. A whitened sepulchre, "A den of thieves and murderers," the

Thomas L. Kane acted as mediator in the dispute that flared between the Mormons and the federal government in the 1850s. His long friendship with Mormon leaders aided his mission.

> emigrants say, but to our eyes alone it would seem to be an abode of purity and happiness, a going back to the Golden Age.

The troops did not remain in Salt Lake City but marched on to Cedar Valley, some forty miles southwest. Within the week church leaders announced that all who wished to go back to the city could do so. The return, involving upwards of 30,000, lasted for roughly two months.

The Mormon leaders undertook several measures designed to ensure a large measure of self-government, despite the imposition of a non-Mormon governor and the presence of federal troops in Utah. The legislative assembly moved criminal jurisdiction from federal district courts to locally controlled territorial courts. The Green River area was annexed to Salt Lake County, to prevent judicial proceedings by federal appointees wintering in that area. Not least, the legislature abolished the federal territorial tax. They further provided that the territorial militia could appoint its own officers. Public works and many civil functions were removed from government control.

Economically, the army's presence proved a blessing in a variety of ways. A flourishing trade developed during the next two years between the Mormons and the 7,000 military and civilian personnel at Camp Floyd in Cedar Valley. A large freighting firm was commissioned to supply the encampment from the East. But the Saints traded extensively with the troops in fresh foods and dairy products. And the church received contracts to supply grain and lumber. Employment opportunities at the camp provided jobs for several hundred Mormons.

One of the greatest windfalls came from the sale of surplus government goods during 1860–61 when the garrison was first reduced, and then abandoned following the outbreak of the Civil War. The 1861 sale involved an estimated $4 million worth of goods for which the Saints paid about $100,000. A supplying firm was also forced to dispose of large quantities of goods at low prices. The largest sale involved nearly 3,500 large freight wagons sold for $10 each. The final result of the occupation has been described thus: "The great Buchanan Utah Expedition, costing the Government millions . . . accomplish[ed] nothing, except making many of the Saints comparatively rich, and improving the circumstances of most of the people of Utah."

Politics, Education, and Culture

Political activity in Utah in the 1860s was characterized by several trends. A high turnover of federally appointed officials meant a measure of instability in formal territorial institutions, particularly during the first half of the decade. Five governors served between 1860 and 1869. And Utah's isolation meant the office was also frequently occupied by acting governors. Furthermore, tension continued between Mormon leaders and federally appointed officials. Attitudes on both sides did little to inspire trust. And the refusal of statehood and passage of the Morrill Anti-Bigamy Act during the summer of 1862 added to ill will.

The State of Deseret continued as a "ghost" state for eight years. Until 1870 this legislature, nearly identical in composition to the territorial body, met each year and formally reenacted the laws passed by the territorial legislature. And it installed Young as governor. Young maintained that, despite Cumming's appointment, he was still governor of the people.

During the 1860s there was a growing conflict between Mormons and the increasing non-Mormon population, who often sought common cause with the federally appointed officials. Crusading ministers entered the territory in the mid-1860s and became active preachers. Above all, non-Mormons feared weakened federal control which they looked to for security and patronage. The conflict was most visible in the appearance of rival newspapers. But the church still remained the most important influence in the daily life of Utah citizens.

Mormon colonization programs resulted in an unusually rapid spread of educational and cultural institutions. Education was an important responsibility of the community. In the first year in Salt Lake Valley, Mary Jane Dilworth opened a school in a tent. Three years later two

tons of schoolbooks were hauled across the plains. School districts had been set up and attendance at lessons was compulsory. By 1854, there were 226 schools with 13,000 students. Adult and higher education also received much attention, and in 1852 Young counselled Saints to form religious study groups. Formal higher education began with the creation in 1850 of the University of Deseret. But the economic crises of the mid-1850s caused its closure for over a decade. Once reopened, the commitment to higher education remained firm.

Mormon officials also supported the development of cultural life. Dramatic productions and concerts began in 1850 and later spread throughout the territory. The

Mormons placed great stress on education and even introduced a new alphabet. This book's title translates as The Deseret First Book. The publication was issued by the University of Deseret, which later became the University of Utah.

Salt Lake Theater, constructed in 1861–62, accommodated 3,000 persons and cost upwards of $100,000.

Life in the Great Basin included a conscious effort to maintain a distance from the "things of the world." In 1852 a campaign began to root out profanity in daily speech, and heavy fines were levied. Constant appeals to avoid the fashions and customs of the world punctuated speeches by church leaders. Commitment and singleness of purpose were expected. Life was austere, but there was little alienation.

The first two decades in the Great Basin showed the determination of the Mormons and the wisdom of their leaders. An overriding commitment to the church and a willingness to submit to the demands of cooperation ultimately secured a substantial measure of success.

Nevertheless, Brigham Young had his detractors. Outside observers claimed that his leadership was characterized by dictatorship, arrogance, and suspicion. But that so much had been achieved was, in many respects, due to his work.

Raised in rural poverty with no formal schooling, he had first become a carpenter and painter. Later in life he was acknowledged for his practical flair. He had courage, determination, and superb organizational skills, and he inspired deep loyalty. Planning and leading the great trek westward, founding Salt Lake City and numerous satellites, and organizing the massive immigration effort were the more obvious accomplishments of this great colonizer.

Brigham Young is shown preaching to his followers at Salt Lake City in this 1870 engraving. By the time of his death seven years later, the number of Mormons living in Utah stood at 140,000.

Chapter 6

EL DORADO ON THE PACIFIC

No sooner had the Mexican hold on California been broken than gold was discovered in the Sacramento Valley. Before long the region was swarming with prospectors from the four corners of the globe. Many had to endure the passage around Cape Horn while others rolled across the continent in a long and wearisome journey by wagon. Still others came singly with heavily laden mules. The Forty-Niners did not intend to settle in California; they simply wanted to win a lifetime's earnings in a few short months. A small number were lucky but for most the dream was elusive. Although the gold rush left a legacy of greed and mob rule, it nevertheless brought a dramatic injection of wealth into California and made San Francisco a major financial center almost overnight.

Conquest and Gold

In December 1845, an American "exploring expedition" arrived in California led by Captain John C. Frémont of the army's Topographical Corps. At this time Colonel José Castro was the military commandant of Mexican California with headquarters in Monterey. Frémont informed him that the men in the expedition were not soldiers. Their purpose was merely to survey a route to the Pacific.

The truth was that Frémont's men were armed and had been recruited because they were expert marksmen. Frémont hoped to participate in the military conquest of California, rather than in its peaceful exploration. He had received encouragement in this plan from his father-in-law, the expansionist Senator Thomas Hart Benton of Missouri. When Frémont's men established their camp only a few miles from Monterey, Colonel Castro angrily ordered them out of California. But Frémont defiantly entrenched them on Hawk's Peak (now Frémont Peak) in the nearby Gabilan Mountains, and raised the American flag. Castro issued a proclamation calling out the militia to repel this "invasion," so Frémont retreated "slowly and growlingly" toward Oregon through the Sacramento and Napa valleys. There he spread rumors among the recent American settlers that Colonel Castro's militia intended to drive them off their lands and burn their homes.

On May 9, 1846, Frémont was overtaken in southern Oregon by Lieutenant Archibald Gillespie of the United States Marine Corps. Gillespie had been sent to California with secret instructions from President Polk and Secretary of State Buchanan to cooperate with Thomas O. Larkin, the American consul at Monterey, in a secret plan. The aim was to persuade Californians to secede from Mexico, set up an independent republic, and seek the protection of the United States and ultimately annexation to it. This was a very promising plan because many Californian leaders, notably Colonel Mariano Vallejo, were disgusted with Mexican rule. But the rash actions of Frémont destroyed the possibility of a peaceful secession from Mexico. Gillespie had also brought personal letters from Senator Benton for Frémont, which he handed to him in Oregon. Frémont later claimed that he had received secret sanction from the highest authorities in Washington to engage in military filibustering in California. But there is no reliable evidence that this was true. Believing that war between the United States and Mexico was imminent, Frémont reentered California. He established his camp at Sutter's Fort on the Sacramento and fomented a "sponta-

John C. Frémont (inset) fomented an uprising against Mexican rule in California. The Rocky Mountains' explorer, after whom Frémont Peak, Wyoming, is named (right), had entered the region in the guise of a peaceful surveyor.

neous'' revolt among the American settlers in the region.

These settlers were mostly rough-and-ready frontiersmen. They were uneasy because they could not acquire legal ownership of their lands unless they became naturalized Mexicans and consequently Roman Catholic. On June 10, under the leadership of Ezekiel Merritt, they seized a herd of horses intended for Castro's militia. Two days later a band of more than thirty of them rode to the town of Sonoma and surrounded the home of Colonel Vallejo. The colonel had once been the military commander of the region, but he was no longer on active military duty and there were no soldiers in the town. Nevertheless the raiders informed him that he was a ''prisoner of war.'' He invited them in to have some brandy and to explain which war he was a prisoner of. After becoming thoroughly drunk the leaders decided to take Vallejo to Sutter's Fort, where Frémont had him confined to a cell—an unnecessary and arrogant act. Before leaving Sonoma the filibusters declared themselves a republic and devised the famous Bear Flag. Like the flag of the Republic of Texas, of which they were obviously thinking, it bore a large lone star. There was also a grizzly bear.

This framed photograph shows Mariano Vallejo surrounded by his daughters. The former Mexican governor of California was detained as a ''prisoner of war'' during the Bear Flag Revolt in June 1846.

As Frémont had intended, the Bear Flag Revolt forced Castro to try to suppress it. This in turn enabled Frémont and his men to come to the aid of the American settlers. Merging his own force with the rebels, Frémont easily won control of the area north of San Francisco Bay. He then crossed the Golden Gate (to which he gave the name), to ''capture'' the long-abandoned presidio of Yerba Buena (renamed San Francisco in 1847). He ceremoniously spiked its ten rusted guns, even though the ancient cannons had never been fired in anger. They had been incapable of action for at least forty years. Then on July 7, Commodore John D. Sloat, commander of the Pacific Squadron, raised the American flag at Monterey, and two days later it replaced the Bear Flag at Sonoma.

The brief episode of the Bear Flag Revolt would probably have resulted in war between the United States and Mexico if this had not already begun in May on the disputed southern border of Texas. The news, however, did not reach California until July. Frémont's actions in instigating the revolt were unauthorized, improper, and of no genuine value. But, as he hoped, they would add to the romantic reputation that later made him a United States senator from California and, in 1856, the first nominee of the Republican party for the presidency.

The Struggle for California

When Commodore Sloat occupied Monterey he had not yet received official news of the declaration of war between Mexico and the United States. He was afraid that he might be repeating the blunder of Commodore Thomas Jones who had raised the American flag at Monterey on the basis of a false rumor in 1842. Sloat issued a conciliatory proclamation to the Californians, assuring them that he came ''as their best friend.'' But he was in poor health, and on July 23, at his own request, Commodore Robert F. Stockton took over command. At once the tone of the American occupation changed to one of arrogance and provocation. Sloat and Larkin had hoped that California would pass into American hands without a shot being fired. But Stockton, like Frémont, was impulsive, politically ambitious, and desired military glory. (In 1844, for example, Stockton falsely claimed credit for designing a huge new naval cannon. He arranged a demonstration of it, but it exploded and killed the secretary of the navy and the secretary of state. Stockton, however, managed to escape responsibility.)

In Monterey, Stockton replaced Sloat's conciliatory proclamation with a bombastic one of his own. He mustered Frémont's Bear Flaggers, now organized as the ''California Battalion of Mounted Riflemen,'' into United States service. Stockton, Gillespie, and Frémont then proceeded to Los Angeles which they occupied peacefully.

Colonel Castro and Governor Pío Pico had satisfied their honor by fleeing to Mexico. Stockton and Frémont returned to northern California, leaving Gillespie with a small garrison in command of Los Angeles. They were to enforce Stockton's proclamation of "martial law" with such irritating and unaccustomed regulations as a curfew. Gillespie soon provoked a rebellion by treating the *Californios* with open contempt. Then a guerrilla force led by Andres Pico, brother of the last Mexican governor, forced the Americans to leave Los Angeles and withdraw to the nearby port of

San Pedro. Meanwhile, Gillespie's courier, Juan Flaco (Lean John) Brown, had managed to ride 500 miles in five days to bring word to Stockton at San Francisco. A relief force of marines and sailors hastily sailed to San Pedro. The Americans then set out to recapture Los Angeles but were driven back when the rebels produced a surprisingly effective old cannon. Originally used to fire ceremonial salutes in the Los Angeles plaza, it was now lashed to a wagon and fired with homemade powder and cigarettes. The cannon inflicted heavy casualties on the Americans

California Historical Society

California State Library

The Bear Flag Revolt proclaimed California's independence from Mexico. On June 14, 1846, the Mexican flag was lowered at Sonoma fort (above) and replaced by the Bear Flag (left) with its red star and crudely drawn grizzly bear. A month later, after the conquest of Monterey, the American flag was raised in Sonoma.

and Los Angeles remained in rebel hands for three months more.

Meanwhile, General Stephen W. Kearny had been ordered by the War Department to occupy New Mexico and then move west to head California's military government. While leading 300 dragoons to California he had the misfortune to meet Kit Carson, the army scout. Stockton had prematurely sent him to tell Kearny that California had been occupied without resistance. Relying on this news, Kearny sent most of his men back to Santa Fe and took only about a hundred on to California. When they arrived near San Pascual, a village not far from San Diego, Kearny's men and horses were exhausted by the long desert journey. Here Kearny was again misinformed by Carson, who assured him that the rebels were poor fighters. He urged him to attack them in order to capture

Courtesy Chicago Historical Society

As commander of the US Pacific Squadron, Robert Stockton assumed control of the American military effort in California in July 1846. He and Frémont finally took Los Angeles six months later.

their horses. But the rebels under Pico were extraordinarily skillful, and expert horsemen. In the subsequent battle in the middle of the night on December 6, using lances against the American cavalry sabers, they killed twenty-two of Kearny's men and wounded sixteen including Kearny, with few losses themselves. At last, with the aid of a relief force, Kearny was able to reach San Diego. On January 10, 1847, Los Angeles surrendered to Stockton and Frémont, and three days later the last Californian resistance was formally ended with the Capitulation of Cahuenga.

There was now complete confusion over the matter of command. Stockton sailed for Mexico to engage in naval action off the coast, but before he did so he appointed Frémont to succeed him as military governor. Frémont was now a lieutenant colonel, but he was outranked by Brigadier General Kearny who carried written instructions from the secretary of war appointing Kearny to the California post. Nevertheless, Frémont defiantly continued to act as governor, apparently thinking that his father-in-law Senator Benton, the powerful chairman of the Senate Committee on Military Affairs, would support him. Kearny could not condone such an act of mutiny without seriously damaging the morale of his officers, most of whom detested Frémont. Finally he ordered Frémont to be placed under military arrest and taken back to Washington. There he was court-martialed and dismissed from the service for disobedience of orders. Yet Frémont remained a hero in the eyes of most Americans and he was well aware of this. His rashness had been due in part to the encouragement of his wife, Jessie Benton Frémont. A gifted woman, deeply frustrated by the limited recognition women of talent received, she had an even more aggressive temperament than her husband.

Rumors of Gold

The Treaty of Guadalupe Hidalgo, ceding California to the United States, was signed on February 2, 1848. The signatories did not know it, but eight days earlier gold had been discovered in the foothills of the Sierra Nevada. Even if this had been known to the Mexican negotiators, their country was in no position to hold out for better terms.

The Spanish, always so eager for gold, never found it in California. This was because when they found gold in other parts of their empire in the Americas it was usually already in the possession of Indians. But the Indians of California were a primitive people without knowledge of the value of gold or of any other metal. Neither Spanish nor Mexican settlement had penetrated far enough into the interior to learn of the gold-bearing streams of the Sierra Nevada foothills.

When it finally came, the discovery was accidental. It was the byproduct of the building of a sawmill on the south fork of the American River, about forty-five miles northeast of Sutter's Fort. The German-Swiss adventurer, John A. Sutter, held large Mexican land grants in the Sacramento Valley. He hoped to make a fortune from the sale of lands, supplies, and particularly lumber to American settlers. He had commissioned a moody and eccentric carpenter, James Wilson Marshall, to build the sawmill. One morning when Marshall was inspecting the newly

On January 24, 1848, James Marshall (below) found
flakes of gold at the site of Sutter's sawmill
(bottom) on the American River near Coloma. Right:
A laborer's diary entry records Marshall's
discovery of a metal "that looks like goald."

dug channel of the millrace he saw the glint of gold. The next morning, in a state of intense excitement, he brought Sutter an ounce or two of gold in dust, flakes, and grains wrapped in a rag. "The biggest piece," Sutter recalled, "was not as large as a pea, and it varied from that down to less than a pinhead in size." After reading the article on gold in the *Encyclopedia Americana*, he spent the rest of the day putting the samples to all the tests he could. Then he told Marshall his verdict: "It's gold—at least twenty-three-carat gold." At this, Marshall became so excited that he rode back to the mill in pouring rain in the middle of the night. He was the first victim of gold mania.

Sutter, on the other hand, was concerned lest the discovery delayed completion of his sawmill. He promised Marshall and his workmen double wages if they kept the discovery secret and looked for gold only on Sundays. But gradually and inevitably the secret leaked out. At first there were few who believed it. Idle rumors of gold in California dated from the sixteenth century. In 1842, north of Los Angeles, there had been a discovery of a small placer deposit that had quickly played out. The young editor of the *California Star*, a one-page newspaper in San Francisco, dismissed the reports of Marshall's new discovery as a hoax, "a supurb [sic] take-in as was ever got up to guzzle the gullible." But on May 12, in a crafty scheme for self-enrichment, the enterprising Mormon elder Samuel Brannan deliberately touched off the powder train of gold mania that would spread all over the world.

Leader of the California Mormons, Brannan had brought a party of 200 by ship from New York in July 1846. Their arrival had tripled the population of the village of Yerba Buena. Though still in his twenties, Brannan became California's first millionaire by shamelessly using the tithes of his church for his own profit through personal investments in real estate and other activities. When Brigham Young sent a deputation from Salt Lake City to recover "the Lord's money," Brannan said that he would turn it over when he got a receipt signed by the Lord.

For such conduct Brannan was officially "disfellow-shipped." But he ignored the order of excommunication and continued to collect the tithes. One of his enterprises was a general store at Sutter's Fort, and there, in March 1848, he first learned of the gold discovery when customers began to offer gold in payment for whiskey and other goods. For several weeks Brannan bought everything in the region that might be useful to gold miners. This he accumulated in a warehouse near his store. He then suddenly appeared in the plaza at San Francisco on May 12, waving a bottle of gold dust and shouting "Gold! Gold! Gold from the American River!"

Typical of the reaction that would soon afflict so many were the emotions described by one man at this time: "I looked on for a moment; a frenzy seized my soul; unbidden my legs performed entirely new movements of polka steps—I took several; houses were too small for

The gold-rush years made businessman Sam Brannan a wealthy man. Once California's leading Mormon, he was excommunicated for using church funds to further his business interests.

me to stay in; I was soon in the streets in search of necessary outfits; piles of gold rose up before me at every step; castles of marble, dazzling the eye with their rich appliances; thousands of slaves bowing to my beck and call; myriads of fair virgins contending with each other for my love—were the fancies of my fevered imagination. The Rothschilds, Girards and Astors appeared to me but poor people; in short, I had a very violent attack of the gold fever."

When the rumors first reached Monterey they were not believed. But on June 6, Walter Colton, the first American *alcalde* or mayor of Monterey, sent a messenger to the American River to verify or disprove the stories. When he returned with samples of gold a few weeks later, Colton recalled that "the blacksmith dropped his hammer, the carpenter his plane, the mason his trowel, the farmer his sickle, the baker his loaf, the tapster his bottle. All were off to the mines, some on horses, some on carts, and some on crutches, and one went on a litter." Within a few days the military and civil governor of California, Colonel Richard B. Mason, Colton, and other officers found themselves doing their own cooking "in a smoking kitchen, grinding coffee, toasting a herring and peeling onions! These gold mines," Colton complained, "are going to upset all the domestic arrangements of society." Colonel Mason could not prevent his soldiers from deserting, especially after one of them returned from a three-week furlough with a quantity of gold worth more than his army pay for five years. By the end of 1848 about 4,000 men from various parts of California and about 6,000 from Hawaii, Oregon, Utah, Mexico, Peru, and Chile were at the California diggings.

Off to the Diggings in Droves

The gold rush became a national and world phenomenon after President Polk confirmed the richness of the discovery in his annual message to Congress on December 5, 1848. Polk was worn out by the strain of the Mexican War and the massive criticism he had received during its progress. Now he was delighted to be able to quote from the report of Colonel Mason that California contained enough gold to pay for the war "a hundred times over."

"The accounts of the abundance of gold," the president wrote, "are of such an extraordinary character as would scarcely command belief were they not corroborated by the authentic reports of officers in the public service." On December 9 the *New York Herald* screamed: "The gold region in California! Startling discoveries! The El

News of the discovery of gold excited the nation. This painting by William Sidney Mount, entitled California News, *portrays a group of people at a Long Island post office reading the latest reports from El Dorado.*

Dorado of the old Spaniards is discovered at last. We now have the highest official authority for believing in the discovery of vast gold mines in California, and that the discovery is the greatest and most startling, not to say miraculous, that the history of the last five centuries can produce.'' Only a few weeks earlier the *Herald*'s editor, James Gordon Bennett, had solemnly cautioned his fellow Americans against the lure of California and ''the mania of hasty money making . . . all the gold in the world will not make you happy; pursue, quietly and steadily, the sober path of regular industry.'' But all such warnings were now forgotten. By January 1849 the *Herald* was noting that ''all classes of our citizens appear to be under the influence of this extraordinary mania. . . . Every day men of property and means are advertising their possessions for sale in order to furnish themselves with the means to reach that golden land.''

Yankee enterprise produced a thriving industry in the manufacture and sale of fanciful machines for gold mining. They were all complicated, expensive, and useless. Fraudulent guidebooks blossomed, pieced together from the reports of Frémont, Mason, and Larkin. And sheet music publishers stole the notes of Stephen Foster's ''Oh! Susanna,'' adapting the song with new words:

Oh! Susanna, don't you cry for me!

I'm going to California with my washbowl on my knee.

The Forty-Niners got to California by three principal routes, across the Isthmus of Panama, around the Horn, and overland. The Panama route was the most attractive in the winter and spring of 1849 because it promised to be the quickest. Congress had recently subsidized a new steamship line from New York to Chagres, on the east coast of the isthmus, and another from the port of Panama on the west coast to San Francisco. But travel across the cholera-infested isthmus, first in small boats poled up the Chagres River and then on mules through a sweltering jungle, proved difficult. And at Panama hundreds of gold seekers waited months for a steamer.

The voyage around Cape Horn covered 18,000 miles and took five to eight months. Many who took this route were organized into joint-stock companies. They bought old ships and hired incompetent captains, for this was the best they could do in so short a time. The crews generally had no more qualifications than an urge to get to the gold mines. Such companies believed they could sell the ships in California. But instead, hundreds of vessels were abandoned at the San Francisco waterfront where they gradually rotted and sank into the mud.

Gold fever gripped the nation once news of the find became known. This cartoon pokes fun at the mad rush to get to California. The artist shows the swiftest possible means—''a grand patent India-rubber air line railway.''

The overland routes included the Santa Fe Trail and various tracks across Texas and former Mexican country. But most routes followed the California Trail by way of the Platte River, South Pass, and the Humboldt. "The hardships of the overland route to California," as traveler and author John Lloyd Stephens recalled, "are beyond conception. Care and suspense, pained anxiety, fear of losing animals and leaving one to foot it and pack his 'duds' on his back, begging provisions, fear of being left in the mountains to starve and freeze to death, and a thousand things which no one thinks of until on the way, are things of which I may write and you may read, but they are nothing to the reality." Along the California Trail were hundreds of graves, mostly the result of a cholera epidemic. There were thousands of skeletons of horses and oxen, dead from the shortage of grass and exhaustion. Altogether about 90,000 people went to California in 1849, half by land and half by sea. It was one of the largest mass migrations in history.

The journey to California by sea—round Cape Horn or via the Panama isthmus—took much longer than by land. The broadside at right advertised a service offered by a Boston agent. In the days before the Panama Canal was opened, passengers had to disembark at Chagres (below) in Central America, travel overland to the West Coast, then resume the sea journey.

CALIFORNIA AGENCY OFFICE.

Persons who wish to secure a passage to California will do well to call on the subscriber, who has opened an office for the express accommodation of persons wishing to embark for the

GOLD REGIONS.

No trip to California was easy for the inexperienced travelers who headed west. "The hardships of the overland route . . . are beyond conception," wrote an Ohio man. "Fear of losing animals and leaving one to foot it and pack his 'duds' on his back, begging provisions, fear of being left in the mountains to starve and freeze to death, and a thousand other things . . . are nothing to the reality." Above: a whimsical view of a well-equipped "Forty-Niner" setting out alone. Above right: Pack mules could ease the journey for a man, but their stubbornness was a drawback. Right: A party of men settle down to a meal on the plains. Buffaloes provided both meat and, in the form of buffalo chips, cooking fuel.

Gold Mining Techniques

Then and for several years afterward most of California's population was concentrated in the foothills of the Sierra Nevada, from the Yuba River in the north to Mariposa in the south. Through this region ran the Mother Lode, a continuous belt of gold about 120 miles long and from a few hundred feet to two miles wide. An ancient network of thousands of arteries were shaped when the Sierra Nevada had been formed by a great crack in the crust of the earth. Molten gold had then flowed up into fissures in the rock. The Mother Lode country referred to the wider area into which particles of gold had later been carried by erosion.

The Spanish had had noticeably more experience in gold mining and its techniques than Americans. But there had been some gold mining in Georgia and the Carolinas. A veteran of those diggings who happened to be at Sutter's Fort in the spring of 1848 was the first to show early prospectors how to use the pan, the rocker, and the cradle instead of a knife and a spoon. For the lucky few thousands in the first months of 1848, getting gold was easy. It was more like harvesting than mining. But after the easiest gold had been taken out, mining the rest became back-breaking labor. It was a cruel disappointment to those who had expected to get rich easily and quickly. In pan-

ning, the miner had to squat or stoop for hours while moving his wrists, arms, and shoulders. He held his pan of dirt under the surface of the water and carefully swirled it about until the clay and sand were washed away and the particles of gold, if any, remained in the bottom.

The next step in the development of mining techniques was the rocker. This was an oblong box mounted on rockers like a child's cradle, and placed on a slant. One miner threw dirt onto a sieve at the upper end and a second man poured buckets of water over the dirt. A third rocked the cradle, so that the dirt was washed through the lower, open end of the box while the gold particles were trapped behind cleats nailed to the bottom. The "long tom" was a much longer box, through which a steady stream of water could pass from a ditch or a wooden flume. In a later development, the sluice, a whole series of such boxes placed end to end, reached lengths of several hundred feet. Sometimes the water was diverted into the sluice from a wing dam built part way across a stream. Occasionally an entire stream was diverted, with the added advantage of exposing the pay dirt in the stream bed below the dam.

Gold could also be separated from dirt and sand by using

A group of prospectors pause for the photographer. The "long tom" shown here developed out of the rocker. Dirt was placed at one end and washed with water from the nearby stream.

Library of Congress

Left: Gold mining on the Calaveras River, near San Francisco. On the most fruitful rivers, hundreds of men worked side by side. But in lesser-known sites, a few would toil away in the hope of stumbling on a bonanza. One pioneer wrote that "this gold digging is no child's play but downright hard labor, and a man to make anything must work harder than any day laborer in the States." Once the alluvial gold had been won, miners turned to extracting the metal from solid rock. The "arrastra" shown above was a device that enabled rock to be broken up by abrasive boulders. Below: A Forty-Niner.

Courtesy of the Bancroft Library, University of California/Camera Press

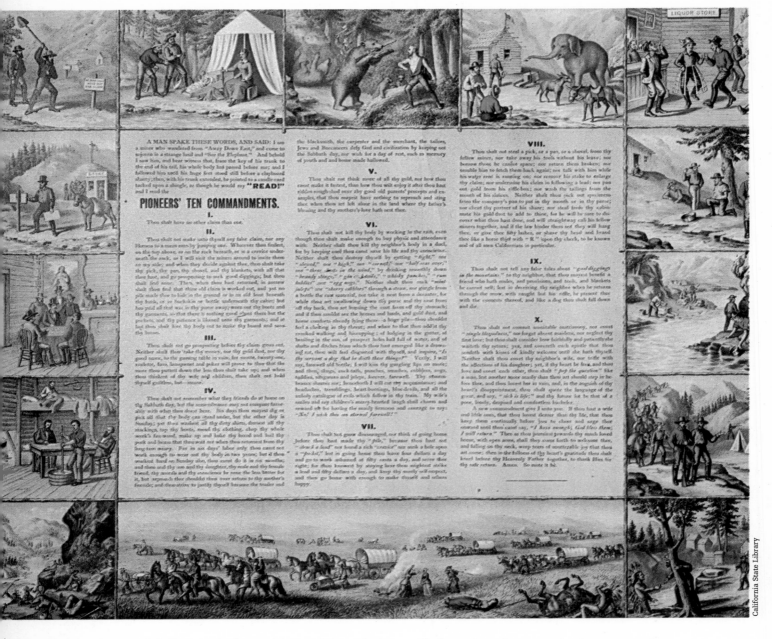

mercury or quicksilver, which combines with gold. By heating the amalgam in a closed vessel the mercury was separated by vaporizing. It was then recovered and re-used as soon as it cooled from vapor to liquid. Through a remarkably lucky coincidence a rich deposit of quicksilver had been discovered in 1845 at New Almaden, a few miles south of San Jose.

The Forty-Niners had to devise their own system of law and self-government. Virtually the entire gold-mining area was on United States public land, but until September 1850 when Congress approved its admission as a state, California had no fully legal system of civil government. In any case there was no federal law relating to mining camps because no gold had ever been discovered before

The letter sheet above was one of many pirated versions of the hugely successful "Miners Ten Commandments." Unlike most miners, the author of the original made a fortune.

on American public lands. Thus each California mining camp had to hold a mass meeting, organize itself as a "mining district," and elect a committee to draw up a code of regulations. Eventually there were more than 500 similar committees based largely on Spanish-Mexican mining codes and customs. The miners acquired no title of ownership to the land, but only the right to use it for mining. The most important regulations were those that limited the size of claims and required that they be con-

entire hillsides were washed loose with powerful streams of hosed water. The water had to be accumulated in large volumes at points much higher than the nozzle of the hose, and it had to pass through miles of ditches and wooden flumes. Not only did this process leave hideous and permanent scars on the landscape, but its cost required large-scale investments.

The Elusive Bonanza

Even before the end of the era of simple placer mining, an individual miner's chances of success declined rapidly after the lush days of 1848. In 1849 average earnings were about $20 a day, but because of inflated prices for food and other essential goods the miner's expenses were about $18. As one gold seeker wrote home to his brother: "The stories you hear frequently in the States are the most extravagant lies imaginable—the mines are a humbug. All hopes of making a fortune in California are lost sight of in ninety-nine cases out of a hundred, and the almost universal feeling is to get home. It is truly heart rending to witness the general despondency which exists among miners, and to see stout-hearted and brave men shed tears at their hopeless condition." And one doctor wrote that he "never saw so many broken down constitutions as during my brief stay in California." Hinton R. Helper, a North Carolinian, wrote an account of his experiences in the gold rush entitled *The Land of Gold: Reality Versus Fiction*. Because so many miners had failed to earn enough to pay for transportation back to their homes, he pointed out, California was full of embittered and desperate men. "Suffice it to say," Helper concluded, "that I know of no country in which there is so much corruption, villainy, outlawry, licentiousness, and every variety of crime, folly, and meanness. Words fail to express the shameful depravity and unexampled turpitude of California society." In only one respect would he qualify this judgment. "California can and does furnish the best bad things that are obtainable in America. I have seen purer liquors, better segars, finer tobacco, truer guns and pistols, larger dirks and bowie knives, and prettier courtezans here in San Francisco than in any other place I have ever visited."

According to legend the prospectors came to California as pioneers and commonwealth builders. One writer has better described the hopes and intentions of most of them: "Five years was the longest period anyone expected to stay. Five years at most was to be given to rifling California of her treasures, and then that country was to be thrown aside like a used-up newspaper and the rich adventurers would spend the rest of their days in wealth, peace, and prosperity at their Eastern homes." And as British historian James Bryce wrote: "The chief occupation of the first generation of Californians was mining, an

"The mines are a humbug," wrote one disappointed miner. For most prospectors, California yielded just a few dollars. Cuban artist Augusto Ferran painted this watercolor entitled Weighing the Dust.

tinuously worked to remain valid. Each district elected a recorder of claims, often called an *alcalde.*

This highly democratic system was quite appropriate in the early stage of the gold rush when the miners worked individually or in small groups. But after two or three years the placer gold that could be mined in this fashion began to be exhausted, and there was a shift to more complicated techniques requiring corporate organization, expensive equipment, and large amounts of capital. One of these was quartz mining—the extraction of gold from solid rock taken from a mine shaft or tunnel. The rock first had to be crushed to a fine powder. The most important device for doing this was the stamp mill, a large mechanized version of the mortar and pestle. Another method was the "arrastra," an Anglicized spelling of the Spanish *arrastre.* This was a device whereby a mule plodded around a circular track pulling heavy abrasive stones over the gold-bearing rock. Sometimes the pulverized rock, mixed with water, was passed over coarse blankets in which the fine gold particles were caught. The huge beds of gravel that lay deep in the hillsides were another source of gold. From 1853 these were attacked with the new method called "hydraulicking" in which

Camp life on the gold fields could be raucous and primitive. Charles Nahl painted Sunday Morning in the Mines (below) which shows miners reading and doing domestic chores while others brawl and a youth lives it up. Nahl came to California from France in 1850 and prospected in Nevada County. Like all mining towns, Nevada City (inset) had a rough, untidy look.

EMPIRE

E. COOK & Cº

industry which is like gambling in its influence on the character, with its sudden alternations of wealth and poverty, its long hours of painful toil relieved by bouts of drinking and merriment, its life in a crowd of men who have come together from the four winds of heaven, and will scatter again as soon as some are enriched and others ruined, or the gold in the gulch is exhausted.''

Such views tend to exaggerate the darker side, and there are many more positive things to be said. The gold rush was, after all, one of the greatest adventure stories in human history. The discoveries of gold greatly increased the money supply, and subsequently stimulated the economic growth of California and the United States. In San Francisco, the commercial and financial center for the new industry, half a century of growth was telescoped into a year. Within five years San Francisco was a financial rival of New York and in some respects a cultural rival of Boston.

In California the traditional view has been that the gold rush was not only the most significant, but also the most fortunate, single factor in the history of the state. Yet it can be argued that in the long run California would have been better off without gold. Though the early growth of its population and economy were greatly stimulated by gold, its climate and other resources would eventually have made it just as populous and prosperous. Its social development, though more gradual, would have been far more orderly and civilized. Had it not been for gold,

Drinking and gambling helped pass the time when miners were not at their claims. Above: A relaxed trio of drinkers sketched by Augusto Ferran. Below: The bar of a Sonora gambling saloon about 1850.

The influx of miners created large, enthusiastic audiences for entertainers. These two fiddlers were photographed in California in 1849.

California Historical Society, San Francisco. Inset: New York Public Library, Stokes Collection

Originally a village called *Yerba Buena*, the streets of which were laid out in the 1830s, San Francisco was a small frontier town on the eve of the gold rush. The painting below shows the settlement in 1847. The population stood at about 800 in 1848; two years later the figure had rocketed to nearly 35,000. The once-sleepy village became a magnet for prospectors from throughout the world—Germany, France, Britain, Italy, Hong Kong, Australia, South America, Canada, Mexico— and the United States. The scene at left shows crowds milling round the post office at the height of the rush. Vigilante committees sprang up to stamp out crime, which was of epidemic proportions. They meted out their own form of "justice" and wielded great power. The certificate at right was issued to a member of San Francisco's vigilante committee.

Oregon would have been settled and ready for admission as a state before California. And the first transcontinental railroad would probably have been built to Oregon rather than to California. But if the Central Pacific route to California had been constructed later, it might have been in the hands of a less piratical group of men. And California might have escaped from decades of economic and political tyranny at the hands of the owners of its monopoly railroad.

A Boisterous Society

The gold rushers were predominantly young and overwhelmingly male. Half of those who came in 1849 were under thirty, and they were likely to describe a man of forty-five as "the old gentleman." Women were few, and virtuous women fewer still. The female contingent was only one-twelfth of the population in the census of 1850. Such a society was certain to be crude, boisterous, and often impulsively violent. Men tried to find relief from difficult conditions in a desperate kind of humor, as in the names they gave to such mining camps as Hell's Delight, Gouge Eye, Poker Flat, or Gomorrah—and in the organization of the Ancient and Honorable Order of E Clampus Vitus, or "the Clampers." The members of this miners' fraternity were "pledged to take care of widows and orphans, especially widows." It is said that there were no records of its meetings because no one was ever sober enough to keep minutes. But there was often more tragedy than humor and romance in the drinking, gambling, and vice through which many miners tried to escape from hardship and anxiety. Later generations got their impressions of the gold rush largely from the stories of Bret Harte, who romanticized it as quaint comedy and sentimental melodrama although he never had any personal experience of mining-camp life. But even Harte's stories often reflected the tragic aspects, including the story that became the basis for Puccini's opera *The Girl of the Golden West*.

For nearly three years the confused conditions of the gold rush intensified the disorder resulting from the delay of Congress in providing a legal form of government for California. During the Mexican War California had been governed under the rules of military occupation, which provided that the previous system of local government should remain. However, some modifications could be made at the discretion of the military commander. Even before the end of the war there was much uncertainty about the powers and status of the "military and civil governors" who rotated rapidly. When five "governors" had served within the first ten months—Sloat, Stockton, Frémont, Kearny, and Mason—a navy captain wrote: "The Californians think . . . that we cannot be much better

than Mexico for they connect the appearance of every new commander-in-chief with some new revolution."

In the previous Mexican system of local government extraordinary power was concentrated in the *alcalde*. This official had not only executive and judicial powers but considerable legislative powers as well. Such sweeping authority shocked many Americans. Walter Colton, after he became the first American *alcalde* of Monterey, wrote that "such an absolute disposal of questions affecting property and personal liberty never ought to be confided to one man." There were many other protests against the "inefficient mongrel" combination of military and *alcalde* rule.

Congress provided for a territorial government in Oregon in the spring of 1848. But such provisions for New Mexico and California became deadlocked in interminable debates over the question of the legal future of slavery in the Mexican Cession. When the Treaty of Guadalupe Hidalgo was ratified in May 1848 and the official news of it reached California in August, the political situation there became acutely embarrassing. The military governor had to continue to rule in time of peace even though he had no legal authority to do so. By February 1849, public meetings of American residents in San Jose, San Francisco, and Sacramento had established forms of local representative government. But the military commanders withheld their recognition.

The impact of California's boom years was reflected in numerous ways, significant and trivial, throughout the nation. This little appliquéd cotton coverlet dates from the 1850s.

In May General Bennett Riley, in his capacity as "civil governor," heard that Congress had once more adjourned without providing a territorial organization. By popular demand he issued a call for a state constitutional convention to be elected and to meet at Monterey on September 1. Obviously California already had, or would soon have, more than the 60,000 inhabitants required for admission as a state. (It was to skip the territorial stage of government entirely, as only four other new states—Vermont, Kentucky, Maine, and Texas—had previously done.)

Although Forty-Niners were a large majority of the population of California they were only a small minority of the constitutional convention. Few gold seekers were willing to take time out. One delegate from the mining district of San Joaquin had apparently already made his fortune, since he listed his occupation as "elegant leisure." But most of the delegates had been in California more than three years. An important exception was William M. Gwin, who had been there less than three months. Gwin was a Democrat from Tennessee. He had lost his federal job in Washington when the administration passed to the Whigs under General Zachary Taylor in March 1849. He had come to California with the announced intention of becoming one of its first United States senators, and he saw a chance to pave his way toward that office by taking a prominent part in the state constitutional convention.

Drafting the State Constitution

Of the forty-eight delegates who attended, only eleven came from the southern districts. They owned ranch lands in what would soon be called the "cow counties." These delegates preferred California to have the status of a territory rather than a state. They knew that taxation of ranch land would be the main source of revenue in a state, while the mines on public land would bring in no property taxes. Moreover, the federal government would pay all the administrative expenses of a territory. But Gwin, who could not become a senator from a territory, introduced a provision for statehood as the first important resolution of the convention. He had the majority behind him. The proposal of Jose Antonio Carrillo of Los Angeles, that southern California be separately organized as a territory, was defeated.

The question of slavery in California, which so agitated the national Congress, was not even a serious issue in the region. The convention voted unanimously to forbid its existence. This was not for humanitarian or idealistic reasons. It was simply because the miners, whether they came from the North or the South, feared and hated the idea of competing with Negro slave labor in the diggings. Great publicity was given to the attempt of Colonel Thomas Jefferson Green of Texas to use his slaves in working several claims at Rose's Bar on the Yuba River. It was widely and accurately reported that Colonel Green had left Texas partly at the demand of his political rival Sam Houston, who described him as having "all the characteristics of a dog except fidelity." The miners of Rose's Bar held a mass meeting, ordered the slaves out of the district by the next morning, and resolved that "no slave or negro should own claims or even work in the mines." The same miners then elected the delegate who was to introduce the convention resolution that "neither slavery nor involuntary servitude, unless for punishment of crimes, shall ever be tolerated in this state." Clearly the opposition to slavery was racist rather than humanitarian.

There was also a serious proposal to exclude free Negroes from California. Such a clause was actually adopted. But it was then removed because of the fear that Congress, considering it a violation of the federal Constitution, would reject California's proposed constitution in its entirety, thus further delaying its admission as a state. Another problem was that of the right to vote. The federal Constitution still allowed a state to deny the suffrage on the ground of race. But there was a potentially embarrassing complication in the Treaty of Guadalupe Hidalgo that permitted former Mexican citizens of California to become American citizens. For centuries the Spanish in Mexico had interbred freely with Indians and the descendants of Negro slaves. Most Californians as a result were partly of Indian ancestry, and many also had considerable African blood. Nevertheless the California constitution restricted the suffrage to white male citizens, and both Congress and the state chose to ignore the question of Mexican non-white ancestry.

Most of the other provisions of the first California constitution were borrowed from the recently adopted constitution of Iowa. Gwin had conveniently arranged to have copies of this printed for each delegate. The design of the state seal, however, was quite original. It featured Minerva, the Roman goddess of political wisdom; the Greek motto "Eureka"; scenes of gold mining and ships on the Sacramento River; and in the foreground was a grizzly bear. A temporary difficulty arose when General Vallejo, an honored delegate to the convention, objected to the bear because it reminded him of the indignities inflicted on him during the Bear Flag Revolt. But he was reassured that no offense was intended.

On November 13, 1849, a month after the Monterey convention adjourned, an election was held to ratify the constitution and to choose the state officials to serve under it. The legislature assembled in December at the first state capital, San Jose, and soon afterward elected Frémont and Gwin as its first two United States senators. For the greater part of a year a *de facto* state government was in operation before California was finally admitted as a free state on September 9, 1850.

California's state seal (above). The design features the Greek word Eureka ("I've found it") which Archimedes supposedly called out when he discovered how to determine the purity of gold.

William Gwin came to California with the intention of representing the new state in the Senate. He played a prominent role in the constitutional convention and later served nine years as senator.

The Dark Side of the Coin

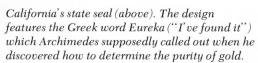

Among the problems of California society in the early years of statehood were racism, confusion over land titles, and vigilantism. Anglo-Americans in California were saturated with a belief in their own superiority. With this convenient justification they systematically oppressed Mexicans, Chinese, Indians, and Negroes. Nearly all of the mining camp codes excluded non-whites from the mines. Mexicans were driven out en masse, often without any distinction in favor of native Californians although the treaty had promised them all the rights of Americans. The Chinese began to come to the California mines in large numbers in 1850. The legislature adopted a "foreign miners' license tax" which nominally applied to all foreigners but in practice was enforced almost exclusively against the Chinese. The population of the California Indians had already declined drastically under Spain and Mexico, largely because of epidemics. Under the Americans they were now subjected to campaigns of virtual genocide under the guise of "Indian wars." And the "free" Negroes, grudgingly admitted under the state constitution, were harassed by a battery of discriminatory laws.

Great disorder prevailed over land titles. In the treaty

with Mexico the United States had promised to respect the previous titles of land ownership in California. Under the Mexican system nearly all the best land in the coastal valleys from San Francisco to San Diego had been parcelled out in more than 800 large rancho land grants. Nearly all were unsurveyed and had very loosely defined boundaries. Many grants were legally doubtful even under the terms of the lackadaisical Mexican administration, and quite a number of claims were fabricated.

Then in 1851 Congress passed a bill introduced by Senator Gwin and intended to favor the American land seekers and squatters at the expense of the Mexican grantees. Under this scheme a Mexican grant had to win approval by a special land commission and then usually by a federal district court. Furthermore, the United States Supreme Court often had to approve it as well. The average length of time required for ultimate establishment of such a land title was seventeen years. In the meantime almost all of the original Mexican grantees had been financially ruined. And the American land seekers had been deterred from buying because of the long uncertainty over whether a particular title would or would not be confirmed. Thus the establishment of small farms in California was discouraged.

A major symptom of the chronic social disorder that stemmed from the gold rush was the spread of "vigilante" committees. This began with the lynch mobs of the mining camps, which later developed into more formal organizations in San Francisco and other towns.

Vigilantism had been practiced in Mexican California even before the gold rush, notably in Los Angeles in 1836. (*Vigilante*, a Spanish word, was first used in California at that time.) There was nothing innately Anglo-Saxon about the practice, and even if there had been, it was nothing to be proud of. For the lynch mob and the vigilance committee were mass exercises in sadistic ritual murder. They were self-righteously disguised as public-spirited concern for the safety of the community.

The true contributions of Anglo-Saxon justice have been on the side of the due process of law, and the tactics of the vigilance committees were parodies of this. They held their "trials" in anger and in haste. There could be no motions for change of venue, and witnesses for the defense were usually afraid to testify. The committees often resorted to hanging because they had no practicable means of enforcing a long sentence of imprisonment. There could be no appeal, and no executive clemency. For a lordly band of self-appointed individuals to take the law into their own hands was a criminal act—especially

after regular courts had already been established. Yet when such committees virtually took over the government of San Francisco in 1851 and again in 1856, the majority of Californians applauded their actions. Such events were to be expected in a society based on the lust for gold and the lawlessness of the mining camps.

Mineral wealth nurtured personal greed, but it also nourished long-term economic advancement. In the 1850s a start was made in exploiting the natural resources of the state, including its land and timber. By 1860 San Francisco had become a center of light manufacturing, shipbuilding, and flour milling. In the same year, the value of California's manufactured goods was estimated at $24 million, more than half the value of gold mining output. The frantic boom years of the gold rush led to disillusionment for many, but the enormous wealth they produced thrust California into the future in a manner no other state experienced.

Vigilante groups arose in San Francisco, partly because thugs were thought to be responsible for several fires in the city. This 1851 engraving shows two men hanged by vigilante action.

Chapter 7

ACROSS THE CONTINENT

When the Civil War began, the American people were poised to conquer one last frontier—the trans-Mississippi West. Between the eastern states and California, separated by some fifteen hundred miles, lay a fabulous expanse of prairies, canyons, and mountains. Inhabited almost solely by the red man, and teeming with wildlife, the West offered a growing nation matchless scope for initiative. With the close of the war, the country was ready to turn its energies in this direction. There were many "conquests" of the West, but first and foremost was the conquest by rail.

Western Panorama

By 1861 the surge of westward advance had already carried America's pioneers some way beyond the Mississippi. The line of settlement ran for the most part along the western boundaries of the tier of states immediately beyond the river—Minnesota, Iowa, Missouri, Arkansas. In places it extended slightly farther west, jutting outward to include the eastern parts of Kansas and Nebraska and outward yet again to take in the west-central parts of Texas. In addition settlement had leapfrogged to the Pacific Coast to create a second frontier line in California and Oregon. Between the two frontiers was a land of varied and breathtaking vistas. Before the frontiersman lay seemingly endless plains, towering mountain peaks, majestic canyons, strange rock formations, parched deserts, and grassy plateaus. In 1861, except for small Mormon settlements in Utah, the Far West was the home only of Indian tribes and of wild animals. But in the space of a single generation the westward surge swept over an area greater in extent than all the territory that had been settled since the landing at Jamestown in 1607. By the end of the century the settlement and the political organization of the continent were complete.

The speed with which this huge undeveloped area filled up is all the more astonishing in view of the fact that settlement required adaptation to new and strange environments. The topography, climate, and soils of the trans-Mississippi region were different from those of the East, so different that the pioneering techniques and agricultural methods that had proved successful in earlier frontiers no longer worked. The ax, the plow, and the rifle, which had enabled the pioneers to subdue the forests and the rolling prairies in the eastern half of the continent, were inadequate and even useless in a tree-less, semiarid region. As the historian Walter P. Webb has put it: "East of the Mississippi civilization stood on three legs—land, water and timber; west of the Mississippi not one but two of the three legs were with-drawn—water and timber—and civilization was left on one leg—land." The environmental problems posed by the Far West required new types of agriculture and only when these had been devised could settlement proceed. For that reason the trans-Mississippi region was initially a miners' and a cattlemen's frontier rather than one occupied by farmers.

This last West was by no means a unit. Within its confines there were three distinct physiographic areas: the Great Plains, the Rocky Mountains, and the Inter-mountain region between the Rockies and the Sierra Nevada-Cascades chain. Of these the Great Plains were the first of the barriers facing frontiersmen as they pushed beyond the 1860 line of settlement. The Great Plains region extended all the way from Canada to

Above: The Badlands of South Dakota, named by
explorers who found them difficult—and
dangerous—to cross. The inhospitable terrain
results from water erosion on soft rock.

Texas, stretching from about the 98th meridian to the foothills of the Rockies and ranging in width from 200 to 700 miles. The Great Plains consisted of a high plateau tilting gently upward to the west. Rarely did the altitude fall below 2,500 feet. At Denver it rose to more than 5,000. Apart from occasional elevations like the Black Hills of South Dakota, the Great Plains were flat and rolling. Except along the rivers and trees, where there were clumps of cottonwoods, it was largely devoid of trees. The light-colored soil was covered with a matting of short grasses, either buffalo or grama grass. Flowing through the region were a number of great rivers like the Missouri, the Platte, the Arkansas, and the Red (of the South) which rose in the Rockies and drained into the Mississippi Valley. These had a number of tributaries like the Canadian, the Cimarron, and the Republican which were longer than most of Europe's great rivers. But only the Missouri carried a substantial body of water all the year round. The rest flowed freely only in the spring and for much of the year either slowed to a trickle or dried up altogether.

*Prior to the Civil War, the Great Plains were
not a goal but an obstacle. Left: Settlers
heading for the Pacific Coast ford the South
Platte in* California Crossing *by W. H. Jackson.*

The climate of the Great Plains was extreme, with blisteringly hot summers and long, bitter winters. There were frequent thunderstorms, blizzards, hailstorms. And there were warm, dry mountain winds known as chinooks. But the most significant physical feature of the Great Plains was the low rainfall. The average annual precipitation throughout the region as a whole was only about fifteen inches, or only about half as much as in the Mississippi Valley. Moreover the burning winds made matters worse by causing rapid evaporation, leaving insufficient moisture for traditional farming methods.

In the first half of the nineteenth century, the Great Plains area acquired such a harsh and forbidding image that most Americans believed them to be uninhabitable at least by white men. In atlases and geographies of the period, the region was described simply as "the Great American desert." This was a name it owed to its early explorers. Lieutenant Zebulon Montgomery Pike, sent out by President Jefferson to explore the Louisiana Purchase, wrote an account of his travels in 1810 that left the impression that the whole area between the Missouri and the Rockies was a sterile waste. This impression was confirmed by the 1823 narrative of the Stephen H. Long expedition. It was Long's opinion that the Great Plains were "almost wholly unfit for cultivation, and of course uninhabitable by a people dependent upon agriculture for their subsistence.'' In the next three decades numerous travel accounts kept alive the notion of a Great American Desert beyond the Missouri. Thomas J. Farnham, a Vermont lawyer who traveled from Illinois to Oregon in 1839, wrote that the Great Plains region was a scene of unparalleled desolation, a ''burnt and arid desert, whose solemn stillness is seldom broken by the tread of any other animal than the wolf or the starved and thirsty horse which bears the traveler across its wastes.'' A decade later Francis Parkman's celebrated account of his journey over the Oregon Trail gave even wider publicity to the notion that the plains were a barren, trackless wilderness.

It was understandable that travelers from more luxuriant regions east of the Mississippi should have been repelled by the aridity of the Great Plains. But it was exaggerated and misleading to refer to it as a desert or as ''one prodigious graveyard,'' which was Mark Twain's description. Vegetation might be sparse but the region teemed with life. The jack rabbit and the prairie dog—

William Cary's painting of a herd of buffalo at a river. Despite its bulk, the buffalo is a strong swimmer, and the great herds frequently crossed rivers during their grazing over the Great Plains.

a kind of burrowing rodent—could survive there virtually without water. Other species, like the antelope, the coyote, and the wolf, found aridity to their liking and in addition possessed the speed and elusiveness essential to safety in such an open country.

These qualities were not, however, possessed by the most numerous and most awesome of the plains animals, the buffalo or American bison. These huge, shaggy beasts were poorly equipped to defend themselves or to detect and escape from enemies. Their shortsightedness, lumbering gait, and ponderous movements made them easy prey for Indian and white hunters. Nevertheless the plains environment was sufficiently favorable to allow immense herds of buffalo to exist. One nineteenth-century naturalist, William T. Hornaday, asserted that ''of all the quadrupeds that have lived upon the earth, probably no other species has ever marshaled such innumerable hosts as the American bison.'' Just how numerous they were is impossible to say. Hornaday believed it would have been ''as easy to count . . . the number of leaves in a forest as to calculate the number of buffaloes living at any given time during the history of the species previous to 1870.'' But for what they are worth, estimates of the buffalo population at the time of the Civil War range from 12 to 15 million.

But the fact that the Great Plains were known to be

capable of supporting an abundance of wildlife did nothing to shake the general conviction that farming could not succeed there. After the Civil War, it is true, the concept of an American Sahara would give way to the more optimistic pictures painted by enthusiastic travelers, townsite promoters, and land and immigration agencies. By the 1870s it would be argued increasingly that there were no geographic or climatic barriers to the advance of the farming frontier. The slogan "Rain Follows the Plough" summarized the widely held superstition that the settlement of the plains would itself produce an increase of rainfall. But although the theory had been heard before 1860, it was not then widely held. On the contrary it was generally assumed that the western limit of traditional agriculture had already been reached. Many people thought that if white men tried to live beyond the 98th meridian they would be forced to adopt a pastoral, nomadic life like that of the plains tribesmen. Similar assumptions guided Congress in passing the Pacific Railroad Act in 1862. The motive for authorizing a transcontinental railroad was not to open up the Great Plains to settlement, but rather to remove a barrier standing between the Mississippi Valley and the settled portions of the Pacific Coast.

On the far side of the Great Plains lay a region which constituted an even more formidable barrier to the west-ward advance of the pioneer. The craggy masses and towering peaks of the Rocky Mountains extended northward from central New Mexico to Alaska to form the backbone of the continent. But although along the rim of the plains the skyline was saw-toothed with jutting granite, the great mountain chain was not as continuous as it may have appeared. Interspersed between the peaks which rose to between 10,000 and 14,000 feet there were numerous plateaus and high grassy valleys suitable for ranching and farming. All the same, large-scale agriculture was ruled out by lack of arable land and the rigors of the climate. Even where rainfall was abundant the growing season was short and, below the timberline, there was a dense and sometimes impenetrable growth of pine, fir, and spruce trees.

In this high country the thick forests sheltered a variety of wildlife. Beaver were plentiful in the streams and lake margins, bear, elk, and bighorn sheep abounded in the higher elevations, and Rocky Mountain goats lived in rocky lairs above the ceiling of tree growth. It was the profusion of wildlife in the Rockies that first lured white men to the region in the 1820s and 1830s—fur traders, trappers, and mountain men seeking beaver pelts and black bear skins. But the intense competition that developed for the fur trade resulted in the destruction of many of the region's fur-bearing animals, especially the

Bruce Coleman

Kenneth Fink/Ardea

The early explorers of the West found a land teeming with wildlife. Above: The puma, or mountain lion, whose territory stretched from North to South America. Left: The massive and ferocious grizzly bear. Below: The bighorn or Rocky Mountain sheep, agile and sure-footed.

beaver, and by 1840 the Rocky Mountain country was completely trapped out. By the time of the Civil War, however, the immense and varied mineral resources of the Rockies were beginning to attract a different kind of pioneer. The discovery of gold in the Pike's Peak district of what would shortly become Colorado Territory started the first of many stampedes of miners and prospectors to the mountains. Within a few years the lure of the gold, silver, copper, lead, and zinc that were so widely embedded throughout the mountain ranges would turn the whole region into a mining frontier.

If settlers found the Rockies unattractive they must have been no less daunted by the last of the Far West's physiographic provinces. This was the huge Intermountain region between the Rockies and the Pacific ranges. Roughly 600 miles wide and about 1,100 miles long this was a region of mountains, high plateaus, basins, and deserts. Taken as a whole it was the driest region of the United States, with an average rainfall of between three and ten inches. It was made up of three distinct sections. In the extreme north lay the Columbia Plateau, located in eastern Washington, Oregon, and parts of Idaho. This was a relatively favored area, receiving sufficient rainfall to become in time an important center of grain and livestock production. But the rest of the region was useless for agriculture.

To the south of the Columbia Plateau lay a great depression centering in Nevada and western Utah and aptly known as the Great Basin. Here the lack of rainfall—only about four or five inches annually—and the saucer-like configuration of the mountain ranges ensured that such streams as existed vanished without ever reaching the sea. The two most important rivers of the Great Basin area, the Humboldt and the Carson, meandered sluggishly eastward from the Sierras through Utah and Nevada before petering out in the sand and salt of the Humboldt and Carson sinks. The only vegetation that could survive in this semiarid and alkaline region was the sagebrush, a low, hardy shrub whose gnarled branches and gray-green leaves formed a thin carpet over the cracked earth. But like the Rockies, the Great Basin was rich in minerals which overnight transformed this barren and inhospitable region into a mining frontier.

Farther south too there would be gold and silver strikes, as well as massive discoveries of copper, after the Civil War. But here in the last of the three sections that made up the Intermountain region there was little else to attract the frontiersman and much to repel him. Embracing southern New Mexico, Arizona, and the southeastern corner of California, this was a bleakly desolate area consisting largely of desert. Within its borders were Death Valley and the Colorado and Mojave deserts of California and the Gila Desert of Arizona. The whole section was one vast expanse of aridity, studded with bare, craggy mountains, interspersed with saline sinks and covered with endless miles of sunbaked, windswept sand dunes. All that would grow here was the creosote bush and certain varieties of cactus. Even the sagebrush found conditions too harsh. In time irrigation would create oases in this unpromising expanse. In the twentieth century, indeed, dams and reservoirs would enable large-scale cultivation to take place. But on the eve of the Civil War this parched wilderness must surely have been among the most repellent areas in the country.

The Indians of the Far West

This then was the natural setting for the western drama that was to be enacted in the generation after the Civil War. But it would not be a drama in which man simply pitted himself against nature. When the miners, the cattlemen, and the ranchers moved into the last frontier they did not enter an empty land but one inhabited by a variety of Indian tribes. The Indians are usually described as an obstacle to white settlement, and so indeed they were. But they ought not to be regarded primarily in that light. They were not merely a problem for the westward-marching pioneer to overcome, like the harsh environment, the unknown distances, the vagaries of climate, and the wild animals. From the Indian point of view the westward surge of frontiersmen was not the triumph of civilization that white men proclaimed it to be but the last sad chapter in the destruction of their ancient and varied cultures. The Indian way of life on the eve of this catastrophe had survived two and a half centuries of contact with the white man. Despite broken treaties and broken promises and successive encroachments by white settlers on his lands, the red man's civilization still flourished. It deserves at least to be described on its own terms and in its own right.

On the eve of the white invasion of the Far West, there were probably 240,000 Indians on the Great Plains, in the Rockies, and in the Intermountain region. In addition tlere were 50,000 or so west of the Pacific ranges and a similar number in the Indian Territory, later to become Oklahoma. Most of the last-named were not indigenous to the West but belonged to the Five Civilized Tribes (Cherokee, Choctaw, Chickasaw, Creek, and Seminole) who had been forcibly removed from their lands east of the Mississippi between 1825 and 1840.

The predominant fact about the western tribesmen was their physical, linguistic, and cultural diversity. The Crow were remarkable for their height, the Utes for being squat and thickset, the California natives for their prominent Mongoloid features. The Sac lived in a bark wigwam, the Kiowa in a tepee made of hide, the Pueblo in an apartment house of stone or adobe. The Mandan inhabited an earthen lodge, the California Indian a brush hut or lean-to,

the Papago a circular thatched hut covered in straw. Some Indians dressed in buckskin and buffalo robes, others in two-piece cotton suits or breechcloth. Others wore nothing at all. Some were sedentary, others nomadic. The Apaches, Comanches, and Sioux were savage and warlike, the Hopi and Zuñi civilized and essentially peaceful. The list of variations was in fact unending. About the only things Indians had in common were black hair, brown eyes, and some shade of coppery skin.

All the same it is possible to divide the Indians of the Far West into three main culture groups: the Plains Indians, the miscellaneous tribes of the Intermountain desert area, and the farmers and herders of the Southwest. Of these groups the last two were relatively few in number, their culture was less well developed, and they were not destined to play a prominent part in the coming conflict with the white man.

In the barren depression between the Rockies and the Sierra Nevada and in the desert region of southeastern California lived the most primitive Indians in the whole of the United States. The tribes which inhabited this harsh environment—the Bannock, Shoshone, Ute, Paiute, Shasta, and Snake—were small, widely scattered, and poorly led. In a region where game was scarce and vegetation scanty, the tribesmen led a miserable existence given over almost wholly to the search for food.

The camp of Kicking Bird, a Kiowa, photographed by William S. Soule. The wooden poles which formed the skeleton of the tepee left a hole at the top for ventilation—particularly necessary when a fire would be lighted in the center.

Scornfully referred to as "diggers" from their practice of grubbing for food, they lived on seeds, berries, roots, and nuts and even on grasshoppers, snakes, reptiles, vermin, and rodents—"anything they can bite," as Mark Twain observed. Their culture, not surprisingly, was as meager as their diet. They made their homes in lean-tos or in holes in the ground. Their clothing was of the scantiest. And they possessed none but the most primitive weapons and implements. Occupied fully with the quest for food, they had little time for religious and other ceremonies and still less for making war on other tribes or on white intruders. Such enfeebled people could offer little resistance either to white encroachment or to disease and already, by the time of the Civil War, their numbers were declining.

In sharp contrast to these unfortunate wretches were the varied groups of Indians who inhabited the dry and desolate uplands of New Mexico and Arizona. This was the home, for example, of the Pueblos, who comprised several tribal groups of which the Hopi, the Zuñi, and the

150

Rio Grande Pueblo were the most important. They were a sedentary and peaceful people with a highly-developed culture. Whole villages lived a communal existence in large, elaborate, fortress-like houses. These dwellings, made of stone and adobe, were situated on lofty mesas or cracks in the cliff and were accessible only by ladders. The Pueblo were skillful farmers, practicing irrigation to grow corn, wheat, vegetables, and fruit. They were also capable artisans, weaving their own cloth and making baskets and pottery.

The other main group of southwestern Indians, the Navajo, had migrated to northern New Mexico and Arizona from the Great Plains several centuries earlier. Their culture was a remarkable blend of elements from the Great Plains and the Southwestern Plateau. They lived both in tepees and mud huts. They were at the same time hunters and farmers. And they combined a nomadic existence in the summer with a sedentary one in the winter. While they ranged widely over the rugged highlands in search of pasture for their sheep, they maintained permanent homes and, besides practicing agriculture, produced intricate silverware, elaborate baskets, and colorful blankets.

The Great Plains Tribes

In 1860, however, nearly two-thirds of all the Indians remaining in the United States lived on the Great Plains. Of the many tribes into which they were divided, the most numerous and powerful in the North were the Sioux of Minnesota and the Dakotas, the Blackfeet of Idaho and western Montana, and the Crow of southern Montana. On the central plains the Cheyenne and the Arapaho were dominant around the headwaters of the Platte, the Pawnee in western Nebraska, and the Osage in western Kansas. Farther south the leading tribes were the Apache and the Comanche of Arizona and New Mexico. In addition there were a number of tribes which, though not in fact inhabitants of the Great Plains, displayed plains characteristics. These included the Mandan and the Omaha of the low plains just west of the Mississippi and the Nez Percé, Ute, and Shoshone who lived in the foothills and valleys of the Rockies.

Above right: A fortress-like Navaho tower sits atop a ridge of the Grand Canyon. Some tribes of the Southwest built cities that could house up to a thousand people. Right: Six young Paiute braves play a game of Ni-aung-pi-kai, or "Kill the Bone," in front of an admiring audience. This photograph was taken at Kaibab Plateau, Arizona, by John Hillers with the Powell Expedition in the early 1870s.

Above left: Two Nez Percés pose in front of their tepee, located near the Yellowstone River in Montana. The French gave the tribe its name because the Indians wore nose pendants. Left: A Crow painted elkskin robe depicting a buffalo hunt; unaffected by the white man's art, Indian primitive artists had developed a unique and vivid narrative style of their own.

George Catlin's view of Plains Indians on a buffalo hunt. The animal was essential to the Indian's way of life: he used the hide for clothing and shelter, the meat for food, and the bones for tools.

The Plains Indians differed from the red men east of the Mississippi in being nomadic and warlike. Both these characteristics were the consequence of their dependence on the buffalo and the horse. The buffalo was to the natives of the plains the source of virtually all the necessities of life. The tribesmen came to depend upon the buffalo's flesh for food, its hide for clothing, shoes, tepees, and blankets. Its bones were used for implements and ornaments, its horns for cups, ladles, and spoons, and its sinews for thread and bowstrings. The buffalo's stomach became a water bottle and even its dung, when dried into chips, was used for fuel.

Originally the Indian had hunted the buffalo on foot. But from the sixteenth century onward the horses introduced into Mexico by the Spaniards wandered northward over the plains in wild herds. By giving the Indian a mobility he had never before possessed the horse transformed his way of life. It now became possible to hunt the buffalo more effectively and to range widely across the plains in pursuit of the great herds. In the course of time the Plains Indians became superb horsemen—the finest in the world in the view of George Catlin, the artist famous for his pictures of Indian life on the plains. The Comanche in particular excited his admiration. "Comanches," he wrote, ". . . in their movements are

heavy and ungraceful; and on their feet one of the most unattractive and slovenly-looking races of Indians that I have ever seen; but the moment they mount their horses they seem at once metamorphosed, and surprise the spectator with the ease and elegance of their movements."

The Plains Indians became not only expert horsemen but, as competition for the buffalo brought them in conflict with other tribes, fierce, and skillful warriors. The weapons they used in hunting and warfare were primitive—bows and arrows and long stone-tipped lances. But mounted on their swift horses they were a formidable foe. They could hang by a heel on one side of the horse, with both hands free to unleash a rapid volley of arrows from under its neck, thus remaining virtually invisible to an enemy. Until the introduction of the repeating rifle, Plains Indians were more than a match for white men. A mounted warrior could fire several arrows while his white adversary was recharging his muzzle-loading rifle. The Colt revolver, introduced in the 1840s, did something

Left: Frederic Remington's watercolor, Pony War Dance, *captures the skill of the Indian rider. The horse, brought to North America by the Spanish, transformed the Plains Indians' way of life. It enabled a tribe to move farther, with more ease, in search of food. In addition, the warriors became formidable light cavalry. Right: Kee-a-kee-ka-sa-coo-way (The Man Who Gives the War Whoop), head chief of the Cree. The artist, Paul Kane, traveled widely in the West in the 1840s, and his sketches and paintings provide a valuable record of the life and customs of many of the tribes.*

to tilt the balance in favor of the white man, but the Indian shield of smoke-cured buffalo hide often proved tough enough to deflect a bullet. Their mobility, moreover, made the tribesmen singularly elusive enemies. With no permanent settlement to bind them to any one locality they could break camp quickly when an enemy approached, and spirit away their villages and their women and children before an attack could be mounted.

Between different tribes fierce enmities could exist, usually in consequence of cultural differences or controversy over vaguely defined hunting grounds. The Utes and the Cheyenne were old enemies. The Kiowa of the Black Hills were for years in a state of continuous warfare with their Sioux, Arapaho, and Cheyenne neighbors before finally being forced to seek new homes to the south. But geographical proximity could also produce friendly relationships between different tribes. So could the common danger in which all Indians were placed by the white advance. Thus the Arapaho were closely associated with the Cheyenne, the Kiowa with the Comanche. There were in addition frequent intertribal contacts for the purposes of trade. It was the practice of Plains Indians to exchange their buffalo pelts and meat for corn and other products raised by more sedentary tribes on the fringes of the plains.

Another factor tending to unite different tribes was similarity of language. But this was not, however, of paramount importance in shaping day-to-day group life.

Nor for that matter was membership of a particular tribe. Occasionally all the members of a tribe would assemble for a tribal festival, a religious ceremony, or a council of war. But the tribal unit was too large and unwieldy to engage in the central activity of the Indians, the buffalo hunt. Hence the all-important social and economic unit was the tribal subdivision known as the band, which consisted of between three hundred and five hundred people. Each band was largely independent and had an elaborate government. At the head was a chief who, with the advice of a council of elders, made all the decisions. These were enforced by "soldier societies" made up of braves who had won renown by their deeds. The different bands ordinarily had little to do with one another. Decisions were taken unilaterally and it was quite common for some bands within a tribe to be at war while others remained at peace. Out of this situation would arise many of the complications and misunderstandings that were to bedevil relations between Indians and whites.

Just as the buffalo hunt formed the basis of social organization so too did it become the main focus of the tribesmen's religion. Like most primitive peoples the Plains Indians believed that the natural world was controlled and guided by supernatural forces and powers. Without their benevolent assistance nothing in the visible universe could prosper. Such aid was always sought in time of sickness, famine, or drought, or when the band

was about to go on the warpath. But it was most frequently and urgently invoked on the eve of a buffalo hunt. Without the aid of the spirits the buffalo herds would stay out of range, the warriors would lack the necessary skill and bravery. Thus to ensure the success of the hunt the tribesmen devoted much attention to religious ceremonies.

Rituals and Religion

Individual braves fasted, prayed, and inflicted torture on themselves in an effort to move the gods to pity and draw from them the needed qualities of mind and body. They consulted medicine men as to the meaning of their dreams, which were seen as guides to future action. They sought from them "medicine bundles"—charms supposed to give the wearer power over natural forces—and advice as to the construction of "medicine signs" to lure the buffalo herds. In addition the warriors performed elaborate ceremonial rites designed to appease the powers that shaped the events of the universe—the sun, the moon, the earth, the sky, the rocks, the wind, and the water.

Of these ceremonies the most important was the sun dance, an eight-day-long ritual which many tribes performed but which was conducted most meticulously by the Arapaho and the Cheyenne. Among the Missouri River tribes it incorporated a self-inflicted torture rite in which the supplicant sought divine favor by exhibiting a willingness to endure extremes of pain. The dancers attached leather thongs to their skins and to the center pole in the sun dance, then danced or pulled away until the thongs were torn free, carrying with them strips of flesh. Such were the lengths to which the braves felt they must go in order to ensure that there existed that harmonious relationship between man and his environment upon which, so they believed, everything else depended.

There was, however, another side to plains life. It was not a constant round of buffalo hunts and religious ceremonies. Plains Indians in fact took a great delight in sport and games. In one sense hunting the buffalo could be classed as sport, but the tribesmen also enjoyed less demanding forms of recreation. They played a kind of lacrosse and a crude form of field hockey known as shinny. They also staged horse races and athletic contests.

But it was warfare that absorbed the greater part of their energies. It also provided the main focus for their aspirations. Indian boys were taught to believe that war was the highest form of activity in which man could engage. It was a reproach, they were told, to live to old age. The highest glory was to die young, fighting bravely in battle. Such a death would ensure for them a happy existence in the spirit world. Meanwhile bravery in

Collection of Mrs Althea Bass/American Heritage

The sun dance was the most important of the Indians' many annual religious rituals. This eight-day-long ceremony, performed with the greatest detail by the Arapaho and Cheyenne tribes, often included self-inflicted torture. Above: Carl Sweeny's watercolor shows Arapaho squaws and braves looking on while the sun dance is performed in the special medicine lodge, built to face the rising sun.

combat, usually measured by "counting coups"—touching an enemy or capturing his horse or his weapons—could also bring recognition and reward in this world. It helped determine social rank and gave warriors the privilege of acquiring additional wives. Warfare, there-

by Carl Sweezy
Sun dance
tribe Arapahoes

fore, although it served the community through defense of tribal hunting grounds, was essentially a means of individual self-fulfillment. This conception of war, so different from that of the white man, explains why the frontiersman was conscious of the Indian mainly as a ferocious enemy. It also goes far to explain the cruel practices which characterized the Indian conduct of war. Torture was seen as a means whereby a captive would acquire a badge of honor and show himself worthy of divine protection. The mutilation of slain enemies was regarded as a safeguard against their becoming threats in the spirit world. Such methods of warfare did not stem, as frontiersmen tended to believe, from uniquely depraved or vicious natures. Rather did they arise and derive their sanction from a particular culture and a distinctive set of religious beliefs.

When the white man's Civil War broke out in 1861 Plains Indians were not greatly affected, and they could have been pardoned for believing that their unique and colorful way of life would go on indefinitely. In fact its days were numbered. Within a generation the Indians' civilization would be smashed beyond repair. The wandering bands of red men, the bellowing herds of buffalo, the swift ponies, the tepee encampments, the ancient tribal rituals, the bow and arrow, the scalping knife, the feathered headdress, the beaded moccasin—all these which had been for so long part of the Western panorama would soon be no more. Their old enemy the white man seemed to have an insatiable lust for land and riches. Even now, in the midst of a great fratricidal struggle, he was poised to span the continent, and his railroad was to change the face of the West forever.

Ribbons of Steel

In the three decades before the Civil War Americans had built a railroad system which fairly well served the eastern half of the nation. By 1861, the western fingers of this iron network were close to the edge of the frontier from Wisconsin to Texas. In the decades following the Civil War, the railroads expanded rapidly west. And in the 1870s and 1880s the westward reaching rail lines were to move well ahead of the frontier, pulling millions of Americans out into the Great American Desert.

As the typical settler moved westward he desired any transportation which would link him with his kinfolk back in the East. He also wanted it to supply his many needs and at the same time to furnish a market for his produce. Between the Civil War and the turn of the century, trans-Mississippi railroads were to help a whole generation of prairie farmers conquer the hostile West.

With substantial help from the government, several railroads were built across the western mountains to the Pacific. In these years the railroad also moved the Texas longhorn from cow town to the Chicago stockyards and made the riches of the mines of Colorado, Nevada, and Montana more accessible.

But in the 1850s, before the coming of the railroads, a variety of other forms of transportation and communication were serving the West. The settlement of Oregon, the Mexican War, and the discovery of gold in California, all made strong demands for some form of overland transport. In turn the slow freight wagon, the faster stage-

The coming of the railroad revolutionized life in the West. Right: An advertisement for the Illinois Central shows the railroad superceding other forms of transportation. Below: The old and the new—stage coaches en route from Concord, New Hampshire, to the Union Pacific's terminus in the West.

The stagecoach provided a service to communities not yet served by the railroad. Above: Teams preparing to leave the Wells, Fargo & Co office at a railroad terminus. Below: A six-horse stage crossing the Arizona desert at full speed.

coach, the Pony Express, and finally the galvanized iron wire of the Pacific and Overland Telegraph companies served western settlements before the Civil War.

Some teamsters with their rugged wagons appeared in the West almost as soon as the first settlements did. The early trade over the Santa Fe Trail in the 1820s and 1830s was soon supplemented by wagon traffic on the Oregon, Mormon, and California trails. Army forts, the Mormon settlements in Utah, and the mining camps in Colorado and Nevada all had pressing needs which could only be met by overland freighting.

In these pre-Civil War years modest federal aid was given for the location, survey, and improvement of western wagon roads. In 1853 William B. Waddell and William H. Russell, both of whom had had some experience in the Santa Fe trade, were given a federal contract to carry military supplies from the Missouri River to western army posts. By 1858 the firm owned 3,500 freight wagons pulled by 40,000 oxen driven by as many as 4,000 men. The coming of the railroads a few years later did away with the main wagon routes. But for much of the rest of the century the teamsters furnished feeder line service until the railway network was complete.

In 1850 stagecoach service of a sort was started between Independence, Missouri, and Salt Lake City. A year later it was extended to California. This service was ill-equipped and so irregular that winter travel was often abandoned. Six years later a much improved service was provided by the new Butterfield Overland Mail.

John Butterfield was a New Yorker who had worked himself up from stage driver to a position where he had financial interests in stage lines, canal packet boats, and express routes. In 1857 Butterfield and his associates were awarded a $600,000 contract by the postmaster general to provide semiweekly service, in each direction, from St Louis to San Francisco. The route ran via El Paso, Tucson, and Los Angeles—a distance of 2,800 miles. This route permitted year-round service and also avoided Utah where the Mormons were being troublesome.

During the early months of 1858, Butterfield built 141 way stations, constructed bridges, and purchased 1,500 horses and mules. He used 250 Concord coaches and stagewagons and hired about 800 men to operate the line. When the first eastbound coach from San Francisco arrived at the railroad terminal at Tipton, Missouri, in a little less than twenty-five days, President James Buchanan wired Butterfield: ''It is a glorious triumph for

THE PONY EXPRESS

On April 3, 1860, the first Pony Express rider galloped out of St Joseph, Missouri, where the railroad from the East came to an abrupt end. Six days after this first rider headed west, his mail pouch reached Salt Lake City. Four days later the same mail was delivered to Sacramento. (Usually the same trip by stage coach took about twice that time.) On the arrival of the first Pony Express, brass bands paraded through Sacramento's streets, and bonfires blazed throughout the night as Californians celebrated their new link with the East.

The Pony Express was operated not by the government, but by the freighting company of Russell, Majors & Waddell. Their postage rate began at an extremely expensive $10 an ounce, which was later dropped to a more reasonable $2 an ounce. The company employed about 200 hard-riding horsemen, who rode 500 ponies kept at more than 150 relay stations along the 2,000 mile route.

Speed was of utmost importance. It was in effect a relay race against time. As one horseman charged into a station, another horse and rider galloped off without delay. Some riders, however, traveled a total of from forty to seventy miles on a series of horses. Often a rider would be absent, and it has been said that on one occasion the fifteen-year-old William F. Cody was in the saddle for more than twenty-one hours, and covered a distance of more than 320 miles.

The work of a Pony Express rider was dangerous and far from glamorous. Riders had to contend not only with the rough terrain and extreme weather conditions, but also with hostile Indians. In San Francisco in March 1860, the company advertised for "Young skinny wiry fellows, not over eighteen. Must be expert riders willing to risk death daily. Orphans preferred."

In November 1860, the news of Abraham Lincoln's election as president was carried from Fort Kearney, Nebraska, the end of the eastern telegraph line, to Fort Churchill, Nevada, at the end of the western line. It took only six days—probably the fastest of all Pony Express journeys.

As the telegraph lines began to converge from east and west, the distance traveled by the ponies became shorter. Even as the first riders started out, they passed new telegraph lines in Kansas and in California. Finally when the two advancing wires were joined at Salt Lake City on October 22, 1861, the nation no longer needed the Pony Express, and it came to an end two days later.

Although more than 34,000 pieces of mail were carried, the Pony Express failed to make a profit. Instead, one of the most exciting and daring ventures of the Old West lost over $200,000 during its brief eighteen-month existence.

Below: Remington's view of the Pony Express. One rider has just come into the station—another gallops off.

civilization and the Union." The four-horse stages carried passengers at $200 for a one-way trip and mail at 10 cents per letter.

The Civil War forced the overland mail and stage line to take a more northerly route. On July 18, 1861, stage-coach service began from St Joseph (via Salt Lake City) to Folsom, California. Early in 1862 much of this route came under the control of Ben Holladay, a freighter from Missouri who had known and served the West since the Mexican War. Holladay expanded his western stage lines during the Civil War. When he sold out to Wells, Fargo & Company in 1866, he was operating nearly 5,000 miles of stage lines stretching from the Missouri River to California, and from Colorado north to Montana and Oregon. On most of these routes he held mail contracts, and soon Holladay was known as the "stagecoach king" of the West. Even after the railroad had replaced the stage over the main routes, the staging business long remained important for the branch line or feeder service which it provided.

Planning the Routes West

Some Americans had been dreaming about western rail lines even as oxen or mule-drawn wagons and stages were still providing what transportation there was. One of the first dreamers was Asa Whitney, a merchant from New York City. Whitney proposed a railroad from the Great Lakes to the mouth of the Columbia River, after a trip to China had convinced him of the great importance of future trade with the Orient.

Whitney made a personal inspection of the eastern portion of the proposed route and in 1845 sent to Congress a request for a charter for such a railroad. His proposal gained only modest support from the lawmakers. Four years later the influential senator from Missouri, Thomas Hart Benton, introduced a Pacific Railroad Bill for a line from St Louis to San Francisco. The project was to be financed by the sale of public lands. Benton had once helped finance a Pacific railroad survey expedition which was led by his son-in-law John C. Frémont.

In the 1850s the maturing railroad industry clearly made the idea of a railroad to the Pacific far more feasible. Benton favored St Louis as the eastern terminus of any Pacific railroad, but other promoters just as actively pushed Milwaukee, Chicago, Memphis, Vicksburg, or New Orleans for that honor. In March 1853 Congress voted $150,000 in the Pacific Railroad Survey Act for the survey of several possible rail routes to the Pacific Coast. US Army engineer survey teams examined four central or southern routes while Isaac Stevens, governor of the Washington Territory, surveyed a far northern route.

The Gadsden Purchase of 1853 helped to make interested southerners certain that the best route was along the 32nd parallel. Secretary of War Jefferson Davis did indeed recommend this far southern route, but this carried little weight with northerners who preferred a central route. Senator Stephen A. Douglas had already in 1854 introduced his Kansas–Nebraska Bill, and soon the flare-up of proslavery and antislavery passions caused the Pacific railway issue to be largely forgotten. The financial difficulties created by the panic of 1857 clearly ended any chance of a railroad to the Pacific in the 1850s. But the industry, on the eve of the Civil War, was ready for such a challenge. A generation of railroad experience had solved most earlier technical and engineering problems. By 1860 American railroads were furnishing a reliable and fairly economical transportation service. More than two-thirds of the 30,000-mile rail network had been built during the previous decade, and the service had basically been extended to the frontier.

In Wisconsin the 900 miles of railroad included two rival lines crossing the state from Milwaukee to La Crosse and Prairie du Chien on the Mississippi. Iowa had a direct rail connection to Chicago via the Rock Island Bridge built over the Mississippi in 1856. Four or five rival lines already pushed one-third of the way across the state. The most western outreach of the national network was the Hannibal & St Joseph, which reached the Missouri River early in 1859. Another 400 miles of railroad, tributary to St Louis, served much of central Missouri.

Trans-Mississippi trackage south of Missouri was sparse and scattered in 1860. The thirty-eight miles in Arkansas consisted of two short segments west of Memphis. Louisiana could claim more than a hundred miles of railway west of the Mississippi, but it was in four widely separated parts of the state. The 300 miles of railroad found in Texas were a hundred miles or more from any connecting eastern lines.

In 1860 the Republicans, who nominated Abraham Lincoln in the Chicago Wigwam, promised the voters a railroad to the Pacific. The short session of Congress in 1861 could only think of the pressing problems of war. The longer session of 1861–62, however, had time to take up such matters as the tariff, free land for the farmers, and the sponsorship of a railroad to the Pacific Coast. With the South no longer in Congress, it was a simple matter to agree on a central location, a route which would serve both Chicago and St Louis.

On July 1, 1862, Abraham Lincoln signed into law the first Pacific Railway Act. This authorized two companies to build a transcontinental railroad. The Union Pacific was to build westward from the Missouri River, and the Central Pacific was to build eastward from Sacramento. Unlike the Central Pacific, which had been chartered and organized in California in the spring of 1861, the Union Pacific was set up under a federal charter. It was

The Union Pacific laid track westward from the Missouri at an average of a mile a day. Right: A crew poses atop No 119—the UPRR locomotive at the Promontory Point ceremony.

provided that the Union Pacific should be capitalized at $100 million, and more than 150 commissioners were selected to obtain stock subscriptions.

Both railroads were to receive ten alternate sections of public lands for each completed mile of track. Furthermore each of the two companies was to receive a thirty-year government loan in bonds. The amount of the loan was to vary with the difficulty of the terrain: $16,000 per mile of railroad across the plains, $32,000 per mile for the plateau and desert regions between the Rockies and the Sierra Nevada, and $48,000 per mile for the rigorous mountain regions. The new road was to be built in standard gauge which was 4 feet 8½ inches. Finally, the federal government was to be given reduced fares and rates on all government traffic over the completed road.

Naturally the Civil War slowed the first efforts to build a transcontinental line. When the entire country in 1862 was given a chance to purchase stock in the Union Pacific, only seven subscribers responded. But by the fall of 1863 the required initial stock had been taken. Major General John A. Dix, who had subscribed for fifty shares, was elected president. Dix, a well-known citizen of New York, had earlier been interested in Iowa railroads, but in 1863 he was kept busy by army administration problems. Thus quite early the real management of company affairs fell into the hands of the road's vice president, Dr Thomas C. Durant. Durant had been more concerned with promoting western railroads such as the Mississippi & Missouri, and the Chicago, Rock Island & Pacific, than he had been in following his own profession. Forty-two years of age, lean and energetic though with a marked stoop, he had known for some years that he had a greater flair for stock manipulation than for the art of healing.

On December 2, 1863, ground was finally broken on the bleak Nebraska prairie when territorial Governor Alvin Saunders dug up a few clods of cold prairie sod.

Federal officials, local politicians, bankers, and editors had all been invited by Durant to the Union Pacific ''gala ceremony and banquet.'' Many in the total crowd of more than a thousand heard the chief orator of the day, George Francis Train, promise that the Pacific railroad would bring millions of immigrants to ''settle in this golden land in twenty years.''

Building The Union Pacific

Labor was hard to find, the connecting rail line east was stalled in the middle of Iowa, and new stock subscriptions were scarce. Months brought very little progress. During the waiting Durant and his friends did get Congress to double the land grant in 1864. Some grading was accomplished, and two loaded barges filled with light 50-pound rail finally arrived from Pittsburgh via the Ohio, Mississippi, and Missouri rivers. The first rails were laid in Omaha on July 10, 1865, but the crews were so clumsy and inexperienced that eleven days were needed to spike down the first mile of track on the cottonwood ties. By November the end-of-track was only some thirty miles west of the Missouri.

Even as the first grading and track-laying was taking place, Durant was having difficulty with his chief engineer, the round-faced but dour Peter A. Dey. Dey had seen Durant project rail lines in Iowa, and the cautious engineer was not happy with the recollection. Dey had made careful surveys of construction costs west of Omaha and estimated that the first hundred miles of Union Pacific track could be built at about $30,000 a mile. Durant argued that he wanted a first-class road and asked the engineer to plan a better road with lower grades, easier curves, and broader embankments. Dey

Union Pacific Railroad Museum Collection/Western Americana

Top: The Union Pacific's end-of-track. Above: Dan Casement, the younger of the Casement brothers, famed builders of the Union Pacific. Right: Inside a rail car, called "The Modern Ship of the Plains."

complied with the request and soon changed the specifications which raised estimated costs to about $50,000 per mile. Durant gave a construction contract to Herbert M. Hoxie, who really represented the corrupt Crédit Mobilier company. The contract called for the cheaper specifications in the original Dey estimate, for which Hoxie and his associates were to be paid at the rate of $60,000 per mile. Dey was naturally indignant when he saw a copy of the contract and soon resigned.

Early in 1866 the Union Pacific selected a new engineer, the handsome Civil War veteran General Grenville M. Dodge. He had earlier helped convince President Lincoln that Council Bluffs, Iowa, would be the best eastern terminus for the Union Pacific. Like Dey, Dodge was a capable engineer, but he was also more amenable to the ways of Durant and false front railroad construction companies like the Crédit Mobilier.

In November 1865 Durant invited General William T. Sherman and a few other guests to a brief inspection trip to the end-of-track. The special train was so primitive that Sherman saw the new road while seated on a

nail keg on one of two flatcars coupled to an engine which bore his name. Sherman was a little skeptical even as he listened to Durant's confident prediction of progress. The general noted the treeless prairie, the slow rate of track-laying, and the threatening Indians.

But things quickly improved once Durant signed a construction contract with the Casement brothers of Painesville, Ohio. The thirty-seven-year-old General Jack Casement and his younger brother, Dan, were small but active men. A friend of the brothers once called the pair "the biggest little men you ever saw – about as large as twelve-year-old boys, but requiring bigger hats." Jack was only 5 feet 4 inches tall, but he had a full beard and, more important, a way with men which quickly gained their full respect. Dan was a wizard with figures and problems of logistics. The two men had laid lots of track before the Civil War, and now in February 1866 the brothers agreed to "lay and fill" track for the Union Pacific at a basic rate of $750 a mile. The company was to supply a graded way plus all needed supplies, materials, and transportation.

As the end-of-track moved on, so did the girls, saloonkeepers, and gamblers who relieved the workers of their money. Right: Bear River "City," one of the temporary towns known as "hell on wheels."

The Casements quickly recruited work crews, many of whom were veterans of the Civil War. Some were Irish, but others were "galvanized Yanks" whose army service had been with Lee, Joe Johnston, or Jackson. Whether army vets, or immigrants recruited in Chicago, the workmen soon knew the effective discipline demanded both by the Casements and the lurking Sioux and Cheyenne. The thud of a feathered arrow could quickly make the rifle more important than a shovel or a spike hammer.

The Casements put together construction trains with cars which provided almost every possible need: dining rooms, kitchens, blacksmith's shop, carpenter's shop, saddler's shop, telegraph office, feed store, and water storage. Each sleeping car held bunks for a hundred men with ceiling racks holding many extra rifles. And a herd of cattle which plodded along the right of way provided fresh meat. The Casement gangs quickly speeded up construction. Singing helped in using shovels or spike hammers. Soon Jack Casement promised his men the prize of a pound of tobacco if they could lay a mile of track in a day. Later, an extra half day's pay pushed the track-laying up to a mile and a half per shift. One month in the summer of 1866 saw sixty-five miles of new iron laid down in the broad valley of the Platte. But it could not be all work and no play. At night, on weekends, and especially after payday, the temporary base camps literally became "hell on wheels." A full complement of saloonkeepers, prostitutes, and gamblers of the roughest sort prompted novelist Robert Louis Stevenson to describe the camps as "roaring, impromptu cities full of gold and lust and death."

By the close of 1866 the end-of-track had reached North Platte, Nebraska, 290 miles west of Omaha. During 1867 construction was pushed to a point several miles west of Cheyenne and the following year found the line in eastern Utah not many miles away from Ogden. When the track passed the 100th meridian, 240 miles up the Platte, the exuberant Durant again felt the need to celebrate. Invitations to VIPs were sent out wholesale. In early October 1866, General Dodge hosted such notables as lawyer and politician Benjamin F. Wade and future president Rutherford B. Hayes of Ohio at a buffalo hunt, a mock Indian raid, and a well-controlled prairie fire.

Toward Promontory Point

More than a thousand miles away in California and Nevada, the Central Pacific was building eastward during these same years. Since the mid-1850s an energetic young eastern engineer, Theodore Dehone Judah, had been sponsoring railroads in California. He arranged for railroad conventions in the Golden State, lobbied in Sacramento and Washington, and during the winter of 1859–60 hoped that he might get a Pacific Railroad Act passed by Congress. He did at least convince some California merchants that his proposed railroad across and through the Sierra Nevada could be more than a dream. Four Sacramento businessmen put up the money and became directors. Governor Leland Stanford was president of the Central Pacific, Collis P. Huntington was the eastern agent and political contact man, Mark Hopkins became the treasurer, and Charley Crocker was in charge.

The first shovelful of earth was turned on the muddy levee at Sacramento, on January 8, 1863. Not long after,

Judah had much the same trouble that Dey was to have with the Union Pacific. After the departure and death of Judah the "Big Four," as the merchants were to be called, built the Central Pacific their way.

Since most men in California were still seeking gold, Crocker had a hard time finding workers until someone suggested the Chinese. Few believed that these small men, with an average weight of about 110 pounds, could really endure the hardship of building a mountain railroad. Crocker employed a few and was so pleased that he began hiring them by the hundreds, direct from China. Soon thousands of Orientals were making fills with handbarrows, drilling the Summit Tunnel, or constructing the much-needed snowsheds.

Work in the mountains was slow, and more than three years was required to push over and through the Sierra Nevada. But during 1868 the hard-driving Central Pacific work crews built as fast over the Nevada flats as the Casement boys had over the Nebraska plains. The Indians of the Far West were less warlike than the Sioux, and the Central Pacific had little trouble with them. Huntington once recalled that Indian braves were generally allowed to ride freight cars while "we gave the old chiefs a pass each, good on the passenger cars."

The engineering problems of the two lines varied on the different ends. Neither base, at least at the outset, had easy access to any supply source. San Francisco manufactured little, and thus rails, rolling stock, and heavy tools all came by the slow ocean route. Back at Omaha-Council Bluffs the Union Pacific did not have a direct rail route to the East until the Chicago & North Western reached Council Bluffs in January 1867. Prior to that

Above: Chinese coolies greet a train as it steams through a series of snowsheds. These coverings were designed to keep the tracks clear of avalanching snow—a constant hazard throughout the mountain sections.

event many Union Pacific supplies came by river steamer, at least from St Joseph where a rail connection did exist. While Crocker and his associates back in California had an abundance of wood and stone, Durant and Dodge built much of their line over a nearly treeless plain. Neither of the merging lines was held down originally to a standard maximum grade—both were anxious to build track which would bring in more land grant acres.

As the rival companies raced toward each other, a compromise meeting place—Promontory Point, Utah—was finally named by Congress on April 10, 1869. The racing groups laid track with new speed. In these last construction days Crocker beefed up his sturdy Chinese crews with some stalwart Irish, and then won a $10,000 wager from Union Pacific officials by laying ten miles of track in a single day.

On May 10, 1869, the Union Pacific (1,038 miles) and the Central Pacific (742 miles) met at the little tent construction town at Promontory Point. Stanford and his guests came in two special trains from California. The Union Pacific train was late because of heavy rains and trouble from unpaid workers. Finally at noon all was ready. After a ceremony with a golden spike, Stanford and Durant tried their hands with an ordinary iron spike. Both men missed, much to the delight of the professionals who had driven spikes from Omaha and the Pacific.

The Central Pacific's route passed through extremely rugged country, which made for slow progress. Right: Construction across the Sierra Nevada in 1865.

Camera Press

As the last spike was tapped into place the telegraph sent the news to a waiting nation. A seven-mile parade started in Chicago, and fire bells rang out in San Francisco. In Utah the assembled officials retired to their private cars to celebrate.

Expansion of the Rail Network

Four more transcontinental lines were built in the quarter of a century after Promontory. The Northern Pacific Railroad received its charter from Congress on July 2, 1864, in legislation which gave the new road forty sections of federal land for each mile completed within the territories. The terrain of the proposed new route was so bleak and unfriendly that General Sherman once described it "as bad as God ever made." The whole project languished until Jay Cooke, Civil War financier and Philadelphia banker, took over in 1869. The first rails were laid in Minnesota in 1870, and by 1873 the track stretched nearly 500 miles westward to Bismarck, North Dakota. The panic of 1873, which ruined Jay Cooke, forced the line into receivership. Meanwhile Henry Villard, Bavarian immigrant and former newspaperman, had become interested in transportation in the far Northwest. With borrowed funds Villard got control of the Northern Pacific and soon had as many as 25,000 men at work on the line. On September 8, 1883, west of Helena and in the presence of President Chester A. Arthur, the last rails were laid on the Northern Pacific Railroad.

A second northern road to the Pacific was built a few years later without the benefit of a federal land grant. James Jerome Hill in 1878 already had twenty years of experience in frontier selling, freighting, and transportation. In that year the canny, one-eyed Jim Hill, along with some Scottish-Canadian associates, bought the rusting and bankrupt St Paul & Pacific Railroad. Building substantially, even though slowly, the Hill group expanded their line, now called the Great Northern Rail-

"It was a bright but cold day," wrote the Union Pacific's chief engineer. "After a few speeches we all took refuge in the Central Pacific's cars, where wine flowed freely...." It was an example followed all over the country when the news of the linking of the two railroads at Promontory Point on May 10, 1869, was received. The nation's first transcontinental railroad was worth celebrating. The Union Pacific wasted no time in advertising the merits of the new service which carried passengers "Through to San Francisco in less than Four Days...."

169

way, both to the north and toward the Pacific. By 1893 the road was completed to Seattle. The "Empire Builder" Jim Hill continued to enjoy fine financial health while nearby competing lines were facing receivership or bankruptcy. In fact the financial trouble of the nearest competitor, the Northern Pacific, became so great that the Hill interests controlled it by the turn of the century.

South of the Union Pacific other roads were also headed for mountain passes and the far Pacific. Cyrus K. Holliday, one of the founders of Topeka, Kansas, in 1863 obtained a land grant for his short Atchison & Topeka Railroad. Twenty-eight miles of track were built in 1869. Three years later, now with Santa Fe added to its name, the road had pushed out to Dodge City, soon to become the biggest cow town in the West. Once the Santa Fe reached Colorado it came into conflict with the narrow gauge Denver & Rio Grande, then being built by General William Jackson Palmer. The Santa Fe lost to the three-foot road in the Royal Gorge of the Arkansas but did beat Palmer's work crews to Raton Pass, the best entrance into New Mexico.

Above: Working in Big Rock Cut, Oregon, a Northern Pacific crew poses with a boulder suspended overhead.

After William Strong became president of the road in 1881 the Santa Fe expanded rapidly. Through a combination of construction, purchases, and leases, the Santa Fe by 1889 had become a 7,000-mile system stretching from Chicago to the Gulf of Mexico and the Pacific. A major reason for the popularity of the Santa Fe was the fine food served in dozens of Harvey Houses. Frederick H. Harvey had founded this service in 1876 and soon was hiring hundreds of Harvey Girls, "Young women of good character, attractive and intelligent, 18 to 30."

The last of the railroads to the Pacific followed the route favored by the South and ran through the Gadsden Purchase. After 1869 the Big Four soon were building coastal lines, both to the north and the south. The southern branch was called the Southern Pacific, but the Big Four used the false front Western Development Company to give themselves most of the construction

*An 1879 advertisement for one of the Granger
railroads. The Rock Island's pleasures
included luxurious dining-car service.*

themselves the chance of an extra profit in a business that at best was filled with great risk. The Crédit Mobilier and the Contract and Finance Company, used by the Big Four and the Central Pacific, made their owners some enormous profits. Dozens of less lucky contractors and construction companies failed, as roads were left unbuilt and profits unmade. Since the contractors were often paid off with bonds and stocks, some observers believed the builders were more concerned with moving securities than in moving dirt. But the dirt was moved, even if the completed roads were not always of first-class quality.

Corruption marred the construction of the Union Pacific and Central Pacific. When Oakes and Oliver Ames, shovelmakers from Massachusetts, joined Durant and Sidney Dillon in rigging the Crédit Mobilier, none of them was thinking about a modest profit. The Ames brothers wanted far more than the profit made by selling thousands of shovels to the Union Pacific. Estimates of the total Crédit Mobilier profits, paid out in cash plus securities, ranged as high as $23 million and some critics claimed that half of the $100 million Union Pacific capital structure was pure water.

The scandal of the Crédit Mobilier came in 1872, after the completion of the line. From his vantage point in Congress, Oakes Ames had passed out Crédit Mobilier shares among fellow politicians, where, as Ames saw it, "they will do most good to us." Soon the careers of such men as Vice President Schuyler Colfax, James A. Garfield, and James G. Blaine were all sullied in the resulting investigation. The Big Four were luckier in concealing the deft financial footwork and profits which came from their Contract and Finance Company. Generally each man —Stanford, Crocker, Hopkins, and Huntington—had subscribed equally to their construction company. Any real investigation was quite difficult, since the books of the construction company had been lost in a fire which destroyed the company offices. Some of the rail kings were indeed rich. Hopkins left a fortune of $19 million in 1878, and a dozen years later Crocker's estate was perhaps $24 million.

Despite the financial corruption, western rail mileage rapidly increased more than fivefold in the 1860s, and far more than doubled in each of the two following decades. Trans-Mississippi mileage, which was only 7 per cent of the national total in 1860, had grown to a third of the total figure by 1880, and nearly a half by 1900.

In many western states, especially Wyoming, Utah, Oklahoma, New Mexico, and Arizona, substantial rail mileage preceded admission to statehood by as much as twenty years. In the four or five years following both the panic of 1873 and the panic of 1893 new construction was quite slow, but it proceeded at a hectic pace during the prosperous 1880s. Much of the new construction, in addition to branch lines, was by the "Granger" railroads of the prairie states or in the new narrow gauge mileage

contracts. Yuma, Arizona, was reached by 1877, but difficulties in crossing the Yuma Indian Reservation delayed further progress until construction there was eventually approved by President Rutherford B. Hayes. In the late 1870s, the line was built across Arizona and New Mexico. In 1882 the Southern Pacific made a junction east of El Paso, Texas, with the Texas & Pacific, a line built by Thomas A. Scott of the Pennsylvania Railroad. Within a short time the Big Four built and purchased a second line across Texas, which gave them their own direct service to New Orleans in 1883.

All these railroads to the Pacific were projected and constructed into desolate areas well beyond the settled frontier. The financial risks in such a situation were great, and it became almost a standard practice to set up and use a "construction company." With this device the directors, managers, and promoters of a railroad gave

popular in several mining states.

The narrow gauge railway was popular in Britain in the early 1870s, and the idea quickly spread to the United States. Those who supported "slim gauge" railroads argued that such lines would be cheaper to build, equip, and maintain than the wider standard gauge roads. Such advantages made sense, especially in mountainous regions where tunnels and expensive rock excavations were so frequent. Many other railroads followed the lead of General William Jackson Palmer who started to build his three-foot gauge Denver & Rio Grande south and west of Denver in the early 1870s.

By 1874 almost 1,700 miles of narrow gauge had been built in the nation. By 1880 the figure had risen to more than 5,000 miles. A few eastern states, such as Ohio, Pennsylvania, Illinois, and Kentucky, experimented with narrow gauge, but the majority of such trackage was in the western mountain states—mostly in California, Nevada, and Colorado. At one time nine short, narrow gauge lines were operating in California. Several other lines were built in the 1870s and early 1880s to serve the gold, silver, and lead mines of Nevada. Before long, almost a third of all track in Colorado was narrow gauge.

When General Palmer found the Santa Fe blocking his original entrance into New Mexico, he quickly turned to build into the mountains west and north of Pueblo, Colorado. Soon he reached the mining mountain towns of Leadville, Durango, and Aspen. The narrow gauge line which John Evans built to Leadville, (the Denver, South Park & Pacific), had so steep a grade that on one occasion a circus train unloaded its elephants to help push the cars into the Leadville station. While economy was a major feature of the narrow gauge lines, the prosperous mining patrons of the little railroads generally demanded—and got—the best of service in the small, red, plush and paneled dining, parlor, and Pullman cars. In the last

years of the nineteenth century many of the narrow gauge lines were converted to standard gauge.

In the Granger area—from Illinois, Missouri, and Kansas north to Canada—four lines were of prime importance. They were the Chicago & North Western, the Chicago, Milwaukee & St Paul, the Chicago, Rock Island & Pacific, and the Chicago, Burlington & Quincy. By 1890 these Granger railroads already had a total trackage of some 18,000 miles. As their names indicated, each of the lines was subservient to Chicago. This was because they carried the prairie products of wheat, corn, beef, and pork to the elevators and stockyards of the important rail center and lake port.

Benefits of the Land Grants

All of the Granger lines, plus four of the first five Pacific railroads, obtained federal land grants. Between the first grant in 1850 and 1871, most western lines sought, and often obtained, such aid from the federal government. The early grants in the fifties were normally offered at the rate of six sections of land per mile of track. But trans-Missouri grants after the Civil War were generally for twenty sections per mile of railroad, with the Northern Pacific even being given forty sections per mile.

When the last significant grant was made to the Texas & Pacific in 1871, the total of all available federal land grants came close to 170 million acres. Many of the more than eighty projected railroads which were offered land were never built or completed in time to receive the aid. Thus millions of acres of land were forfeited and returned to the government. The completed roads received full and final title over 130 million acres. (Texas, which retained control of her own land, obtained no federal land grants,

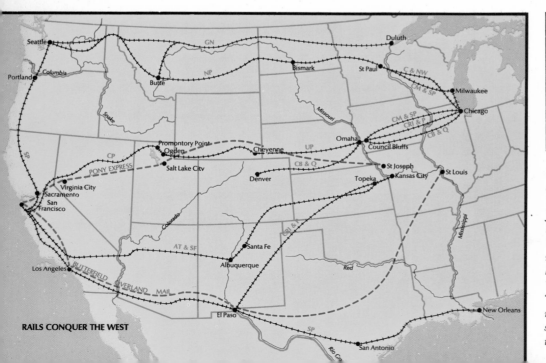

RAILS CONQUER THE WEST

UP	Union Pacific
CP	Central Pacific
GN	Great Northern
SP	Southern Pacific
NP	Northern Pacific
C & NW	Chicago & North Western
AT & SF	Atchison, Topeka & Santa Fe
CB & Q	Chicago, Burlington & Quincy
CRI & P	Chicago, Rock Island & Pacific
CM & SP	Chicago, Milwaukee & St Paul

Right: "The Scourge of the West," an 1885 cartoon. Honest citizens are held to ransom as Industry and Justice are swept aside by the locomotive ridden by William H. Vanderbilt—representing the ruthless railroadmen. The locomotive carries as its motto Vanderbilt's cynical remark, "The Public Be D——!" Left: A map of the railroad lines which stretched through the plains and the mountains to the West.

nor were there any in Indian Territory.)

The land grants helped in the construction of more than 18,000 miles of line. Without such aid the construction would often have been delayed or postponed. Certainly the Golden Spike ceremony in May 1869 was hastened by the land grant. The Hannibal & St Joseph in Missouri, the Kansas Pacific in Kansas, and the Burlington, west of the Missouri River, all had a faster construction rate because of the help provided by the federal government. The real contribution made by the land grants to the prairie and mountain railroads was that they furnished an early basis of credit which allowed construction to start. Generally, the projected road with a land grant mortgaged its land long before receiving final certification and title.

As far as benefits were concerned in the land grant issue it was far from a one-way street, since the federal government also gained. For one thing the alternate sections of land retained by the government in the grant area immediately were raised from the normal price of $1.25 to $2.50 an acre. Furthermore the government was to receive a substantial discount on the fares and rates charged for government personnel and freight moving over the land grant lines. The courts subsequently deter-

mined that government shipments and travel should receive a deduction of 50 per cent. These discounted rates for federal traffic were in effect from 1850 to 1945. In the latter year a congressional committee report estimated that the total savings to the government amounted to about $900 million. Early railroad observers even before the Civil War thought the government had made a good bargain. Recalling the continued movement of troops and government freight across Iowa in 1859, Charles Russell Lowell, the young Burlington land office agent, wrote: ''It may be found that even with the most liberal construction of the grant, the government has not been so 'munificent' as sharp.''

In their use of land grants the western railroads were not faultless. The Union Pacific avoided local taxation in Nebraska for years by being intentionally tardy in applying for the patents for their land grants. And some railroads allowed favored company officials to make profits by selling land grants to insiders or affiliated groups.

In summary the land grants did not by themselves build the first western lines, but they were of almost immeasurable assistance. The completed lines greatly reduced the cost of overland transportation, and more importantly

provided transportation to unsettled regions. As a result, in only a generation the moving edge of settlement filled in much of the Great Plains and the mountain West.

The Railroad's Impact on the West

The trans-Mississippi region in the generation after the Civil War was largely rural, and much of the early opposition to railroads came from farmer; folk. No doubt James C. Clarke, president of the Illinois Central, was thinking chiefly of farmers when he wrote in 1883: "The people are in favor of building a new road and do what they can to promote it. After it is once built and fixed then the policy of the people is usually in opposition." The shift in the farmer's attitude concerning railroads naturally came earlier on the eastern prairie than it did farther west. And the hard times which followed the panic of 1873 increased the hostility toward railways in all parts of the West.

The prosperity of the western farmer depended to a great degree upon his ability to send his produce to market at a reasonable cost. The farmer living west of the Mississippi was no longer a self-sufficient producer but was producing for a distant eastern market. Thus the farmer was most concerned with railroad rates. The complexity of railroad freight rates was very great, but to many farmers it seemed that the principal rate theory used by railroads was charging as much as the traffic would bear. One rail executive told the Interstate Commerce Commission that his line's rate policy was: ". . . we get all we can, and even that is too little."

The farmer felt that the rates charged for the shipment of his grain and livestock to the Chicago market were excessive. He heard the story about the Iowa farmer who burned his corn crop for fuel because at 15 cents a bushel it was cheaper than coal—and at the same time corn in the East was selling at $1.00 per bushel! He hated the discrimination of the long-and-short-haul, which

As a prairie schooner stretches toward the frontier, its path crosses the railroad heading in the same direction. Thomas Otter's painting On The Road *symbolizes the westward migration.*

resulted from the fact that the average mid-western prairie hamlet was served by only a single railroad. And he was quite certain that the prices he paid at the general or country store had been hiked up because of the high local freight rates.

Effective railroad regulation at the state level came to the western states with the appearance of the National Grange of the Patrons of Husbandry. Organized and founded in 1867 by Oliver H. Kelley, Minnesota farmer and clerk in the Bureau of Agriculture in Washington, the Grange had grown to 800,000 members by 1875. In 1871 the Grangers succeeded in passing effective railroad legislation in Illinois. Comparable laws and regulation came to Iowa and Minnesota in 1874, and to Missouri, Kansas, and Nebraska a few years later. The western or Granger style of railroad control used regulative commissions, whose schedules of reasonable maximum rates and fares were generally upheld in the resulting judicial proceedings.

While freight rates seemed high to the western farmer, in fact they were dropping rather rapidly during the last three decades of the nineteenth century. Increased competition plus the new state and federal regulation was

responsible for much of the decline. The total freight bill on a carload of steers from western Nebraska to Chicago might still seem high to the farmer at the turn of the century. But it was a simple confirmation of the fact that the greater distances typical of the last frontier really made transportation costs an unavoidable tax upon the farming operations of the trans-Mississippi West.

In the generation after the Civil War, the rapid expansion of the railroads and the settling of the nation's last frontier were in many ways simultaneous developments. In the 1870s and 1880s the newly-built lines had drawn tens of thousands of new settlers and pioneers out into raw territories that soon would become states. The railroad depot, whether it be a small South Dakota station or the giant Union Station at St Louis, was serving both rural and urban westerners. The railroad station at the end of Main Street was the focal point of contact with the outside world. It had a telegraph office, an express and mail service, and a full schedule of freight and passenger trains. The iron network was nearly complete, and by the end of the century few inhabited places in the West were far removed from the piercing sound of the locomotive whistle.

Nelson Gallery-Atkins Museum, Kansas City, Missouri (Nelson Fund)

Chapter 8

THE CATTLE KINGDOM

Herds of longhorns had roamed the vast grasslands of Texas for decades. But bringing them to the hungry cities of the East was difficult and financially risky. It was only the coming of the railroad that made it possible for the cattle to reach the East in good condition. Once there, they might fetch for their owners up to ten times their cost. Thus began the brief era of the cowboy, the cattle trail, and the cow town. Railheads like Abilene, Wichita, and Dodge City boomed with saloons, gamblers, and girls—and made a reputation for drama and excitement as the "Wild West."

"Head 'em North"

In 1865 some 5 million cattle roamed the vast grasslands of Texas. Fierce descendants of Spanish breeds, long-legged and lean, and armed with horns that might spread as wide as a man's reach, they hardly seemed worth rounding up. The drive to cities, where there was a great demand for beef, led far to the north through hostile lands. So Texans slaughtered thousands of these "long-horns" just for tallow and hide.

Long before the War of Independence the cattle business had thrived on the frontier. Here stretched the prairies not yet torn by the plow—ideal grazing lands for large beef herds. But the difficulty had always been in getting them to city markets. As early as 1802 cattle raisers in Ohio and Kentucky began driving their livestock to Baltimore, Philadelphia, and New York City. Butchers bought most of these beeves. Others went to nearby farmers who made profits by fattening trail-worn cattle, usually on hay or corn or the refuse from distilleries, and then selling them.

As the agricultural frontier inched westward a more elaborate chain of transactions arose to speed the cattle on their passage east. From cattlemen in Illinois, Iowa, and Missouri, pioneer corngrowers in the Ohio River valley bought in stock to feed up during the winter; they were kept in enclosed fields or on open pastures. In spring, when they were fat and marketable, the cattle were led over the mountains to the slaughterhouses.

The coming of the railroads dramatically disrupted this arrangement. Now that livestock could be carried east by rail, the cattle industry fled westward. Illinois and Iowa, new centers of corn production, emerged as feeder states. The source of young beef cattle shifted to Texas. From 1850 to 1865 the estimated tally of beeves ranging the remote prairie empire increased tenfold.

Rising beef prices in the 1850s enriched many Texas cattlemen, especially those on the coastal plains of the Gulf of Mexico with easy access to New Orleans by water. But steamships could accommodate only a small fraction of the longhorns not sold in local markets, and south-western railroads were still just a gleam in a promoter's eye. One determined Texan drove a herd to Ohio as early as 1846. A few others had prodded their cattle to Missouri before the Civil War. By the end of the war, Texas swarmed with stray cattle that had multiplied on the range. Worth only $3 to $5 a head on their native pastures, they could fetch ten times that price in the towns of the Northeast. "The big Texas problem," as one historian has phrased it, "was to link a four-dollar steer to a forty-dollar market."

Transporting the cattle was only one part of the problem. Longhorns carried splenic fever—commonly

Longhorns in Frank Reaugh's The Herd.
They were not prime beef but tough animals
that could survive the rigors of the trail.
In 1865 millions of them roamed the Southwest.

called "Spanish" or "Texas" fever. They were practically immune to this, but it invariably wrought havoc among northern herds whenever improved breeds came into contact with southern stock. Texas drovers dismissed northern concern about infection. They claimed that it was merely a front for postwar discrimination against them as southerners, but midwestern stockmen had correctly identified longhorns as the secondary source of the disease. Experience had shown that only in winter, when the minuscule tick that transmitted splenic fever was dead, could Texas cattle be safely imported. By the summer and fall of 1866 Texas drovers found the way north barred by quarantine laws forbidding entry into Kansas and Missouri. In some places local vigilante groups enforced these laws with violence. Sky-high beef prices beckoned in the North, but overland routes to market were closed.

The Growth of the Cattle Business

Americans honor a young Illinois livestock dealer named Joseph G. McCoy as the originator of the frontier cattle market. Indeed, in his own account, McCoy credited no one but himself. But it is now known that a small group of dealers from Kansas, interested in the cattle business, had paved the way for McCoy's remarkable venture. They successfully lobbied the Kansas legislature against the law forbidding summer entry to longhorns. As a result, early in 1867, the legislature passed a bill that opened the western third of Kansas to Texas cattle. It also authorized shipment east from central Kansas via the newly laid tracks of the Kansas Pacific Railroad. For some reason those who had achieved this victory then lost interest. Not so McCoy, who established himself at the frontier village of Abilene in June 1867.

The liberalized quarantine law still blocked longhorns from reaching the railroad as far east as Abilene. But during a brief visit to Topeka McCoy persuaded the Kansas governor to write him a "semi-official" endorsement of the project. Back in Abilene McCoy set up a large stockyard, a barn, an office building, a set of livestock scales, a hotel, and a bank. He also sent an agent deep into Indian Territory to contact startled and initially skeptical Texan owners of northbound herds. By mid-August longhorns nibbled the upland grasses surrounding Abilene. In early September the first twenty carloads moved out, bound for the Chicago stockyards. By the year's end some 35,000 head had funneled through Abilene, about 20,000 of them leaving McCoy's loading pen. The great Texas cattle drives had begun.

Some truly spectacular profits in the early days of trail driving inspired Texas cattlemen of succeeding seasons. In 1868, for example, one of them bought 600 steers in

Texas at $8 to $10 a head, for a total of $5,400. Trailing them to Abilene without much loss, he sold the herd for $16,800. Reckoning his expenses at $4 a head, his net profit was about $9,000—a snug sum in those days for one season's work. Another Texan drove a mixed herd of around 750 to Abilene the following year, also earning a $9,000 profit. Drovers of later years made up for lower profits per head by trailing larger herds.

Railroads operating beyond settled territory also found Texas cattle profitable. Not all animals sold at Abilene and other cattle towns were shipped east by rail. Many trekked to ranches in Colorado, the Dakotas, Wyoming, and Montana. Here a demand persisted for yearlings and two-year-olds as stock cattle. According to McCoy, it became quite as usual to drive cattle northwest from Abilene as to transport them east by rail. In 1871, for instance, cattlemen sold some 190,000 head at Abilene, of which only 40,000 went out by rail. In 1882 buyers at Dodge City purchased approximately 200,000 head, but only about 65,000 of this number left town on the cars. But the railroads' commercial involvement in livestock remained considerable.

The railroads sorely needed the eastbound traffic that western livestock provided. Typical of "underdeveloped" regions, the West imported more goods than it produced. Many freight cars, fully loaded on the westbound run, returned empty. This loss could be eliminated only when western states and territories became fully settled and productive. Meanwhile, railroad officials grasped eagerly at anything resembling a fairly stable source of freight going east.

Mainly because of this, in 1867 extremely cautious railroad officials granted McCoy some help in his Abilene project. The Kansas Pacific's report to stockholders in late 1868 observed enthusiastically that the Texas cattle trade "already adds largely to the east-bound freight of the road," though it was only half the tonnage that headed west. Figures from the Atchison, Topeka & Santa Fe reveal much the same traffic imbalance. Vigorous cattle commerce at Wichita, Dodge City, and other Kansas cattle towns, however, helped to alleviate this.

A handful of trails from the longhorns' home breeding grounds in Texas became important highways over which the great herds trudged north. The oldest of these major routes, the Shawnee Trail, was followed by drovers as early as the 1840s. Originating in south-central Texas, it swung north through the frontier town of Dallas toward Missouri, finally crossing into that state from the northeast corner of Indian Territory. Here the trail fanned out, with branches running to St Louis, Sedalia, and Kansas City. Agricultural settlement and Missouri's quarantine law closed the Shawnee Trail at the Missouri border soon after the Civil War. Many herds, however, followed it to the south-eastern Kansas border where they were sold and shipped out.

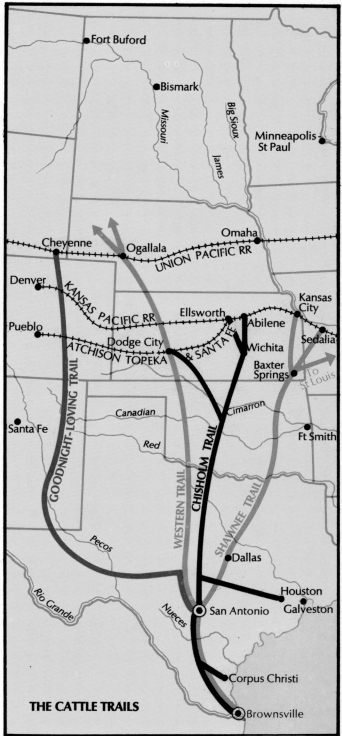

THE CATTLE TRAILS

Another route—the Goodnight-Loving Trail—circled west out of central Texas through New Mexico Territory. Laid out in 1866 by Charles Goodnight and his partner Oliver Loving, it gave cattlemen access to the isolated markets provided by the mining camps and ranches of Colorado and Wyoming.

A third important route, the Western Trail, came into being in the 1870s. It struck north along the western edge of Indian Territory toward Dodge City, where herds could be sold and shipped east on the Santa Fe. They could alternatively be walked northwest to Ogallala, Nebraska, a major cattle town on the Union Pacific line. Here the Western Trail split. One branch extended up to Fort Buford in northern Dakota Territory. The other branched west to Wyoming and Montana.

The Chisholm Trail was the most famous of them all. On a map it resembled a great tree, with numerous feeder trails leading in from Brownsville, Corpus Christi, Houston, and other points. These met at Red River Station on the northern border of Texas. From here the trunk of the tree crossed Indian Territory to the Cimarron River, where branches spread out toward Dodge City, Caldwell, Abilene, and other Kansas shipping centers. In later years oldtime trail drivers would argue over the trail's correct name. Many insisted that the Chisholm Trail was only that segment of the route laid out during the Civil War by the halfbreed Indian trader Jesse Chisholm. It was supposedly intended to serve as a link between central Indian Territory and the temporary native settlement that in 1870 would become the town of Wichita. They remembered the route from Wichita to Abilene, marked by McCoy's agents, as the Abilene Trail, and called the

Above left: Jesse Chisholm laid out a supply trail from Texas to Kansas during the Civil War. The trail later gained fame as the route to the railhead at Abilene. Above: A map of the West showing the location of cattle trails, towns, and the railroads linking them with the East.

westward-leaning branch to the cattle market at Ellsworth the Ellsworth Trail. The latter-day cutoff toward Dodge City they termed the Eastern Trail. But history gave to roots, trunk, and branches the name Chisholm.

The Cowboy and His Herd

Many cattlemen made small or large fortunes in the livestock business, but there was no such thing as a rich cowboy. In 1880 McCoy reckoned the average cowhand's wages at $25 to $30 a month. Indeed the latter figure is usually applied to the years between the late 1860s and the 1880s. The typical herd arriving at Abilene was said to have been two months on the trail. Ten years later, when many herds came into Kansas from nearer points McCoy estimated their marching time at thirty-five days. Most cowboys probably signed on before the actual drive began. Some were retained after the drive to hold the

herd while the owner bargained with buyers. So two or three months' wages—between $60 and $90—seems a probable financial return for any cowboy's cattle driving season.

Pay may not have been high—and most of it was squandered on fancy clothes and high times at the shipping head—but the drive itself was rich in excitement and hardship. Pitting oneself against experts in the rigors of the trail, comradeship in an exclusive male society, and the life of freedom, all combined as an alluring challenge to footloose types ready for adventure.

Managing the longhorns was a feat in itself. "The longer he lived, the meaner he became," wrote one plainsman. "While in an ordinary frame of mind, he was always much of a blusterer and went swaggering around and threatening destruction to everything that came near him. His temper became ungovernable when he was aroused and made him a dangerous animal." Nevertheless, the breed was particularly suited to the journey. Goodnight claimed that their equal as trail cattle had never been known. "Their hoofs are superior to those of any other

Courtesy Amon Carter Museum, Fort Worth, Texas (detail)

Charles Russell's Cowboy Camp During The Roundup *depicts the colorful action on a ranch in the 1880s. Russell painted the view from real life, and the cowboys were delighted when they saw themselves and their friends on canvas.*

cattle. In stampedes, they hold together better, are easier circled in a run, and rarely split off when you commence to turn the front. No animal of the cow kind will shift and take care of itself under all conditions as will the Longhorns. They can go farther without water and endure more suffering than others.''

Herds ranged in size from a few hundred to the largest known—150,000 head—that hit the trail in 1869. Two or three thousand was the best size at stream crossings and water holes. Goodnight figured that one steer required thirty gallons of water per day and ten acres of prairie grass when the grass was good, twice that if the vegetation was poor and dry. One cowhand per 250 to 400 head was the usual ratio. Crews were expected to chivy the mass of cattle eight to twenty miles a day, blizzards, hailstorms, Indians, and stampedes notwithstanding.

Of the million or so head trailed from the end of the Civil War through the mid-1880s, roughly half followed the Chisholm Trail. The middle part of the route had been established by Chisholm for transporting his wagonloads of trade. It was a straight and level track that offered easy river crossings. In time, beaten by wheel and hoof to a width of about 400 feet, and eroded by rains, the roadbed sank below the level of the surrounding prairie. Even on such a carefully planned and well marked route, natural and human hazards plagued the drive. A stream that was a trickle could in one day, if fed by spring runoffs, become a boiling torrent that churned hoofs, horns, and cowhands together in fatal confusion. The famous drover Abel H. ("Shanghai") Pierce once said that his herds did so much swimming on the way to Kansas that they merited being called sea lions. Herds sometimes had to be detoured twenty-five miles to avoid flooded streams or quicksands.

Somewhere along the way extremes of weather were almost sure to take their toll. Spring blizzards frequently caused severe losses. Colonel Ike T. Pryor took a herd, worth half a million dollars, along the trail and after one night's snowstorm found himself with a remnant worth only $65,000. In 1874 one outfit on Hell Roaring Creek in Indian Territory was hit with a night of sleet and wind-driven snow that froze seventy-eight relay horses to death. Hailstorms were particularly damaging on the treeless plains. They felled cattle and cowhands alike, and stripped the skin from animals that soon dropped in their tracks. Even when Nature smiled, there could be a problem. Heavy rains sometimes produced a quick overgrowth of prairie grass that was luxuriant but poor in quality. The herds might graze abundantly but still arrive at the railhead suffering from malnutrition. It was then necessary to fatten them before sale.

Life on the Trail

As for human hazards, there were Indians, settlers, and the hair-trigger tempers of overworked fellow cowhands. In 1870 Cheyennes stampeded and drove off an entire herd—a total loss of $18,000. Bill Poage asserted that there was as much to fear from friendly Indians as from

Thomas Gilcrease Institute, Tulsa, Oklahoma

A charging herd was the cowboy's greatest danger. The slightest noise on the prairie or a frisky steer could set hundreds of cattle thundering across the plains. Above: Remington's Stampeded by Lightning.

those who were hostile: "The wild ones would stampede our horses and try to get away with them. The friendly ones would run them off at night and come back the next day to get a reward for returning them." Many owners gave away a head of cattle a day to Indians to forestall them from helping themselves. The natural antipathy between trail crews and settlers anxious to protect their field crops also produced trouble. "There was scarcely a day when we didn't have a row with some settler," recalled Poage. "The boys took delight in doing everything they could to provoke settlers. The settlers paid us back, with interest, by harassing us in every way they could think of. The boss was arrested twice in one day for trespassing. A settler would plow a furrow around his claim. According to the laws of Kansas, this was a fence. Any loose stock that crossed it was trespassing, and the owner was liable for damages."

Although cowboys worked off much of the tension of the drive through horseplay and practical jokes, there were violent incidents. In 1873 a crew from Texas was sleeping peacefully beside the trail when a cowboy snatched up an ax and beheaded four dozing companions. A fifth woke up to see the ax raised over his head and gave the alarm, but the murderer escaped. To avoid clashes among the crew, many outfits banned liquor on the trail and even fined cowhands who used profanity.

The most widely known and prevalent hazard was the

stampede. The herd was more likely to be spooked during the first few days of the drive. Theories differed as to whether to tire the herd by pushing it hard at first, or to begin with short, easy drives in an attempt to keep it from getting edgy. "After a month or two," said Goodnight, "the cattle became gentler." Even so, anything or nothing might set the herd stampeding and scatter it as widely as a hundred miles. One cowboy wrote, "While I was looking at him, this steer leaped into the air, hit the ground with a heavy thud, and gave a grunt that sounded like that of a hog. That was the signal. The whole herd was up and going—and heading right for me. My horse gave a lunge, jerked loose from me, and was away. I barely had time to climb into an oak. The cattle went by like a hurricane, hitting the tree with their horns. It took us all night to round them up. When we got them quieted next morning, we found ourselves six miles from camp."

Herds might stampede a dozen times a night, leveling everything—even fullgrown trees—in their path and generating great heat in their rush. "The faces of the men riding on the leeward side of the herd," said Goodnight

An early or late winter blizzard sometimes played havoc with a herd. Left: A cowboy rescues a Hereford calf during a raging plains snowstorm.

183

A photographic record of the early cattle business. Above: The trail boss, who bore full responsibility for the herd and crew. Above right: A rider "cuts out" a cow and her unbranded calf. Opposite: His bunk and some of the tools of the cowboy's trade. Inset: Cowpunchers prepare to bed down for the night. Below: Cowboys at the chuck wagon pause for one of their three hot meals of the day. Right: The cowboy's most important possession: his saddle. The Western saddle evolved from the Spanish saddle and was specially designed for the cowboy's rough riding. The high cantle at the back protected him against falling off, and the horn at the front was used for roping. The stirrups allowed the cowboy to keep his legs straight—for greater stability.

Wild Horse Hunters *by Charles Russell.*
Cowboys became adept at roping steers and
wild horses. The mustangs in the painting
would later be "broken"—tamed—then used
as cow ponies on the trail.

of one stampede, "were almost blistered, as if they had been struck by a blast from a furnace." Once a stampede had started, all hands tried to "mill" the animals. The herd was surrounded and driven into a turning mass that eventually wore out its momentum. One crew was unable to get its rampaging herd to circle, and it poured over the edge of a ravine known thereafter as Stampede Gulch. Of the 2,700 head lost, only the horns and the hides could be salvaged.

The trail boss—typically paid three or four times more than a common hand—was the key man. It was the boss who, as Bill Poage said, "must see that there are enough provisions, as short grub does more toward dissatisfying the cowboy than anything else. He must assign each man to his proper duty. He must be the first up in the morning to wake the men. He must ride ahead to see that there is water at the proper distance. He must know where to stop for noon. He must count the cattle at intervals to see that none have been lost. He must settle all difficulties among his men." It was the trail boss who waked the cook. He in turn put the coffee on the boil for half an hour "until it could float a pistol," and then gathered the men for breakfast at 3.30 in the morning. The cook was likely to be the oldest member of the crew. The wrangler

—the most inexperienced hand and the one who tended the horses and served as general errand boy—was the youngest. The working day began before dawn and ended after dark and sometimes even later, for many drew guard duty. Every job was tough. It was not an uncommon practice for cowboys to rub tobacco juice into their eyes to keep awake.

While it was still dark, the pointers—a couple of reliable men who led the drive—moved to the front of the herd. Swing men came behind them, followed by flank riders, with drag men bringing up the rear of the herd at a distance of perhaps half a mile. Positions were sometimes rotated to even up the burden of dust-eating and the heavier chores. Each company had spare mounts, mostly mustangs, along with quarter-horses, an eastern breed trained for quarter-mile racing. Cow ponies were selected on the basis of intelligence, training, and reliability. Some cattle dealers bought up to a hundred horses

Courtesy Amon Carter Museum, Fort Worth, Texas (detail)

drive. Late each day the herd increased its speed as the cattle grew thirsty, anticipating the water holes. Their appetite for grass was strong in the evening, but by sundown they were ready to settle for the night. At around midnight they would stand up to stretch and then lie down again, only to repeat this an hour later. On moonlit nights they were most restless and needed closest supervision by the night shifts. "To ride around the big steers at night," reminisced one cowhand, "all lying down full as a tick, chewing their cuds and blowing, with the moon shining down on their big horns, was a sight to make a man's eyes pop."

On the Chisholm Trail the drive to the Red River crossing covered the roughest country, and the Red River itself, often in flood, remained a major hazard. After moving into Indian Territory, the route lay across open country where tree-lined streams were relatively easy to ford and campsites inviting. Farther north the wood supply gave out and the cook and wrangler collected dried buffalo or cow dung for the campfire. Large prairie dog villages had to be avoided since they were traps for longhorns' legs. Shawnee or Skeleton creeks vied with the Red River as a dangerous crossing, again because of flooding, quicksand, and the appearance of an occasional Indian raider. But once the herd had crossed into Kansas, the perils of the trail subsided. These were replaced by a need for extra caution in passing through settlements and agricultural areas.

"Entertaining" the Cowboy

At the journey's end, drovers and livestock buyers gathered at small urban centers, the strategic junctions of trail and rail. These were scattered across the Great Plains from southern Kansas to Montana. Here also lived many who sought the subsidiary profits of the cattle business: bankers, grocery and dry goods merchants, innkeepers, and a small host of business and professional men of every type.

Of chief importance to the average cowboy just off the trail was each cattle town's "entertainment industry." Wrote McCoy: "The barroom, the theater, the gambling room, the bawdy house, the dance house, each and all come in for their full share of attention. . . . Such is the manner in which the cowboy spends his hard-earned dollars." Others verified this statement. "The cowboy spends his money recklessly," observed a visitor to Dodge City. "He is a jovial, careless fellow bent on having a big time regardless of expense. He will make away with the wages of a half year in a few weeks. . . ." An oldtimer who drove cattle to Caldwell, Kansas, in 1882 and 1884 recalled, "Like most of the boys of the early days, I had to sow my wild oats, and I regret to say that I also sowed all of the money I made right along with the oats."

for a drive, from which they would "end up fat and in good condition. That way, each man would ride six or seven horses on the trail." The horses were then sold when the cattle were delivered.

The idea was to keep the cattle in a fairly loose but controllable pack. They would be moved at a pace that kept them calm, allowed for some grazing on the way, and still made good progress on the trail. The animals each took positions on the first day and generally maintained them for the whole trip. Those in the front of the group became lead steers that guided the rest up to the loading pen. Some of these proved so proficient in this role, that they were taken home again and used as leads for subsequent drives. Animals from several spreads might be banded together for the drive, when they were given a common trail brand. Mixed herds traveled slower than herds of mature male animals, since cows and calves tended to wander and linger. Calves born on the trail were usually slaughtered, as were weak and diseased animals that could not keep pace.

Each morning at eleven the men dismounted and headed for the chuck wagon. The cattle were allowed to graze until, having eaten their fill, they began to lie down for a collective nap, only to be roused for the afternoon

Cattle owners could be just as reckless as their employees and had more money to spend. Texas drovers, said McCoy, "do not hesitate to squander tens, fifties, and hundreds for the gratification of their appetites or passions." In 1871, for example, John James Haynes and his partner drove a thousand head of yearlings bought on credit. "We reached Abilene, Kansas," Haynes recalled, "with our yearlings in good shape, and we sold them for eight dollars per head. We found ourselves in possession of $8,000, and had started out without a dollar. But any old trail driver who found himself rich in Abilene in 1871, knows the rest."

Much exaggeration inflates the "wild and woolly" image of cattle town life. What is known of the cattle towns of Kansas serves as a guide to separate folklore from reality. In Abilene's busiest cattle season, 1871, the town had eleven taverns, including bars operated in the Drovers Cottage and the Planters Hotel. Dodge City's saloons numbered eight in 1878, fourteen in 1879, and thirteen in 1882, when the resident population was around 2,000. As for the "painted ladies" who served the cattlemen, cow-

Abilene, Kansas, in 1879. For years the site of the railhead to the east, the town was the center of the cattle business. But when the railroad moved farther west, Abilene lost its prominence.

boys, and gamblers, the legendary numbers also seem overblown. In 1869 Abilene harbored but three brothels and twenty-one whores. Caldwell's police court docket, which listed all resident prostitutes, displayed the names of only twenty-five in the shipping season of 1880.

The legendary cattle town homicide rate also bears reduction. Dodge City—the longest-lived of the Kansas cattle towns and a full-fledged "cowboy capital" for fully ten seasons after 1875—serves as an example. It was actually before its role as a cattle town that Dodge City experienced its most violent era. Probably fifteen buffalo hunters, gamblers, and assorted frontier riffraff were interred on the lonely slope of "Boot Hill" in its first year as a community. But with the arrival of the cattle trade came the establishment of courts. Disorderly conduct and guntoting within the city limits were heavily penalized, and a police force of several officers was formed. From then on, despite a continuous explosive mixture of liquor, gambling, loose women, and guns, homicides never came near the astronomical figures suggested by the Dodge City of fiction.

Many famous desperadoes and gunfighters paraded through Dodge City at one time or another, but few took part in any slayings. The overall homicide total at Dodge City during its ten years as a cattle town reached only fifteen. Three of its seasons were completely devoid of deaths by violence. Of the fifteen deaths recorded, the 1878 shipping season accounted for five, and citizens that year rightly considered matters to be out of hand.

Cattle Town Controversy

Taking all the major Kansas cattle towns together—Abilene, Ellsworth, Wichita, Caldwell, and Dodge City—the average number of homicides per cattle trading season amounted to only one and a half per year, for a grand total of just forty-five. In at least six cases it is doubtful that the incidents were connected with the cattle trade. A drunk murdered his wife, for instance. Another conventional murderer was himself lynched by local residents.

The state of Kansas outlawed the sale and consumption of liquor (except for "medicinal purposes") in 1880, four

decades before prohibition descended on the United States as a whole. But both Dodge City and Caldwell were to remain cattle trading centers for five more years. No cattle town could hope to attract Texas drovers and their herds without offering a drink at the end of the trail. At these two places, therefore, the first half of the 1880s witnessed increasing hostility to "moral reform" elements for the Texas cattle trade. Antidrink enthusiasts included both men and those legendary pillars of frontier social uplift, mobilized housewives. But rumor credited the men with far greater fanaticism on the prohibition question. Violence finally erupted. At Caldwell a bootlegger was found one morning swinging from an overhead beam at the local cattle pen. A note pinned to his shirt warned all such types to get out of town. For a few scary days all-out warfare threatened, but the town's business leaders hastily negotiated peace.

Dodge City was troubled with similar guerrilla warfare, and terrorism on both sides nearly resulted in death. The widening gulf between pro- and antiliquor supporters culminated when a moral reform arsonist twice set the business district ablaze. He successfully leveled saloons and brothels, as well as shops, restaurants, and newspaper offices. Such displays of social division always alarmed the prosperous business and professional men who made up the local cattle town power structure. They feared that adverse publicity would kill a frontier community's chances for attracting population and commercial investment. At such moments strong figures were propelled into office as mayors.

Alonzo B. Webster was such a leader to strife-torn Dodge City in 1881. A tough former cavalryman who had once killed a man in a gunfight, Webster was a dry goods merchant who later branched out into groceries, and then followed the lumber business exclusively. No prohibitionist (within two years he would abandon lumber for the saloon business), Webster yielded to the moral reform impulses to the extent of offering strong law and order. His first official act was to order out of town all "thieves, thugs, confidence men, and persons without visible means of support." Three weeks later the police were provided with dapper blue uniforms. He regularized an assessment of monthly fines on gamblers and prostitutes so as to pay for the cost of the police force. This "taxation" of disorderly elements had been a cattle town institution ever since its introduction in Abilene by McCoy. By the end of Webster's first term as mayor his version of reform proved so popular with taxpayers that he was reelected without opposition. Early in 1886, with conflict on the liquor question again threatening the town's good name, businessmen once more nominated him to office. And once again Webster compromised with the moral reformers, ordering all saloons closed on Sundays.

"Respectable" citizens' dislike of saloons, brothels, dance houses, and gambling halls grew at every cattle

center as wives and children increasingly inhabited what had been male-dominated towns. In the end, however, it was mainly the westward pace of the agricultural frontier that forced the cattle towns of Kansas—as elsewhere on the plains in the 1880s—to give up their unique cattle trade.

After 1875 railroads penetrated nearly every corner of the trans-Missouri West. The long drive in its classic form gradually came to its end. It was replaced by shorter drives from ranch to nearest loading pen. And from Texas to Montana, from Arizona to the Dakotas, the practices of the great cattle kingdom took a standard form.

Still far beyond the farmers' advance, western ranches were relatively vast stretches of empty land. For the most part they were owned by cattlemen only in the informal sense of occupancy. An exception was Texas itself, where a land system originating from the days of Spanish ownership still allowed individual purchase of large tracts. Another exception was Indian Territory (soon to become the state of Oklahoma). Here, corporations of ranchers leased huge ranges from various tribes that were settled there on government reserves. But in the main, the American system of land disposal was still based on the sale of 160-acre plots to small farmers. Most ranchers, therefore, simply "squatted" on a public domain that would sooner or later fall to the plow.

By the 1880s the cattle business was coming to resemble the kind of corporate enterprise then emerging everywhere on the American scene. As in any growing business, the larger owners—the cattle barons—transformed their operations into joint-stock companies and sought investment funds in the capital-rich cities of the East. They were aided by a vast flood of promotional literature from the pens of western editors, governors, and professional boosters. From 1880 to 1900, the number of incorporated cattle companies in Montana, Wyoming, Colorado, and New Mexico rose to 879, with a total value of nearly $285 million.

Like many notorious industrialists of that age, the organized cattle barons frequently clashed with the public interest. In Colorado, for instance, the Arkansas Valley Cattle Company erected a fence around more than a million acres of publicly owned land. This was intended to keep out legitimate settlers. Complaints of similar unpopular activities—barbed wire springing up to prevent mail deliveries and making whole towns inaccessible—deluged Washington from all regions of the Great Plains. "Some morning we will wake up to find that a corporation has run a wire fence about the boundary lines of Wyoming, and all within the same have been notified to move," wrote a newspaperman from that state.

The US Department of the Interior, with jurisdiction over the public lands, finally authorized bona fide settlers simply to cut illegal fences. This brought threats of violent retaliation from cattlemen. Congress urged President Grover Cleveland to action. "There is not another nation on the earth that would permit such outrages," argued the House Public Lands Committee. Cleveland had to agree. He ordered federal prosecution of illegal fencers, and barbed wire on the public domain began to come down.

The cattle barons had better luck with another device. They ordered their cowhands to blanket the ranges with homestead claims. These could then be legally transferred to themselves after individual titles had been secured. This, too, brought outraged complaints from frontier farmers and small stockmen.

The End of the Open Range

Amidst all the commotion over the advance of the farmers' frontier, the old "open-range" cattle business slowly collapsed. But its demise was a product of several forces, in which growing public criticism played only a minor part. For one thing a widening split developed among the western cattlemen themselves. Everywhere on the ranges of the West in the early 1880s northern ranchers were improving their herds with young breeding stock and stock steers brought in from the East. Special use was made of grade and purebred Hereford bulls. But the dreaded splenic fever continued to be as mysterious a destroyer of improved cattle as in the years immediately after the Civil War. The cattle raisers of the central and northern plains increasingly demanded limitations on the movement of livestock from Texas. They began to lobby both in Congress and in the various state legislatures for restrictions.

Early in 1884 Congress passed a bill creating a Bureau of Animal Industry. It was headed by a commissioner who had the power to prohibit the interstate transportation of diseased stock. Under the influence of the Wyoming stock growers, the bill was made to cover splenic fever. But the senators from Texas, stubbornly insisting that splenic fever existed only in northern imagination, succeeded in having "the so-called splenetic [sic] fever or Texas fever" removed from the operations of the act.

Meeting in Dodge City, the Western Kansas Cattle Growers' Association called for an end to summer driving of Texas cattle into the state. "We have spent years of care and labor," the assembled cattlemen argued through their executive committee's report, "and have expended thousands of dollars in the purchase of high grade and thoroughbred bulls, to bring our herds to their present high degree of improvement, by which very improvement they are rendered more susceptible to the contraction of disease." On the other hand they claimed, "The business of driving Texas cattle northward is now confined to hardly more than a score of men, and these few men claim to make but a small margin of profit on the purchase and driving of their cattle to be sold in this and other northern markets."

Above: In 1885 homesteaders in Nebraska pose while cutting a fence blocking their access to water. Fences were erected by cattlemen and often led to "barbed-wire wars" with farmers.

Cattle ranches could attain immense proportions. The Prairie Cattle Company, for instance, owned over 150,000 head that roamed over 5 million acres. Below: Four company officers.

HICKS STOCK CAR   ED CATTLE CAR 3896

The cattle trail ended at the railhead. Left: In Montana cattle hands prod steers up a ramp and into a specially-built cattle car for shipment to market in Chicago.
Below: At the East St Louis stockyards, cattle were unloaded from the rail cars and kept in pens until they were slaughtered.
Right: Sketches showing the slaughterhouse and meatpacking facilities at Chicago. The beef was then moved to railroad cars for shipment to the East and Europe.

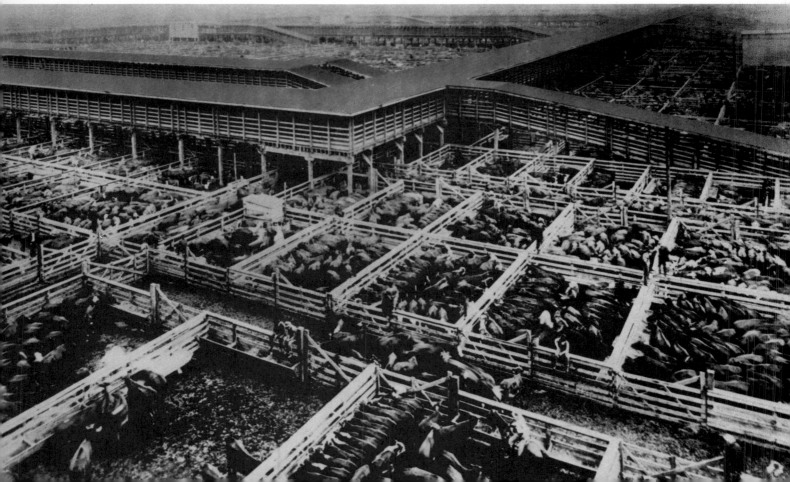

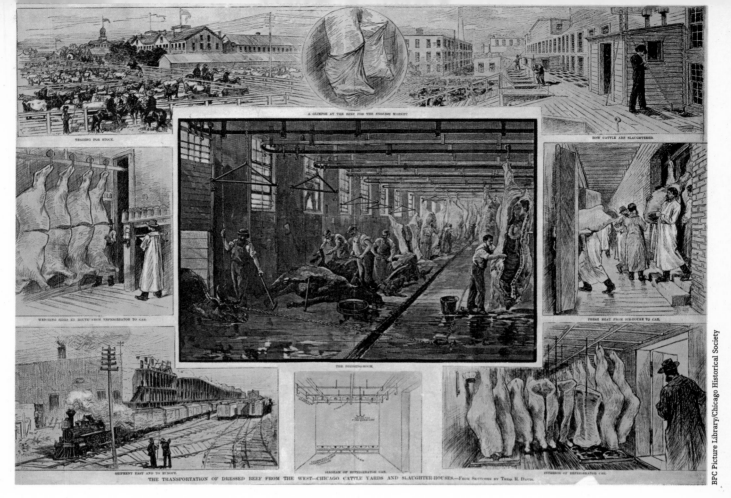

A GLIMPSE AT THE BEEF FOR THE ENGLISH MARKET.

TRADING FOR STOCK.

HOW CATTLE ARE SLAUGHTERED.

WEDGING SIDES EN ROUTE FROM REFRIGERATOR TO CAR.

FRESH MEAT FROM ICE-HOUSE TO CAR.

THE DRESSING-ROOM.

SHIPMENT EAST AND TO EUROPE.

DIAGRAM OF REFRIGERATOR CAR.

INTERIOR OF REFRIGERATOR CAR.

THE TRANSPORTATION OF DRESSED BEEF FROM THE WEST—CHICAGO CATTLE YARDS AND SLAUGHTER-HOUSES.—From Sketches by Theo. R. Davis.

That summer splenic fever broke out among improved herds in the stockyards at Kansas City, St Louis, and Chicago. The state of Illinois threatened to embargo all cattle shipped from Kansas. Drastic action seemed imperative. In August, at the urging of alarmed livestock firms, stockyard companies, and railroad managements, the governor of Kansas summarily forbade further imports of southern cattle for the rest of the season. On the Western Trail below Dodge City officers of the law turned back suspect herds and their crews at the Kansas line.

That autumn a national convention of stockmen met at St Louis. It adopted a resolution proposed by a Texas delegate asking Congress to lay out and maintain a "national trail" from the Red River to Canada. A committee then sped to Washington to lobby for a highway that would swing wide of Kansas through eastern Colorado. Early in 1885 Texans introduced the proposal in both houses of Congress. The Texas legislature adopted a supporting resolution, and the Texas Live Stock Association and a few similar groups urged its passage. But the hostility of northern cattle associations had its effect and the bills died in committee.

Congressional inaction proved fatal to the trail drive. The Kansas legislature, responding to the farmers' interests, finally closed the state permanently to summer importation of southern livestock. This action was soon imitated by other western legislatures. By 1887, with the northern ranges overstocked, livestock prices in decline, and a part of southeast Colorado open for permanent settlement, large-scale trailing fell off abruptly. Homesteaders' fences quickly closed the Colorado route, and few northern ranchers found themselves in a position to complain.

Meanwhile the weather hit the overstocked northern ranges a series of disastrous blows. An initial warning of the destruction to come occurred during the winter of 1884–85, when a severe snowstorm struck the central plains. "Most of the cattle," wrote a Kansas census reporter, "died for want of food and not being acclimated and for want of shelter." An even worse winter the following year, and on its heels the great northern blizzard of 1886–87, laid on the finishing touches. In this last disaster losses varied between 30 and 80 per cent of the herds.

The open range cattle industry of the northern plains, tied as it was to the annual influx of southern stock, came to an end. At some places the traditional routines persisted. Montana cattlemen held the last of their old-style roundups as late as 1906. But the "new" cattle kingdom was an empire of stockmen-farmers possessing fenced, individually owned spreads equipped with sufficient shelter, feed, and water to resist a hostile climate. "Scientific" beef producers replaced the intrepid cattlemen of old even as cowboys became primarily posthole diggers and hay cutters. All would retain the wide-brimmed Stetson hat as a proud badge of their profession. A Winchester might hang in the place of honor over the ranchhouse fireplace, but an era had come to an end.

193

Courtesy Amon Carter Museum, Fort Worth, Texas (detail)

The Wild West

The wagon team toiling through the rocky defile; the beautiful innocent girl, the penniless widow, and the dispossessed farmer; the lone crackshot outlaw, silhouetted against the sky; and the cloud of dust above the trail that signals the approach of the sheriff and his men—all this is familiar to anyone who has read a dime novel or seen a Western movie. Yet they would have been just as familiar six centuries ago in England. Make the year 1322, the outlaw Robin Hood, the place Sherwood Forest; let the sheriff ride out from Nottingham Town—and the story is unchanged.

The necessity to turn the outlaw into a mythical hero is born of certain well-defined social conditions. What motivation was it that could turn the near-moronic teenage killer William Bonney into the ''devoted, gallant, generous'' Billy the Kid? How could the treacherous and coldblooded railroad robber Dingus James grow into the Robin Hood of St Jo? Who found, in the drunken nymphomaniac Martha Jane Cannaray, the touching wide-eyed innocence of Calamity Jane? These myths can only grow in certain places and at certain times.

The Wild West is such a place and such a time. It begins with the conclusion of the Civil War and ends with the close of the western frontier—which coincides roughly with the close of the nineteenth century. It is peopled by alienated ex-Confederates at a loose end and ex-Union soldiers with a taste for adventure—and easy money. There are homesteaders in collision with railroad kings and cattle barons—and there are miners besotted with dreams of instant riches. And of course there are the men who recognized that the western myth was another sort of ore to mine.

Edward Zane Carroll Judson, discharged dishonorably from the Union army in 1864, headed westward looking for stories for the *New York Weekly*. Ex-jailbird, a founder member of the Know-Nothing party, ex-sailor, Judson wrote under the name of Ned Buntline. He was one of the fathers of the dime novel, and in William Frederick Cody, former Union scout and supplier of buffalo meat to the Union Pacific construction crews, he found his ideal hero. Within three years ''Buffalo Bill'' was the star of *Scouts of the Plains*, a roistering drama playing to packed houses in New York, and the legend of the swaggering, sharp-shooting Wild West was born.

Another contributor to the fiction was George Ward Nichols, who arrived in Springfield, Missouri, in 1866, and described the revelation he experienced in *Harper's Monthly*. He looked into a ''quiet, manly face; so gentle in its expression as to utterly belie the history of its owner. And eyes as gentle as a woman's . . . you would not believe that you were looking into eyes that have pointed the way to death for hundreds of men.'' Nichols had made the

In Without Knocking by Russell. Such a scene was by no means typical. But it is America's—and the world's—image of the Wild West.

195

William F. Cody, popularly known as "Buffalo Bill." Cody was ideal material for the making of a legend. He was a former army scout, Pony Express rider, and buffalo hunter for the crews laying the transcontinental railroad.

he had made for himself. Appointed marshal of Abilene, Kansas, in 1871, he lasted only a month or two, before he shot his own deputy by mistake. He joined Buffalo Bill's touring company, then left it to marry Mrs Agnes Thatcher Lake, the proprietor of a rival Wild West show. After a short honeymoon, he set off in 1876 for Deadwood, South Dakota, where gold had been found the year before.

But Wild Bill was not in Deadwood to prospect and dig. He was a professional gambler, and he was there to win a living from his cards. With him was Calamity Jane, a hard-drinking twenty-five-year old who had spent most of her time since adolescence dressed as a man among the railroad gangs and mule skinners—when she was not swimming naked with them in the creek. Within a few weeks Wild Bill was dead, shot through the back of the head by cross-eyed Jack McCall, for no apparent reason.

acquaintance of James Butler Hickok.

"Wild Bill," another former Union scout, had acquired some notoriety as a gunman in the so-called McCanles Affair. He had shot down David McCanles from behind a curtain, shot James Woods from behind a door, and gunned down M. R. Gordon as he ran for the underbrush. The jury in Jefferson County, Nebraska, found that Hickok and his accomplice, Horace Wellman, had done all this in self-defense. But by the time he sat down in that saloon in Springfield with Nichols, the story had changed a little.

Singlehanded, said Wild Bill, he had met McCanles and his gang of "desperadoes, horsethieves, murderers, regular cut-throats." With his six bullets he killed six of them, cut four more to pieces with his knife, and walked away unharmed except for eleven bullet holes and thirteen stab wounds. Warming to his theme, he described his exploits at Wilson Creek, where he brought down fifty men with fifty shots. Nichols believed it all. Later biographers made even more of it. O. W. Coursey had Hickok shoot one man in front of him with the gun in his left hand, while at the same moment he pointed his right hand over his shoulder to shoot another man behind him.

Unhappily, Wild Bill could not live up to the reputation

James Butler "Wild Bill" Hickok, left, confessed to being so afraid at times that his face turned as white as chalk. Wild Bill claimed to have killed over a hundred men, all of them—he said— for good reasons. Hickok was himself shot in Deadwood, South Dakota, in 1876.

Above: Russell's When Guns Speak, Death Settles Disputes. *A melodramatic view of the West—but many cattle towns took the threat of lawlessness seriously. Ordinances were passed prohibiting the carrying of firearms, with stiff penalties for offenders.*

As for Calamity Jane, she drifted on and down. The heroine of the dime novelists was hired by the dime museums. Dismissed for drunkenness, she cadged from bartenders by offering them free copies of her ghosted memoirs.

When Wild Bill died, the Wild West was still in its heyday, and Abilene, a small town on the advancing Kansas Pacific Railroad, was its first "metropolis." The drovers came into town after as much as six months on the trail, their thoughts exclusively occupied with hot water, cheap whiskey, and cheaper women. They all carried guns, against rustlers and Indians, and it is no wonder that bullets flew in the shabby streets. McCoy brought in Tom Smith as town marshal, and when Smith was shot in the back Wild Bill Hickok took the job. But by then the town was relatively quiet, because the railhead had moved on to Ellsworth.

Here Wyatt Earp comes on the scene. According to his own story of the event, the twenty-five-year-old bison hunter walked alone from the Kansas Pacific depot to Brennan's saloon to take a gun from Ben Thompson, the Texan gambler. Afterward Earp traveled to Wichita. The Santa Fe, driving south across Kansas, was draining all the beef traffic from the Kansas Pacific. A year after his arrival in the town, "Policeman Erp" (as the newspapers persisted in describing him) was appointed to serve under the marshal and assistant marshal. He lasted a year before he was arrested, fined, and fired for violating the peace.

Following the westward movement of the railhead, Earp appeared next in Dodge City, "Queen of the Cowtowns." Here he served two terms as assistant marshal, but most of the time he banked faro in the Long Branch Saloon. So too did "Bat" Masterson, another former bison hunter and Earp's long-time friend, who earned his nick-

Left: "Calamity Jane" Cannaray was Hickok's great friend in Deadwood. She dressed like a man and rode with cavalry units in 1875 until it was discovered that she was a woman.

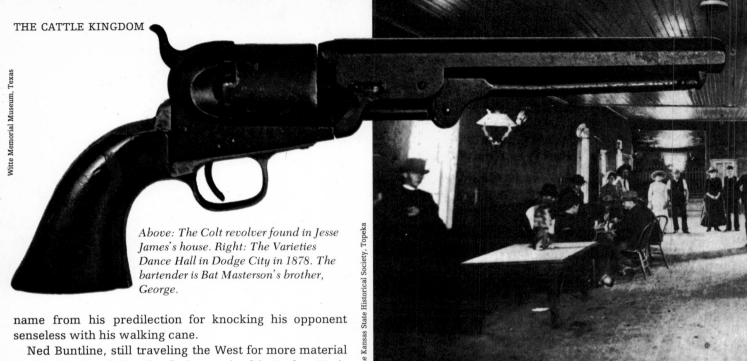

Above: The Colt revolver found in Jesse James's house. Right: The Varieties Dance Hall in Dodge City in 1878. The bartender is Bat Masterson's brother, George.

name from his predilection for knocking his opponent senseless with his walking cane.

Ned Buntline, still traveling the West for more material for his blood-and-thunder fiction, arrived in Dodge. He is said to have presented Earp, Masterson, and three other local peace officers—Bill Tilghman, Charlie Bassett, and Neil Brown—with special single-action Colts fitted with 12-inch barrels and detachable walnut stocks. None of these five guns appears to have survived, although others, some with 10-inch barrels and others with 16-inch barrels and rifle sights, are known to collectors as Buntline Specials.

Certainly these weapons would have had greater accuracy than the old Colt Civilian model, with its 4¾-inch barrel, which was the pistol carried by the average gunman. In fact, nearly all the stories told of the gunmen's sharpshooting exploits must be discounted. Even with its action fined down for a quick draw, the Civilian single-action, loaded with .45 cartridges which were notorious for their high rate of failure, could not be relied on to hit its target at a range of much more than six yards.

Indeed, the man who drew his gun and fired first was frequently at a disadvantage. Wes Hardin survived as long as he did because he took his time and coolly aimed to kill. In Comanche, Texas, "as I turned around I saw Charles Webb drawing his pistol. He was in the act of presenting it when I jumped to one side, drew my pistol and fired. In the meantime Webb had fired. . . . My aim was good, and a bullet hole in the left cheek did the work."

By 1879, the law had the upper hand in the cow towns. The railroads had driven farther westward, and the great cattle drives were diluted over a much wider area. When news spread of the silver strike at Tombstone in the Arizona Territory, the dance halls and the faro games, the gamblers, the girls, the pimps, and the gunmen, all moved west in search of easier victims and richer pickings. Wyatt Earp's brother Virgil was appointed deputy marshal for southern Arizona in November 1879 and assistant

town marshal in Tombstone in October 1880. Wyatt, with brothers Jim and Morgan, arrived there in December 1879, followed by "Doc" Holliday, the tubercular ex-dentist gambler, and his common-law wife, "Big Nose" Kate Fisher. The cast was assembled for one of the most famous legends of the West.

The trouble started on the night of March 15, 1881. Bandits held up a stagecoach which had left Tombstone. The driver and one passenger were killed, and the gunman, according to the local newspaper, *The Nugget*, (supported by a statement from Big Nose Kate) was Doc Holliday. And Ike Clanton, another local gunslinger, maintained that Wyatt Earp had offered him $6,000 to implicate some other members of the Clanton outfit.

On the morning of October 26, Ike Clanton was back in Tombstone, with his younger brother Billy, Frank and Tom McLowry, and Billy Claiborne, all men with reputations as cattle rustlers. Virgil Earp, now assistant marshal, deputized his brothers Wyatt and Morgan, and the three patrolled the streets, apparently trying to pick a quarrel with the Clantons: Virgil struck Ike with his pistol barrel, and Wyatt punched Tom McLowry. When the Clantons went to the OK Corral to collect their horses and leave town, the Earp brothers followed them. Doc Holliday tagged along with a sawed-off shotgun under his frock coat.

In the corral, Virgil called out, "You are under arrest." Somebody fired. In less than a minute, Billy Clanton and the McLowrys were dead, Ike Clanton and Billy Claiborne had run for their lives, Morgan Earp had a bullet in the left shoulder, Virgil one in the leg, and Holliday one in the left hip. When the Clanton and McLowry bodies were laid out in their caskets, citizens hung a large notice over them: "Murdered in the streets of Tombstone."

Left to right: Tom McLowry, Frank McLowry and Billy Clanton, victims of the McLowry-Earp feud.

Above: Members of the Dodge City Peace Commission. The moustachioed Wyatt Earp sits second from left, while Bat Masterson stands on the right.

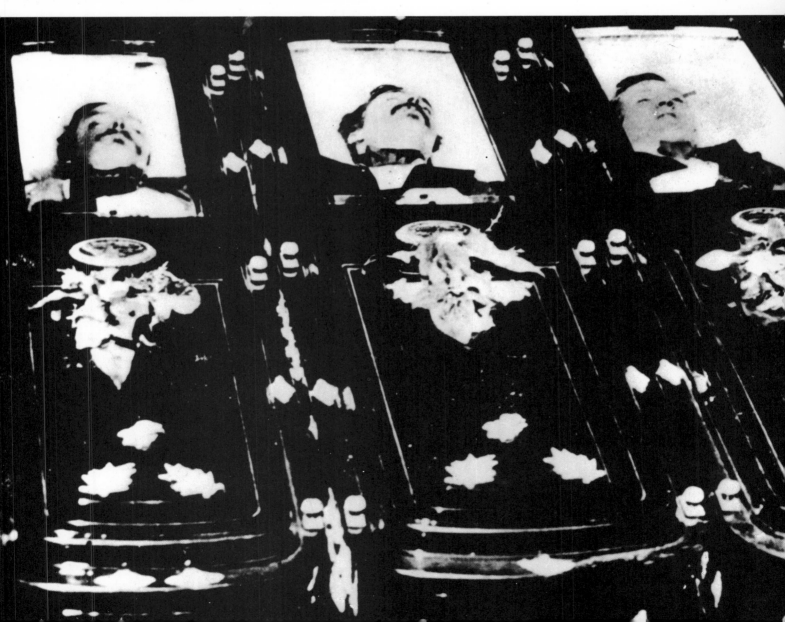

And that nearly ends the Earp epic. Someone crippled Virgil with a burst of gunfire in December and someone killed Morgan with a lucky shot through the back window of a poolroom in March 1882. Wyatt managed to get himself deputized by a federal marshal, gathered together a posse, and rode out of Tombstone never to return. He later made his way into the state of Colorado with Doc Holliday, and in Denver they joined forces again with Bat Masterson. Holliday died in Glenwood Springs sanitarium three years later. Masterson ran a faro game at the Arcade, while Earp ran one at the Central. In 1902 Masterson was ordered out of Denver and went to New York, where he ended his life as a sports writer on the *Morning Telegraph*, dying at his desk in 1921. Earp lingered on in retirement in Los Angeles until 1929.

For all their lawlessness, Hickok and Earp, Holliday and Masterson, and all their hard-gambling, gun-toting friends were overtly on the right side. The eagerness with which they went after jobs as marshals shows that. There were, of course, many others who deliberately chose a life outside the law.

The *National Police Gazette*—a sensational illustrated weekly that began publication in 1877 under the inspired editorship of Richard K. Fox—can claim some of the responsibility for the glorification of at least one. When William Bonney was shot on July 14, 1881, he cannot have imagined the fame he would achieve as "Billy the Kid."

Even his real name is shrouded in obscurity. It is likely that he was born in the New York slums in November 1859, and his mother called herself Mrs Catherine McCarty. In 1873, she married a miner, William Antrim, in Santa Fe. The following year she died in Silver City.

Seven years later William Bonney, Billy the Kid, was gunned down by Sheriff Pat Garrett of Lincoln County, Arizona, and the book that gives most likely details of his life was later written by Garrett. It is not surprising that, in the process, the Kid should have been inflated by the sheriff into a merciless killer and a worthy adversary.

According to this account, the Kid killed his first man at the age of twelve. By 1877 he reputedly had fifteen killings to his name. In that year he became involved in the Lincoln County War, which included several skirmishes and at least one pitched battle. The two sides were respectively the small ranchers and settlers, represented by Major L. G. Murphy and J. J. Dolan (backed by US attorney Thomas Catron), and cattle king John Chisum, with his representatives Alexander McSween and the Englishman John Tunstall. Chisum had taken over some 27,000 acres of squatter and homestead rights along the Pecos, where he soon had 100,000 head of cattle. Billy joined Murphy and Dolan, who were raiding Chisum's herds for meat.

Some time later Billy, then eighteen years old and no doubt impressionable, met John Tunstall and immediately

Sheriff Pat Garrett (top) achieved fame by killing one of the West's most notorious outlaws, Billy the Kid (right). Garrett and the Kid at one time were close friends.

transferred his loyalties to the Chisum side. "That's the finest lad I ever met," said Tunstall, "he's a revelation to me every day and would do anything on earth to please me!"

Because of the scandalous situation in Lincoln County, a new governor was appointed. He was Civil War general Lew Wallace (who later wrote *Ben Hur*). He proclaimed an amnesty for all those who would lay down their arms. But the amnesty excluded those already under indictment, and the Kid was wanted for the killing of Sheriff William Brady. He offered to give evidence against Dolan and his associates in return for a pardon, and on March 17, 1879, surrendered to the governor. He was confined in Lincoln, but not in the jail, and after a week or so broke parole and rode off to Fort Sumner, where he joined up with a number of men, all wanted for various offenses.

Pat Garrett, newly-elected county sheriff, determined to capture the Kid. In the course of his campaign he killed Tom O'Folliard in an ambush, got Charlie Bowdre in a stakeout, and finally shot Billy from the bedroom of a ranch house while two deputies kept the young man in conversation on the porch outside. It was July 14, 1881.

Within a month, the first book was published: "The history of an outlaw who killed a man for every year of his life." After that, the fiction grew thick and fast and has not stopped to this day.

The Kid was dead. Hickok was dead, and Holliday was dying. Earp and Masterson and Cody had gone their separate ways to gambling hells and carnivals. Wes Hardin was in jail for twenty-five years hard labor. Billy the Kid was the nearest the mythmakers had come to creating a Robin Hood for the struggling homesteaders of Missouri, Kansas, and the territories. But the stunted, weasel-faced lad was not the most promising of material. Hickok and Cody had the necessary panache, but they were law-and-order men. Besides, they lacked one final requirement—they had not fought on the Confederate side. They were not downtrodden and defeated rebels.

One man still lived who had all the necessary qualifications. As a boy of sixteen he had ridden with Quantrill's Raiders during the Civil War, taking part in the massacre at Lawrence, Kansas. At the Centralia massacre in 1864, he had been party to the killing of over two hundred federal prisoners of war. Riding into Lexington, Missouri, under a flag of truce in 1865, he had been shot through the lung and given up for dead. As an ex-Confederate soldier, he was denied the practice of any profession in the state of Missouri, which was his home. With his brother and cousins he had adopted a life of crime, robbing banks and railroads, which (perhaps) he regarded as symbols of the encroaching Yankee way of life. After ten years of insolent exploits that had made him infamous around the world, he was now living modestly with his wife in a little house on the outskirts of St Joseph. His name was Thomas Howard.

Frank and Jesse James (who rode with Quantrill's Raiders during the Civil War) became the West's best-known bank robbers. Right: An 1881 offer of $5,000 for the arrest of the James brothers.

At least, that was how he was known locally. The world knew him as Jesse James. Six years before, on September 7, 1876, he and his brother Frank had escaped from a bungled bank robbery at Northfield, Minnesota, leaving their cousins, the three Younger brothers, to be caught and jailed. After that it had been difficult to find new gang members prepared to offer their devotion and loyalty to Jesse. The new recruits fought among themselves, and young Bob Ford shot one of his companions. Jesse shot another for talking too much.

By now, the various rewards proclaimed for the capture or death of Jesse James totaled little less than the gang had stolen in all sixteen years of its existence. The James gang is believed to have committed seventeen successful robberies, with a total haul of $200,000—less than $2,000 per year for each man. Stories of the riches they captured are unjustified, as are the theories that they invented the bank robbery and the train holdup. The Reno gang made the first famous train raid in Indiana seven years before the James gang held up the Rock Island train at Adair, Iowa. And in 1864 a Confederate officer, Lieutenant Bennett Young, had robbed three banks of $170,000 in fifteen minutes.

Pinkerton's Inc

PROCLAMATION
OF THE
GOVERNOR OF MISSOURI!
REWARDS
FOR THE ARREST OF
Express and Train Robbers.

STATE OF MISSOURI,
EXECUTIVE DEPARTMENT.

WHEREAS, It has been made known to me, as the Governor of the State of Missouri, that certain parties, whose names are to me unknown, have confederated and banded themselves together for the purpose of committing robberies and other depredations within this State; and

WHEREAS, Said parties did, on or about the Eighth day of October, 1879, stop a train near Glendale, in the county of Jackson, in said State, and, with force and violence, take, steal and carry away the money and other express matter being carried thereon; and

WHEREAS, On the fifteenth day of July 1881, said parties and their confederates did stop a train upon the line of the Chicago, Rock Island and Pacific Railroad, near Winston, in the County of Daviess, in said State, and, with force and violence, take, steal, and carry away the money and other express matter being carried thereon; and, in perpetration of the robbery last aforesaid, the parties engaged therein did kill and murder one WILLIAM WESTFALL, the conductor of the train, together with one JOHN McCULLOCH, who was at the time in the employ of said company, then on said train; and

WHEREAS, FRANK JAMES and JESSE W. JAMES stand indicted in the Circuit Court of said Daviess County, for the murder of JOHN W. SHEETS, and the parties engaged in the robberies and murders aforesaid have fled from justice and have absconded and secreted themselves:

NOW, THEREFORE, in consideration of the premises, and in lieu of all other rewards heretofore offered for the arrest or conviction of the parties aforesaid, or either of them, by any person or corporation, I, THOMAS T. CRITTENDEN, Governor of the State of Missouri, do hereby offer a reward of five thousand dollars ($5,000.00) for the arrest and conviction of each person participating in either of the robberies or murders aforesaid, excepting the said FRANK JAMES and JESSE W. JAMES; and for the arrest and delivery of said

FRANK JAMES and JESSE W. JAMES,

and each or either of them, to the sheriff of said Daviess County, I hereby offer a reward of five thousand dollars, ($5,000.00.) and for the conviction of either of the parties last aforesaid of participation in either of the murders or robberies above mentioned, I hereby offer a further reward of five thousand dollars, ($5,000.00.)

IN TESTIMONY WHEREOF, I have hereunto set my hand and caused to be affixed the Great Seal of the State of Missouri. Done
[SEAL] at the City of Jefferson on this 28th day of July, A. D. 1881.

THOS. T. CRITTENDEN.

By the Governor:
MICH'L K. McGRATH, Sec'y of State.

Four of the West's most notorious outlaws spare a few minutes for a relaxed group portrait. Cole and Bob Younger stand behind Jesse and Frank James. Below: Bob Ford, the assassin of Jesse James, displays his six-shooter.

Bob Ford could not resist the temptation that the rewards offered. On April 3, 1882, he shot Jesse James in the back of the head, as Jesse was standing on a chair to straighten a picture. "Is it Jesse? the Question on Every Tongue," reported the *Kansas City Daily Times*. Within days it was said of him that he was not really dead, that he would return in time to free the West from the domination of the cattle baron and the railroad king. Not even treachery could destroy a man who had defied not one but many sheriffs. Nevertheless, a stone was raised on what was supposed to be his grave: "Murdered," it said, "by a Traitor and Coward Whose Name is Not Worthy to Appear Here. And there, despite the many rogues who have since claimed to be Jesse—the last as recently as 1961, which would have made him 114 years old— there he undeniably lies.

There were, of course, other outlaws, but time was now against them. In the year Jesse died, the great midwestern land boom had started, and Congress imposed the first head tax on the 5 million immigrants who were to arrive within the next ten years. The first Labor Day celebration was held in New York City, and John L. Sullivan won the heavyweight championship. But although the Wild West was tamed, its legend would live forever.

Chapter 9

RICHES OF THE LAND

The West was a land of opportunity not only for the cattleman and cowboy, but for the miner and farmer as well. In the mountain regions, recurrent discoveries of gold, silver, and copper exerted a magnetic pull on ambitious (or merely foot-loose) prospectors, and boom towns like Virginia City sprang up almost overnight. In their wake came the giant companies which turned mining into big business. At the same time, millions of acres of virgin land on the Great Plains beckoned the optimistic homesteader. Could he, too, strike it rich—or at least make a living—on the "Great American Desert"?

The Mining Bonanza

California gold fired men's imaginations. More than that, it indirectly set in motion a restless frontier. From the Sonoran Desert north to Alaska and from the Pacific to the eastern spurs of the Rockies, the mining kingdom sprawled. After the California Mother Lode became more difficult to mine, the pull of the elusive yellow metal cast countless prospectors adrift. With pan and burro they ransacked the dusty arroyos and the high mountain valleys of most of the Far West. Like water seeping into crevices, miners penetrated the most remote regions. As if by magic, the discovery of a few nuggets or a little dust panned in some icy stream spawned hell-roaring camps that teemed with humanity. The virus of gold fever was as incurable as it was contagious. "What a clover-field is to a steer," wrote an editor in 1862, "the sky to the lark— a mudhole to a hog, such are new diggings to a miner."

But Fortune was fickle. Placer gold was soon exhausted and mineral veins pinched out. The makeshift towns faded away. Their inhabitants had come to "git and git out." Now they vanished quietly, perhaps to repeat the process anew at some other time and in some other setting. Or if mineral deposits proved more enduring, as at Washoe, Nevada, the Black Hills of South Dakota, or Butte, Montana, a more complex industry emerged and would be sustained.

As early as 1849 California-bound travelers had found gold in the Washoe Mountains, just east of the Sierra Nevada. But who would stop for a pittance when everyone knew the "true" El Dorado lay just over the range? But a few settlers filtered into Washoe. Among them were the Grosch brothers who, before their deaths in 1857, probably realized that they were onto something of value. Two years later, two Irishmen found dirt on the northern slope of Mt Davidson which paid so well that the gaunt, boastful Henry T. P. Comstock thought it worthwhile to bluff his way into a partnership. But it was curious dirt. It left the miners' rockers clogged with a "damned blue stuff," which had to be laboriously shoveled aside. After a few months a curious settler had the "blue stuff" assayed and found it rich in silver. The rush to Washoe was on.

Within the year the new town of Virginia City contained 10,000 people thrown helter-skelter onto the side of the mountain. J. Ross Browne, world traveler, author, and

One of the first—and most important—buildings to be erected in a new mining town was the assay office. It was there that a hopeful miner would bring samples of ore to be tested for precious-metal content. Below: The assay office in Roosevelt, Idaho.

ASSAY OFFICE

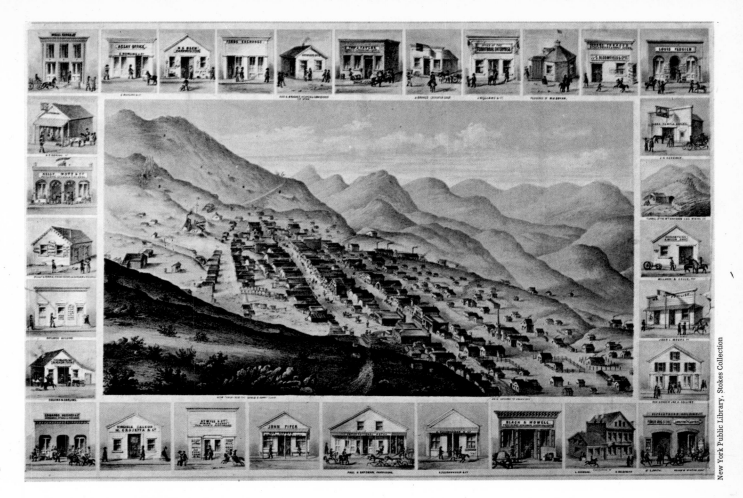

mining expert, surveyed the scene in 1861:

> Frame shanties, pitched together as if by accident; tents of canvas, of blankets, of brush, of potato-sacks, and old shirts, with empty whisky barrels for chimneys; smoky hovels of mud and stone; coyote holes in the mountain-side forcibly seized and held by men; pits and shafts with smoke issuing from every crevice; piles of goods and rubbish on craggy points, in the hollows, on the rocks, in the mud, in the snow, every where, scattered broadcast in pell-mell confusion, as if the clouds had burst overhead and rained down the dregs of all the flimsy, rickety, filthy little hovels and rubbish of merchandise that had ever undergone the process of evaporation from the earth since the days of Noah.

Still boisterous and raw, Virginia City matured as its mining experts moved in. Sixteen rich bonanzas were ultimately found on the Comstock Lode. The greatest of all, the "Big Bonanza," was struck in October 1873 at a depth of more than 1,100 feet. It was a vein so large "a blind man driving a four-horse team could have followed it in a snowstorm." Some $340 million in silver came out of the incredible Comstock between 1860 and 1890, when the area rapidly declined. Other Nevada strikes overlapped, but none matched the one focused in a narrow circle drawn around Mt Davidson.

Meanwhile another story was being written in the

"Virginia City, Nevada Territory, 1861"—a lithograph of the greatest of the mining towns at the time when it was riding the crest of its first boom. Already—just two years after silver was discovered on the Washoe—the city had a population of some 15,000 people.

Colorado Rockies. This beautiful, rugged area was also lightly prospected by impatient souls heading for gold in California. In the summer of 1858, with the depression of the previous year firmly fixed in their minds, several parties returned. Most left discouraged. But enough pay dirt was found to send the cry of "gold" echoing eastward in ever-widening circles. An estimated 100,000 "fifty-niners" headed west for Pike's Peak, as the diggings were called, even though the "mines" were 80 miles from that summit. Blood brothers to the forty-niners, they came along one of the river routes with "light hearts and a thin pair of britches." Half never reached their goal. Some were buried in rude graves along the way, and many turned back before they even saw the Rockies. Of the 50,000 who did reach the mountains, perhaps half returned home immediately. Disillusioned, they damned the rumormongers and the writers of guidebooks by condemning them in rhyme:

> Here lies the body of D. C. Oakes,
> Killed for aiding the Pike's Peak Hoax.

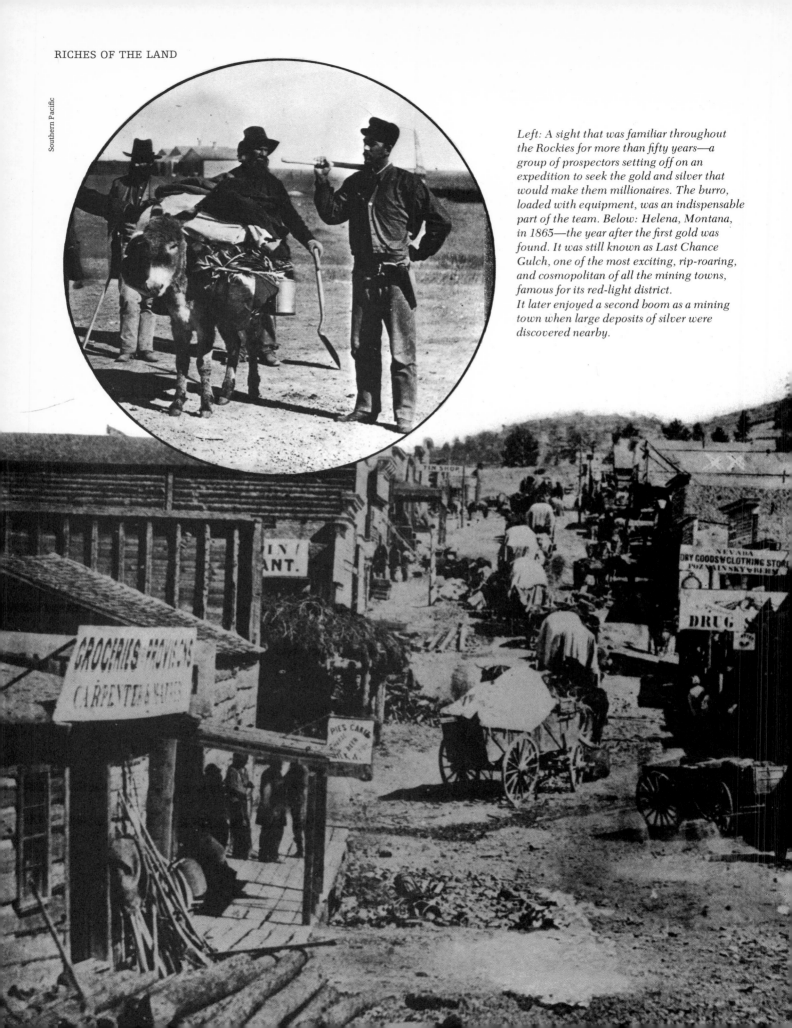

Southern Pacific

Left: A sight that was familiar throughout the Rockies for more than fifty years—a group of prospectors setting off on an expedition to seek the gold and silver that would make them millionaires. The burro, loaded with equipment, was an indispensable part of the team. Below: Helena, Montana, in 1865—the year after the first gold was found. It was still known as Last Chance Gulch, one of the most exciting, rip-roaring, and cosmopolitan of all the mining towns, famous for its red-light district.
It later enjoyed a second boom as a mining town when large deposits of silver were discovered nearby.

But new discoveries revitalized Colorado. Miners flocked to Idaho Springs, to Gold Hill, and to the site of Black Hawk. At the junction of the South Platte and Cherry Creek, a number of small settlements grew together to form Denver. (The town was named for the governor of Kansas Territory, of which it was then a part.) Denver, east of the Rockies, nourished and outfitted the mountain camps as they were born, lived, and died over the rest of the century. There were many of them, Georgetown and Caribou for example, where silver was discovered in the 1860s. There was La Plata, Silverton, and Lake City in the 1870s. And Ouray, which blossomed momentarily between 1870 and 1881, but which was abandoned because of its isolation, then reopened in 1895 with dazzling success.

The mountain camps also included the "Cloud City" of

Montana Historical Society, Helena

Leadville (altitude over 10,000 feet) in California Gulch. It was there that an excited Georgian had shouted in 1860: "By God, I've got all of California in this here pan." However it was not gold, but rich carbonate silver that made Leadville a national byword in the late 1870s. Aspen came into being in 1880. With Creede, it enjoyed real prosperity in 1891–92, a prelude to the last major Colorado rush at Cripple Creek. There, after initial strikes by a local cowboy, prospectors flocked in during the early 1890s. Many were farm lads unfamiliar with mining and were said to have "mined with pitchforks."

Major Strikes Throughout the West

Farther north, British Columbia's Fraser River mines had attracted thousands in 1858. Two years later, prospectors hit gold on the Clearwater in what would become Idaho. From the swarming new camps of Oro Fino and Pierce City a transient population moved on to the Salmon River valley in 1861–62. Since all of these discoveries were on Indian lands, treaty lines had to be redrawn in June 1863 to secure the prize areas. Much farther south, beginning in 1862, miners stampeded to the rich, easily worked placers of Boise Basin. In the mid-1880s came the discovery and exploitation of the rich and very important silver-lead deposits of the Coeur d'Alenes in the Idaho Panhandle.

Eager Coloradans heading for the north Idaho diggings in 1862 found gold on Grasshopper Creek and founded Bannack, in what was to become Montana. In 1863 discoveries on the Stinking Water River brought a boom to Virginia City and a year later to Helena (Last Chance Gulch) and Silver Bow, just south of what would become Butte. The latter town was revived in 1875 as a silver camp, but in the end its reputation rested upon the non-precious metal, copper.

Major strikes dotted other western areas also. Although Mormon leaders were slow in opening mines in Utah, there was the Emma, located in Little Cottonwood Canyon. The Ontario, another Utah property, was as rich a horn silver mine as seen in the West. On the southern edge of the Arizona desert, a drifter named Ed Schieffelin in 1877 made a discovery that precipitated an onrush to Tombstone, the "town too tough to die."

Two government expeditions, one under Lieutenant Colonel George A. Custer, verified the existence of gold in the Black Hills of Dakota in 1874 and 1875. The metal was found on land set aside to the Sioux for "as long as the waters run and the grass grows green." After half-hearted attempts to keep the interloping gold-seekers out, federal authorities gave up in defeat. While the Sioux took to the warpath, white miners swarmed into the Black Hills. Custer City and Deadwood boomed. Four miles

*A facsimile of Francis Bret Harte's popular
parody in verse,* The Heathen Chinee.
*Originally published in 1870, these tales of
mining camps were at first entitled*
Plain Language from Truthful James.

southwest of Deadwood, at Lead, the Homestake vein was discovered. In 1876 it was sold for $70,000 to a trio of shrewd Californians, George Hearst, James Ben Ali Haggin, and Lloyd Tevis. Thus began the Homestake Mining Company, the giant of Black Hills producers.

Wherever or whenever located, whether at Mt Davidson in 1859, on the Stinking Water River a few years later, or on Cripple Creek twenty years later, western mining communities had much in common. To begin with, their population was diverse and cosmopolitan.

Eastern "tenderfeet" rubbed elbows with "yon-siders," as Californians were labeled. Illiterates and college graduates swung picks together. Abolitionists and former slaveholders did the same. All nationalities were there, from the Cornish "Cousin Jacks" to Bret Harte's "Heathen Chinee." Most towns had their *Café de Paris.*

Denver in 1860 had its German newspaper. Higher in the Rockies Englishmen played cricket matches. Even in a settled, conservative, industrial-mining town, the work force would show a striking assortment of national backgrounds.

These were fluid, mobile populations. In the spring the sap began to flow and wanderlust often took hold of mining men, whether prospectors or wage-earners. Californians, especially, were in evidence throughout the mining kingdom. Horace Greeley estimated that out of every ten miners in Colorado prior to the Civil War, three had spent time in California. Californians "have swept in successive waves over every adjacent district from Durango to the Yellowstone," said an Idaho newspaper in 1865. "She is the mother of these Pacific States and Territories." Jim Wardner, who signed himself "of Far Western Mining Fame," is an example. He tried stock speculation in San Francisco, mining in Arizona, and a wide gamut of enterprises in the Black Hills. Eventually he made $100,000 as a partner in the discovery of the Bunker Hill & Sullivan mine in Idaho. He promptly lost it and spent the remainder of his life trying to recoup his fortune in South Africa, Nevada, British Columbia, the Klondyke, and Alaska.

Life In The Mining Camps

The raw mining towns themselves were much alike. If the mines held out, their rowdiness perhaps diminished somewhat, and physically they assumed at least an aura of permanence. Tents and shacks gave way to brick, stone, or frame buildings with the inevitable false fronts —what a Montana visitor called "Queen Anne in front and Crazy Jane behind." Of whatever era, they all seemed cut from the same cloth:

They had narrow streets with a few stores, eating places run by Chinese who knew how to cook, sometimes a bank, not often an "opera house," but always saloons and gambling places. A few homes were built on narrow streets away from the main drag; their number was small and often the owners took in boarders, mostly hard-rock stiffs who worked at the nearby mines. There was always the "line" or "stockade" with its dance halls, parlor houses, and cribs.

Scenic mountain settings to the contrary, mining towns were not necessarily pleasant places. "Boulder is a God forsaken little hole," wrote a Colorado visitor in 1860. "I would hate to live there." The copper town of Bingham, Utah, was later described as "a sewer five miles long." Too often, the traveler could smell or hear such a town before he could see it. Abandoned prospect holes, unsightly tailing dumps, and the grotesque frames of

*Right: An 1876 photograph of Deadwood City,
Dakota Territory. A well-organized crew poses
beside its work, drifting for gold below
Discovery Point.*

A shortage of women (respectable or not) did not prevent prospectors from having a good time. This engraving shows a Saturday night dance in progress in a rough and ready mining town. Below: The main street and surprisingly impressive court house of Nevada City, California, photographed in 1866.

rusted machinery desecrated the landscape. The dull booms of underground blasting could be felt as well as heard. Worse yet, the lack of general sanitation facilities and sulphuric smelter fumes created an appalling waste-land devoid of vegetation.

Except for the well-regulated Canadian Yukon, western mining camps were noted for their turbulence and law-lessness. Browne probably exaggerates a little when he describes some of the Washoe citizenry as "the roaring, raving drunkards of the bar-rooms, swilling fiery liquids from morning till night; the flaring and flaunting gambling-saloons, filled with desperadoes of the vilest sort." But in most new towns "the sky was the limit." Like Deadwood in 1876, with its single street lined with brothels and drinking and gambling houses, they "had no Puritan prejudices to overcome," and mining was hard work. Quick wealth attracted not only prospectors and merchants and craftsmen who supplied them, but people who would "mine the miners" in more iniquitous ways. They were the slick gamblers, the purveyors of bad whiskey, and the hurdy-gurdy dance girls. A cross section of thieves, swindlers, and cutthroats represented the dregs of human society accumulated from several continents.

These towns differed only in degree from more established towns farther east. What was most remarkable was not the presence of the undesirable elements, but the speed and the thoroughness with which responsible citizens brought them under control. Miners' meetings laid down the ground rules for mineral claims. Stern, self-righteous (and occasionally mistaken) vigilante justice usually brought law and order until legal government could do so. The early Montana camps of Bannack and Alder Gulch were examples. Here, late in 1863 and early in 1864, vigilantes completely overwhelmed and eliminated Henry Plummer's outlaw band, shooting or hanging at least twenty-two. In most cases, as large bodies of population shifted rapidly ahead of the machinery of organized government, residents took matters into their own hands, then quickly petitioned Washington for the creation of a new territory or state. "Congregate a hundred Americans anywhere beyond the settlements," wrote an onlooker in 1860, "and they immediately lay out a city, form a State constitution and apply for admission to the Union, while twenty-five of them become candidates for the United States Senate."

Early Virginia City had a reputation as a "city of stove-pipes and single men's wives," but the town soon boasted schools, churches, theaters, and an opera house as fine as any in San Francisco. Colorado miners paid homage to John Barleycorn and beefy German girls, but by 1860 they had also underwritten a school in Denver taught by "Professor" O. J. Goldrick. (He had earlier arrived cracking a whip over a team of oxen, and wearing yellow kid gloves, a glossy black hat, and a black broad-cloth suit.) Miners in Leadville and Butte caroused and cheered their favorite bare-knuckled prize fighters, but they also whooped it up and stomped their feet when Oscar Wilde lectured about the early Florentines, and when Edwin Booth played the title role in *Hamlet*.

Western miners spent time "bucking the tiger" and sitting around the gambling table, but they still formed debating groups, mock legislatures, and literary and poetry societies. They were captivated with the home-spun humor of newsmen like Mark Twain and by the ventriloquists, hypnotists, and other pseudo-scientific "experts" who wandered by. If a grizzled old Colorado veteran expressed surprise when he heard a new church bell pealing—"I'll be damned if Jesus Christ hasn't come to Leadville too"—he must not have been very attentive. From the first, the gold-seekers had held religious services in saloons if necessary, and then moved swiftly to have churches built. In Austin, Nevada, for example, mining men in 1865 donated mineral property to be sold to provide a church building, public library, and lecture and reading rooms. If men worshipped free-milling gold ore or carbonate silver, their concern with a more conventional religion always surfaced in good order.

As they moved about from one major mining center to another, or to short-lived camps, the miners brought with them technology and institutions. They brought and modified the basic mining codes and courts, based on Germanic and Mexican-Spanish traditions, which the Californians had established to fill the void. Meeting informally in the new camps, they set down rules defining mining claims, their acquisition, and transfer. They created courts to hear disputes and even criminal matters. When effective legal government was achieved, these codes were written into the statutes. The territorial courts insisted that since their mineral laws were drawn ultimately from those of California, interpretations by the California courts must also be followed. As a prelude to national mining laws, Congress in 1866 would recognize the local mining codes and in 1872 would begin to incorporate their provisions into a more unified set of federal statutes.

Early Mining Techniques

In most mining districts, early methods and milling processes varied little. They were simple techniques calling for low capital and much labor. Generally the first discoveries in an area were of placer gold. This was easily handled by the classical but inefficient methods of panning, "cradles," or sluice-boxes. Free-milling quartz found in outcrops on or near the surface could readily be crushed with a stamp mill and the gold separated with mercury, but this brought a great loss of precious metal.

Top: A watercolor of a sluice miner by O. C. Seltzer. Above: Panning for gold, from the same series of paintings. Right: The glare of shining magnesium provided the light for this photograph taken in the Comstock Mine, Virginia City, in 1868. Inset: Stiffly-posed miners stand at the top of the shaft.

The days of these elementary techniques were numbered however. In most regions free-milling ore was scarce and the gold-bearing gravels of the streams were worked out quickly, often within a year or two. Miners then followed the outcroppings deep into the ground, but capital requirements mounted as this type of transition was made. Tunneling and shafting were expensive. Blasting was costly as well as dangerous, for power drills soon came to replace hand models. Heavy expenditures went for ventilating, moving the ore while still underground, and hoisting it to the surface. In addition, hundreds of thousands of board feet of timber shored up the mines' interior. By 1881 the deeper shafts on the Comstock were down to 3,000 feet, and the total length of underground workings and interconnections was somewhere between 180 and 190 miles. Clearly, as projected on this scale, deep-level quartz mining had to be big business.

With time and place, the nature of the ore changed so that the standard processes of separation no longer worked. The methods used in California at the end of the 1850s, and on the Comstock a few years later, were wasteful but functioned reasonably well. But deeper in Nevada and in parts of Utah, Montana, and Colorado, ores were more complex. Silver as well as gold was often in combination with base metals or sulphur, and these "refractory" or "rebellious" ores did not respond to the normal milling procedures. Many believed that the general mining slump in Colorado and central Nevada in the mid-1860s was the direct result of the inability to work these stubborn ores.

Big Business Takes Over

When westerners came in contact with the "refractories," the treating of metals was in its infancy. Coping with them proceeded on a trial-and-error basis, rather than on a strictly scientific one. "Process mania" swept the West in 1863 and 1864. Peddlers of dozens of "sure-fire" new approaches became more of a nuisance than snake oil vendors and lightning rod salesmen. In one part of Colorado, "everything from superheated steam to tobacco-juice" was tried on "rebellious ores," according to the United States commissioner of mineral statistics.

Combined with this process mania was a flurry of wild speculation in both mines and mills. The net result was a sharp mining depression in 1864. The slump left in its wake thousands of investors with shattered dreams and a landscape littered with the hulks of abandoned machinery. Fortunately this emergency was relatively short-lived. By the late 1860s, chemist Nathaniel Hill had adapted European advances to Colorado smelting. A remarkable group of metallurgists, many of them

European-born and German-trained, were solving the riddle of complex ores throughout the West.

But these solutions required a heavy outlay of capital. So did new mass production techniques introduced from time to time. Hydraulic mining was an example. A California innovation, this new method involved diverting a stream of water, dropping it through pipes to build up pressure, then shooting it through a nozzle with force enough to wash away a mountain (or to kill a miner who ventured into its path). Loosened by this jet, the gold-bearing dirt was then run through long sluices to separate the metal. Well established after 1857, hydraulic mining was a large-scale, high-capital operation of reasonable efficiency until the mid-1880s. At that time, California farmers succeeded in restraining the dumping of hydraulic debris into the rivers.

Dredge mining, which came into its own shortly before the end of the century, was another of the mass production approaches. The dredge scooped gravel from the river bottom, processed it for gold, and dumped the tailings as an unsightly ridge over land which had sometimes been worked twice before—once by white prospectors and then by Chinese.

Throughout the mining kingdom, simple mining, sustained by blister-and-callous labor, soon gave way to high-capital corporate mining. The independent miner was cast adrift. He could, and many did, go his way, panning new streams and dreaming new dreams. Or he could become a company employee. He was paid $3 per shift-day for shoveling ore into one-ton cars or as part of a double-jack drilling team. One man held and turned the drill, the other struck it rhythmically with an eight-pound sledge at fifty strokes a minute. Or after 1875 he might be a pneumatic drill specialist.

Western mining has always been built on unbounded faith. Corporate mining broadened the base of that faith, adding to that of prospectors and discoverers, that of promoters, capitalists, and investors. In the early mining camp, every man was a potential millionaire. Every pocket was full of samples from the "Wake-up-Jake," the "Root-Hog-or-Die," the "Let-'er-Rip," or other valuable properties not yet developed, but in which the individual owned hundreds or even thousands of "feet." These interests were invariably in "the richest mines on earth," but as Mark Twain pointed out, the owners were in debt to the butcher and had no credit with the grocer.

When companies took over, new importance was assumed by the mine promoter, that imaginative and persistent midwife in the transfer of property to a corporation with capital. Eternally optimistic, not always burdened with scruples, some only bore out the old assertion that a mine was "a hole in the ground owned by a damned liar." Promoters were a dime-a-dozen. They ranged from professionals like William J. Sutherland, described as "expansive and expensive," to amateurs like

the Reverend Calvin A. Pogue. He financed several Arizona mining companies in the 1870s with investments from other clergymen and their flocks. ("A Saintly Syndicate," sneered a skeptical editor. "Presbyterian Preachers in a Prodigious Pool.")

The Craze for Investment

One of the occult sciences connected with the sale or promotion of mining property was "salting." With ingenuity (and luck) interested parties might create the illusion of greater riches than were actually present. Precious metal could be provided by firing a shotgun full of gold into the face of the "vein." Or it could be accomplished by doctoring the samples taken by the examining expert. His samples might be stolen and replaced with rich specimens from another mine. Or it could be achieved by injecting a silver solution from a syringe through the side of his burlap sample bags. Even in the twentieth century, "salting" had not become a lost art. Most mining men came up against it in one form or another during their careers. Enough of it was successful that companies in practically every part of the mining West were occasionally fleeced.

On the whole, however, western mining was based on legitimate investment and optimistic but not fraudulent appraisals. Much of the capital was generated internally. It came from the East Coast, the Midwest, or San Francisco. And much of it was plowed back from profitable mine or mill operations. Dotted here and there were concerns like the Mining Company Nederland in Colorado, a Dutch firm with some Russian capital and the Société Anonyme des Mines de Lexington, a French company operating in both Utah and Montana. More obvious were several hundred British joint-stock companies. Between 1860 and 1901 they invested as much as £50 million in western mines, not including California's. But the bulk of the capital was American.

Like prospecting, mine investment and speculation became a disease. Wild manipulation by insiders at home and among the curbstone brokers of San Francisco might cause violent fluctuations on the market. Both millionaires and paupers were created over the course of a few weeks or even days. Shares of the Alpha mine, for example, soared to $1,570 in February 1868 but had plunged to $33 by September of the same year.

Investors came from all walks of life and from most parts of the country but especially middle-sized and large cities. "The market extends everywhere," noted a San Francisco editor in 1870. Participants included "the millionaire and the mendicant, the modest matron and the brazen courtesan, the prudent man of business and the gambler, the maidservant and her mistress, the banker

Hydraulic mining painted by Mrs Jonas Brown.
The process involved piping water down an
incline, shooting it at high pressure,
then separating the ore in sluices.

and his customer." They included Vice President Garret Hobart and industrialists Samuel Colt (inventor of the revolver) and Cyrus McCormick (manufacturer of the reaper). Others were novelist Owen Wister and "Colonel" Jack Haverly, proprietor of Haverly's Mastadon Minstrels, who played at President Garfield's inaugural ball.

Whether many of these investors reaped much profit is doubtful. Some did, but the real money was made by shrewd entrepreneurs who had the ability to judge men and mines and to invest capital when an opportunity arose. These were generally neither run-of-the-mill investors nor the original discoverers of property. There were always exceptions like "Sandy" Bowers, who struck it rich on the Comstock and eventually ran the full cycle back to poverty. Central City, Colorado, had its Pat Casey, legendary nouveau riche, who was once asked to contribute money to buy a chandelier for the new opera house. "Sure," said Pat. "I'll buy the chandelier. But who will you get to play it?"

Every camp had its examples of the rags to riches success story, but it had far more examples of discoverers who sold out for a pittance to men who subsequently made millions out of the property. Henry T. P. Comstock sold his portion of the lode that bore his name for $11,000 and two jackasses, beasts which in terms of later yield cost him $1.5 million each. Comstock died in 1870, a

California Historical Society

Left: Mansions on Nob Hill in San Francisco. Much of the city's wealth was based on western mining, as well as on railroads and commerce. Below: Virginia City in 1877—dramatically changed since its first days as a mining town. By this time it boasted a famous opera house and a six-storey hotel with the only elevator west of Chicago—as well as over a hundred saloons.

dejected and penniless suicide.

At Butte, that "island of easy money completely surrounded by whiskey," old Bill Parks struck a vein of copper ore so pure it could be "shipped to hell and back for smelting and still make a profit." But he sold out for a mere $10,000, then settled back to watch the new owners take $1 million from that "richest hill on earth."

The Changing Face of Mining

The rise of industrial capitalism brought with it a highly impersonal relationship with labor. This was true in western mining as well. Indeed some of the most militant unions in the country would come out of the mineral West. Even in the 1860s, small impotent unions had formed to protest wage cuts or the introduction of "giant powder" (dynamite), which made it possible for one man, single-drilling, to do the work formerly done by two. They always lost their causes, as they did at Leadville in 1880. In that year, workers lost a strike against mines owned by H. A. W. Tabor and Marshall Field, the Chicago mercantile king. But in the 1890s came the first real federation of hard-rock miners and a series of bitter, violent labor wars that shook the West. In the Coeur d'Alenes of Idaho and at Cripple Creek in Colorado, mine-owners organized and hired detectives to infiltrate union ranks. When strikes came, as they did in 1893 and again in 1899, they imported strike-breakers and benefited from troops brought in to keep order. As a result, the power of the Western Federation of Miners was broken, its members were blacklisted and scattered.

In many ways the mining kingdom was tied in to the larger global mining scene. Its early population was a mingling of nationalities, and there were enough foreign mining firms to be noticeable. Its technology, too, was an international matter. From the beginning crude equipment like the *arrastra* for crushing ore and processes like the *cazo* or *patio* for reducing them had been part of the Mexican heritage in the West. The richest ores or concentrates were sometimes sent to Great Britain for smelting until Cornish and German techniques were applied to western plants. Prior to about 1880, there were relatively few technically trained mining engineers and metallurgists in the West, but most of those had been educated abroad—in Paris, London, or more likely, Frieberg in Saxony. Subsequently American schools of mining became important, notably those of Columbia University and of the University of California.

Of whatever background, this growing corps of engineers, this "lace boot, tack-hammer brigade," became increasingly vital. The "by guess and by God" approach to mining gave way to a more scientific assessment of potential and development. Centering in the American West, these were a versatile lot, inveterate travelers who were as much at home in Coolgardie, Australia, or Antofagasta, Chile, as in Denver or Salt Lake City. As they examined or managed mines and smelters the world over, they carried in their baggage the latest in mining technology. They took Deidesheimer's square-set timbering to Mexico and the flat-hoisting cables manufactured in San Francisco to the El Callao mine in Venezuela. In the 1890s they invaded the gold mining area of South Africa and brought back new ideas, including special modifications of the cyanide process, a Scottish contribution. They took the gold dredge, a New Zealand development, and built the most advanced dredge technology in the world. Within a few years Yankee dredging machinery and know-how was exported as far as Siberia and Malaya.

If the mining kingdom had its international implications, it fitted the mood and pattern of national economic growth. It was part of what one historian has called the "great barbecue," the rapid, often ruthless exploitation of natural resources that characterized the United States in the late nineteenth century. It provided the copper for a new era of electricity and, soon, of automobiles. As American industry and transportation expanded rapidly after the Civil War, the outdated and rigid banking structure could not meet the country's financial needs. But the flow of precious metals from the West eased this situation, contributing to inflation and generally high prices. Without the influx of western gold and silver, the depressions of 1873 and 1893 would no doubt have been more severe and more prolonged. The new metal supply made it possible for the United States to export gold to help finance imports like steel for railroads. On the other hand, the great outpouring from the Comstock Lode had the effect of destroying the ratio between the value of gold and silver. The desire to fix a new ratio at sixteen to one would be one of the focal points in the movement for cheaper money so dear to Populists and Democrats in the 1890s.

Each new discovery also meant opportunity for non-miners. Mining towns demanded foodstuffs and services. The mines themselves supported a variety of auxiliary industries. Even after minerals had played out, a few towns, at least, would survive as centers of agriculture, lumbering, or transportation.

Western mining nabobs plowed part of their gains into other enterprises. The Comstock region was a kind of industrial suburb to San Francisco, and the city by the Golden Gate benefited greatly. William Ralston used money from the Washoe silver to build the Pacific Woolen Mills. Before he went broke, Horace Tabor financed opera houses in Leadville and Denver. Sam Hauser invested in railroads and ranchland in Montana. A few of these wealthy men, including James Fair and William A. Clark, used their money to win seats in the United States Senate.

Since mercury was essential in a number of separation

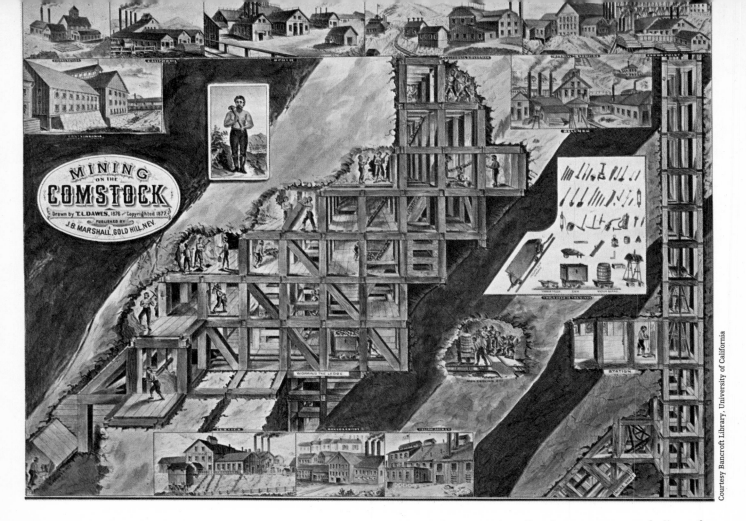

More silver was taken from the Comstock Lode than from any other mine in America. Above: A diagram of the mine revealing the interior of Mt Davidson. Masses of timber were used to shore up the roof and prevent cave-ins, a constant threat.

processes, quicksilver mining in California was kept alive to fill the needs of gold mining. Thus it was said that it takes a mine to run a mine. Chemicals, blasting powder, candles, and timber were also used in profusion in the mines, and separate industries grew in response. Over a thirty-year period, the Comstock swallowed up 800 million board feet of lumber, enough to build 50,000 modern houses. To meet these huge requirements, companies sometimes built flumes ten or a dozen miles long, down which to skid logs to the Virginia City mines. Or where possible, they took what they needed from the public domain. (According to a federal investigator, one British firm operating in central Nevada cut down more than $6 million worth of timber from government land in the fifteen years following 1873.)

Like lumbering, litigation might also be regarded as an auxiliary industry. Frequently claims overlapped. "Everybody's spurs were running into everybody else's angles," it was said. Mining law proved incredibly complex, its interpretation difficult, confusing, and expensive.

A poor mine—a mine "as barren as a mule," as the expression went—posed no problem. But a successful property could be counted upon to produce a crop of lawsuits directly proportional to the richness of its ore. Too often litigation became a form of blackmail by adjoining owners who wished to be bought out at exorbitant prices. In five years, the twelve big mines on the Comstock were engaged in a total of 245 lawsuits, which consumed about 10 per cent of their total production. During the peak of his "war" against Anaconda, "Fritz" Heinze employed thirty-seven lawyers and filed 133 lawsuits. Legal fees drained much of the profits of both sides. But attorneys and experts who testified were given fees, and many a western politician first became known as a mining lawyer.

Above all, mining drew people to the West. Directly or indirectly, it provided an economic base. Some of the rip-roaring camps of the boom eras matured into modern regional centers like Helena, or major cities like Denver. A few, like Butte, are still dominated by the industry. Others, gaudily refurbished, capitalize on their past glories. Virginia City, Tombstone, and Cripple Creek no longer measure their wealth in gold or silver bullion but in the jangle of the cash register as tourists tramp along their wooden sidewalks. And most of the once-bustling camps are now quiet ghost towns marked by lonely graveyards and crumbling, but still eloquent ruins.

The Farmer on the Plains

As Americans pushed westward during the 1840s and 1850s, they avoided or went beyond the Great Plains. The outer edge of settlement in 1860 roughly followed a line from St Paul, Minnesota, southwest to Fort Worth, Texas, and then southward to the Rio Grande. A few settlers had pushed into eastern Kansas and Nebraska in the 1850s, and into southeastern Dakota in the 1860s. But most of the area between Texas and the Canadian border, and between Kansas City and Denver, still awaited the settler's plow at the end of the Civil War.

It is not surprising that farmers had not moved farther west by 1860. There were still millions of acres of good land available in Iowa, Missouri, Arkansas, and eastern Texas. Moreover, most Americans were still convinced that the Great Plains were a desert where agriculture could not possibly flourish. Following a trip westward from Fort Kearney, Nebraska, in 1866, General W. B. Hazen wrote that the area was useless for farming. It could be of value only to ranchers, he insisted, and no railroad promotion, colonization schemes, or governmental encouragement could "ever make more of it." General John Pope wrote in the same year that the Great Plains "is beyond the reach of agriculture, and must always remain a great uninhabited desert. . . ." Writing at about the same time from northeastern Colorado, General W. T. Sherman declared that "the government will have to pay a bounty for people to live up here till necessity forces them."

Despite these and other gloomy reports about the potential of the Great Plains, the idea that farmers could not succeed very far west of Kansas City was in retreat. Travelers, newsmen, and transportation officials reported that agriculture was already a success in some parts of the Great Plains, and that prospects were good in others. A Dakota legislative committee declared in 1869 that, "the capacity of our territory for raising immense herds of cattle, and for the production of large crops of corn, wheat, oats, rye, barley, buckwheat, potatoes, sorghum, melons, fruits and vegetables, demonstrate the ability of our country to sustain a dense population." One traveler, following a trip to the Red River valley of northern Dakota the same year, wrote: "the soil is of the richest sort and easily cultivated for there is neither stone nor stump to bother the plow." The editor of the *Kansas Farmer* journeyed to Fort Harker, some 200 miles west of Lawrence, Kansas, in the summer of 1867, and reported that he had been struck by the "vast areas of unimproved land, rich as that on the banks of the far famed Nile." He saw "land before us, land behind us, land at the right hand, land at the left hand—acres, miles, leagues, townships, counties—

Above: Winslow Homer's The Veteran In a New Field. *Thousands of Civil War soldiers took advantage of the Homestead Act's offer of free land.*

oceans of land, all ready for the plough, good as the best in America, and yet lying without occupants.''

By the late 1860s, the agricultural image of at least the eastern edge of the plains was changing. Publicity by railroads, town site promoters, land speculators, immigration agencies, and the local press combined to create a new image. Soon all these, as well as a few people with scientific credentials, were foolishly declaring that rainfall followed the plow. Some warnings were given about the true nature of the plains—the low rainfall, cold winters, hot summers, and high winds—but these were lost.

How Land Was Obtained

Behind the growing publicity and propaganda about opportunities on the central frontier was one indisputable fact: the availability of free, or at least reasonably cheap, land. For generations there had been a love affair between Americans and the land. The millions of acres on the western prairies and the Great Plains held a compulsive attraction for people farther east and for countless Europeans. In 1872 a young man who had settled some fifty miles southwest of Lincoln, Nebraska, wrote to his mother in Indiana: ''Ma, you can see just as far as you please here and almost every foot in sight can be plowed.'' With $500 and proper management, he added, any man could have a comfortable home within a few years. Other settlers in Kansas, Nebraska, and Dakota were writing similar reports to friends and relatives ''back home.'' In the late 1860s and early 1870s, thousands of farmers swarmed to the new frontier. The Sioux City *Times* reported on June 3, 1869, that ''eight hundred Norwegians are enroute between Chicago and Sioux City bound for Dakota. . . .'' The open land drew settlers like a magnet.

There were two principal methods of acquiring land. A settler could get land at no cost under one of the federal land laws, or he could purchase it from private or public owners. Under the Homestead Act of 1862, a settler (who had not borne arms against the government) could apply for 160 acres of the public domain at no cost except a small filing fee. He was required to build a house and live on the land for five years before the government granted title. If a settler did not want to fulfill the residency requirement, he could, after six months, pay $1.25 an acre and gain title. Settlers could also obtain land under the Preemption Act of 1841. That law permitted a qualified person to buy 160 acres of the public domain for $1.25 an acre. In 1873, Congress passed the Timber Culture Act which granted 160 acres free to any qualified settler who would plant forty acres (later ten acres) of trees on the property. The federal government wanted to encourage tree planting on the western prairies and Great Plains. It was hoped this would reduce the wind, bring increased rainfall, and supply lumber and fuel. It was permissible for a single farmer to get land under each of these laws, making a total of 480 acres.

The second principal method of acquiring land was by purchase. The federal government had withdrawn large areas from the public domain, thereby denying settlers access to it under the land laws. This included land acquired from the Indians, territory set aside for education, and millions of acres given to the railroads. Such lands had to be purchased. In the 1870s, raw land in eastern Dakota, Nebraska, and Kansas generally brought from $2.50 to $10.00 an acre.

Despite the fact that millions of acres were held by agencies of government, corporations, and speculators and could only be bought, there were huge quantities

Freighting by wagon trains from the East brought to the farmer the goods he could not make himself. Below: A sturdy woman driver displays her whip in the Black Hills of South Dakota in 1887.

Land claims frequently changed hands, and the lawyer and surveyor were essential for settling disputes. Above: The proprietors stand outside their office, located west of Court House Square in Round Pond, Oklahoma Territory, in 1894.

available for homesteading and preemption. The first homestead was filed on January 1, 1863, near Beatrice, Nebraska. However, it was not until the late 1860s and early 1870s that homesteading really gained momentum. In 1871, for example, there were over 20,000 entries filed for 2.5 million acres of land under the Homestead Act on the Minnesota-Dakota and Nebraska-Kansas frontiers. In 1871 and 1872, more than 9,000 homestead entries were filed each year in Kansas alone. In other words, in the early 1870s thousands of farmers acquired a free farm. As they pushed farther west onto the high plains in the 1880s, even more of them filed for homesteads. During the boom years of 1885-87 in Kansas, there were 43,000 homestead entries and in 1883 more than 22,000 in Dakota.

The Homestead Act has been criticized on a number of counts. It has been charged that it was superimposed on an already complicated and confused land system. Critics said that it encouraged speculation and monopoly, that it did not achieve its democratic goals of giving people a greater economic stake in society, and that the 160 acres provided for in the law was not enough land on which to make a living in much of the region still available for homesteading. While the law did have weaknesses in both content and administration, it was much more successful than critics have realized.

Any valid evaluation of the Homestead Act must consider the time during which the law was passed and the areas it was to affect. When Congress enacted the law in 1862, there was little thought that farmers would move west of the 100th meridian. Millions of acres of good land were still available east of the 98th meridian where the soil was fertile and rainfall generally adequate for grain farming. Moreover, in that area and at that time, 160 acres was adequate for a single family. The agricultural technology which existed then did not permit many people to cultivate even that much. So long as farmers remained east of the 98th or 99th meridians,

they had a reasonable chance of succeeding on a homestead. The number of farms acquired under the Homestead Act testify to its importance and relative success. A little more than half of the approximately 242,000 new farms established on the Minnesota-Dakota and Nebraska-Kansas frontier between 1863 and 1880 were homesteads acquired through residence and cultivation.

The situation after about 1880 is another story. When farmers pushed into the arid high plains, the Homestead Act did not meet the goals of the law's framers or the expectations of the settlers. On the plains, 160 acres was too small a unit on which to make a living because livestock was a vital part of the farm operations. In the areas of western Kansas and Nebraska, for example, many of those who filed for a homestead were tempted to sell some of their rights for cash. In other words, the law encouraged petty speculation. Despite the fact that the Homestead Act was not suited to the high plains, thousands of settlers established successful farms there under the law.

Glories of the New Land

Multitudes of farmers moved west after the Civil War. However, emigration was not considered substantial enough by state and territorial governments, the railroads, local businessmen, and other promoters. Since people were the key to economic growth, special agencies or commissions were established to promote settlements. Dakota, Nebraska, and Kansas all had active immigration programs. Dakota's first commissioner of immigration wrote: "Immigration is the life of business in a new country. It gives patronage to the railroads; it encourages manufacturers. . . . It builds up cities and towns, and makes a market for the products of the farmer." *The Free Lands of Dakota* was one of the most popular pamphlets distributed by the commissioner. Literally millions of copies of promotional literature were distributed throughout the eastern part of the United States and in Europe. It was published in English and several foreign languages. There were also large numbers of newspaper advertisements which stressed the opportunities for farmers in the West.

Western railroads were also very active in promoting immigration. The Northern Pacific in Dakota, the Burlington & Union Pacific in Nebraska, and the Santa Fe in Kansas were among the main lines which penetrated the plains. With their liberal federal land grants, these railroads had millions of acres for sale. The owners saw clearly that increased settlement would stimulate land prices and provide business for the lines.

The promotional activities of the railroads complemented those of the state and territorial governments.

Many of the western states promoted themselves in an effort to woo settlers. Left: South Dakota proudly offered free homes, public institutions, and modern transportation.

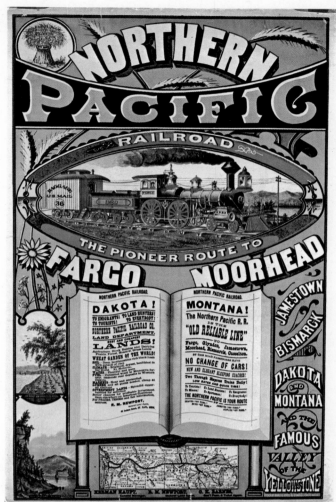

For the railroads, more settlers meant more business. Above: The Northern Pacific promotes the Western territories and proclaims the advantages of its "Pioneer Route."

They distributed millions of pamphlets, circulars, and news stories in the East and in Europe which pictured the West as a Garden of Eden. In 1882 alone, the Northern Pacific sent out more than half a million copies of its promotional pieces which were printed in English, Swedish, Dutch, Danish, and Norwegian. Railroads also sponsored tours for newsmen who published glowing accounts of what they saw. In 1875, the Santa Fe arranged a trip into central Kansas for 225 editors. After the trip, one of them wrote that he had never seen a "finer country in the world than that part of Kansas passed over by the Atchison, Topeka & Santa Fe Road." Another who hailed from Illinois reported that what he had seen in south-central Kansas exceeded "anything I have ever seen elsewhere."

But railroads did not confine their activities to advertising and promotion. They helped farmers locate good land. They sold farms to settlers on credit. They provided so-called "exploring" tickets at reduced prices. And they furnished transportation to many settlers who

223

took up new homes in the West. While railroads later came under severe attack by western farmers, in the 1870s railways were considered absolutely essential to the economic development of the farmer's frontier. In 1872, the editor of the St Paul *Daily Press* wrote that railroads were the "primary and indispensable agencies" for the development of a new country. A writer for the Minneapolis *Tribune* declared in 1873 that the territory between St Paul and Fargo, Dakota, was "utterly unfit for the residence of man" before the construction of the Northern Pacific.

Thanks to free or cheap land, an increasing amount of railroad transportation and promotion, and advertising by state and territorial governments, farmers had settled most of eastern Kansas and Nebraska during the decade

after 1865. By 1875, settlers were beginning to venture onto the high plains. Within another five years, farmers were pushing much farther west. Writing in the fall of 1878 from Edwards County, Kansas, one correspondent reported that settlers could be seen in dugouts and sod shanties "as contented and happy as a preacher, as comfortable as a king." By 1880, a number of farmers had moved into Ford County near Dodge City, an area previously reserved for cattlemen. Settlers were pushing with equal speed into southwestern Nebraska.

A Nebraska family sits outside its prairie sod house. As well as being cheap to build, these houses provided insulation from the extremes of weather found on the plains.

While dry years in the early 1880s slowed and even reversed the immigration to the high plains, increased rainfall and better crops in 1883 and 1884 produced a boom in western Kansas and Nebraska. In the spring of 1885, the Larned (Kansas) *Optic* reported that "the largest immigration ever known in the history of the state is now steadily flowing into southwestern Kansas." In one six-week period in Nebraska during the spring of 1885 some 2,000 settlers filed for homesteads.

Meanwhile a similar boom was occurring farther north in Dakota. The railroads, immigration agencies, and other promoters encouraged settlement in the most vigorous manner. "This is the sole remaining section of paradise in the western world," one observer wrote of Dakota, and "all the wild romances of the gorgeous Orient dwindle into nothing when compared with the everyday realities of Dakota's progress." The *Dakota Farmer* reported in 1884 that "the Almighty seems to have preceded us and prepared a quarter section already to sow. . . ." Another writer declared that "a million plows are wanted in the Territory of Dakota." While this was typical frontier exaggeration, there seemed to be land for all who wanted it. From 1880 through 1889, a total of over 41 million acres were entered under public land laws in Dakota, an area larger than the state of Iowa. In the decade following 1880, the number of farms rose by some 550 per cent.

The boom in the Red River valley of northeastern Dakota centered around large-scale farming operations. These were established on land purchased from the Northern Pacific Railroad. The huge bonanza farms were

entirely different from the 160-acre units of the average pioneer settler. The Grandin farm, for example, contained thousands of acres, was highly mechanized, employed hired labor, and raised thousands of bushels of wheat annually. One writer declared that the production of food was being revolutionized.

By the late 1880s, settlers were also pushing onto the arid plains of eastern Colorado. Sufficient rainfall for good crops in 1887, along with the usual promotional efforts, drew thousands of farmers who acquired land under the Homestead and Timber Culture acts. Some optimistic but naive promoters declared that rainfall was following the plow, and that a "rain belt" had settled over Colorado's eastern plains. One local editor wrote in the spring of 1887 that "the question of moisture is no longer a speculation, but it is an assured fact. . . . All that is needed is to plow, plant and attend to the crops properly; the rains are abundant."

By 1889 and 1890, the agricultural boom on the Great Plains frontier was at an end. It left in its wake broken farmers and bankrupt town speculators. Severe drought, a natural condition of the plains, returned with a vengeance to ruin hopes and dash expectations. Writing from Grant County in western Kansas in late 1889, one citizen said that "most all the people here that could leave have done so. . . ." The next year was even worse. A farmer wrote that he did not raise a grain of wheat from fourteen acres and "we won't get a bushel of corn." Referring to eastern Colorado in January 1891, Denver's *Rocky Mountain News* declared that "hundreds of families are on the verge of starvation." Suddenly the true nature of the Great Plains was discovered by farmers who had been bamboozled by promoters and speculators and lured into hardship by their own desire for free or cheap land.

Farther south a few farmers were moving into the Texas Panhandle in the late 1880s and 1890s. That area, however, as well as the rest of western Texas, remained part of the cattle kingdom until after 1900. On the other hand, there was strong pressure after about 1880 for Congress to open up parts of Indian Territory to white settlement. In 1889, Congress did assign certain lands in the central part of Indian Territory to the public domain. Later organized as Oklahoma Territory, this area was opened for settlement on April 22, 1889. At noon a mad rush for land began. Hundreds of settlers ran pell-mell to stake out a farm or locate a town lot. Within a few hours, claims had been made to thousands of acres. Thus, by around 1890, most of the best lands that could be farmed successfully without irrigation or special dry farming techniques had been occupied between Texas and the Canadian border.

For the most part the farmers who settled the Great Plains frontier were native Americans. Thousands of ambitious and energetic young men and women, as well as many older people, from Missouri, Illinois, Indiana, and states farther east moved to the new frontier. They were in search of land and other economic opportunities. For example, in 1890 there were 138,000 people in Kansas who had been born in Illinois. However, large numbers of foreigners also took up homes on the Great Plains. These included Germans, Scandinavians, Russian Mennonites, Bohemians, Irish, and English. Dakota received especially heavy immigration from the Scandinavian countries. By 1890 about 44 per cent of the people in North Dakota and 27 per cent in South Dakota were foreign-born. The percentages were lower in Nebraska and Kansas, but they were still highly significant. These immigrants went to the farmer's frontier both individually and in groups. In one of the most significant group migrations the Russian Mennonites settled Marion and surrounding counties in Kansas in the mid-1870s. Kansas was also the recipient of an important Negro migration in the late 1870s.

The rapid influx of people onto the Western prairies and Great Plains demanded proper political organization. Kansas had become a state in 1861, but Nebraska did not achieve statehood until 1867. Colorado, largely because of the mining booms following 1859, drew more than enough people to warrant statehood, but did not enter the Union until 1876. The Dakotas, organized as a territory in 1861, did not achieve statehood until 1889. Congress passed the Omnibus Bill in February of that year which created the four states of North Dakota, South Dakota, Montana, and Washington. The next year Congress organized Oklahoma Territory to provide government for the six counties opened to white settlement in the central part of what in 1907 became the state of Oklahoma. By 1890 the Dakotas, Nebraska, Kansas, and Oklahoma Territory had over 3 million people. Some 87 per cent were classified as rural, mostly farmers, and 13 per cent urban.

Pioneer Farmers on the Great Plains

Farming operations on most of the Great Plains frontier, as had been true on earlier frontiers, were small and simple. After acquiring land, the first tasks of a family were to build a shelter and obtain water. Some settlers had sufficient money to build a frame house from lumber shipped to them. Those in eastern Kansas and Nebraska often found enough timber along the creeks and rivers to construct a log house. However, as farmers moved onto the treeless prairies and plains, most of them lived in dugouts or sod houses. In southwestern Minnesota, the Dakotas, and central and western Kansas and Nebraska, thousands of sod houses dotted the landscape by the 1870s and 1880s. Other than windows, a door, and a few poles or rafters to hold up the ceiling, a sod house

THE OKLAHOMA LAND RUN

On March 23, 1889, President Benjamin Harrison announced that in a month's time 2 million acres of unassigned land in Indian Territory would be opened to claim under the generous provisions of the Homestead Act. This land had been purchased from the Creek and Seminole tribes by the government for about $4 million.

Throughout the 1880s, there had been considerable pressure on the government from farmers and railroad officials to open these lands to white settlement. Dissatisfied homesteaders in drought-stricken areas wanted this fertile soil for themselves. Hordes of ''boomers''— illegal settlers—periodically migrated into Indian lands only to be thrown out by federal troops. And the railroads, seeking to increase their business along the route through Indian Territory, lobbied government officials in Washington.

The news that the land would be opened prompted thousands of eager farmers to abandon their settlements in surrounding states and journey to the borders of Texas and Kansas.

A few days before April 22, thousands of prospective settlers were allowed to cross into Indian Territory and line up on the edge of the unassigned land. As noon approached, the crowd became more and more restive. People fought for places along the line until at last starting guns cracked, bugles blew, and flags signaled the opening of the territory. Between 50,000 and 100,000 people rushed forward, leaving behind them a cloud of black and red prairie dust. Men on horseback. families in wagons, and sophisticated speculators on trains raced for their parcel of land. Some who had illegally crossed the border the previous night had already staked out their home sites. These premature settlers were to earn for Oklahoma the nickname of the ''Sooner State.

By the time the sun set, tent cities could be seen along the horizon. Eleven miles from the starting line, 10,000 people pitched their tents and set up camp at the site of present-day Oklahoma City, and another 10,000 spent the night where Guthrie later developed.

The frantic activity of the 1889 land run was repeated in 1893 when 6 million acres of the Cherokee Outlet were opened to settlers. By the turn of the century a territory that had been totally devoid of white settlers only a few years before contained a population approaching a million.

Below: Guthrie shortly after the 1889 run. Tents stretched for miles in the first section of Indian Territory opened for settlement. Inset: The dramatic scene at the 1893 run.

cost little or nothing. For fuel, farmers initially relied on twisted hay or on dried buffalo or cow manure, commonly called cow chips. They dug wells for water. In many parts of the Great Plains water could be found at less than a hundred feet, and often as little as thirty feet below the surface. Until a farmer could afford a windmill, he drew the water up by bucket or hand pump

The typical farmer would start by breaking a few acres of prairie sod in preparation for planting his first crop. On the Dakota frontier wheat was the principal grain grown. Farther south in Nebraska and Kansas corn was the primary crop. Many farmers grew both crops, plus other grains such as oats, rye, and barley. Vegetables for the family table were also cultivated. Most farmers had a few head of livestock, mainly cattle and hogs, and some poultry. Receipts from butter sold in the local town or village were an important item of family income.

Since farming operations were small, incomes were meager. Pioneers on the prairies and plains handled very little money in a year. Farmers raised much of their own food and earned a small amount of cash by selling butter, a few bushels of grain or some livestock at nearby towns. But in the early years of settlement it was not uncommon for settlers to have no more than $100 to $200 a year in cash income. As time passed, however, farmers broke more land, bought more machinery, cultivated greater acreages, and added to their herds. In this process, they often added new houses and outbuildings for livestock, constructed additional fences, and in

general added to their standards of living and capital.

An example of how one farmer progressed can be seen in the career of a young Minnesotan who settled in Brown County, Dakota, in 1880. He acquired 480 acres of land under the Homestead, Timber Culture, and Preemption laws. During the next few years he expanded his wheat operations until in 1885 he harvested 215 acres. That year he raised 5,176 bushels which brought 70 cents a bushel. By that time, his land had increased in value until it was worth $20 an acre, or $9,600 in all. His other property brought his total assets to well over $10,000. Starting with nothing but a team and wagon and a great deal of determination, he had built a comfortable living in only five years. Many, of course, were not so successful, but thousands worked their way into fairly good circumstances.

The extent to which particular farmers succeeded depended on a number of factors. If the pioneer had good crops during the first years of settlement, he was much more likely to succeed. This gave him an opportunity to build up his capital, and some reserves before any calamity (such as drought) might strike. Thus, success was determined to some extent by the vagaries of the weather. He also had a better chance if he began operations when prices were reasonably good. It was also important for a farmer to know what was best to plant in his area and what combination of crops and livestock would be most profitable.

One of the greatest challenges to western farmers was

Showing THE ROSS SPECIAL LITTLE GIANT CUTTERS No. 11A, 13A, 14A, & 17. with Carrier Delivering to the Left for Elevating all kinds of Ensilage or Dry Fodder.

CARRIER CAN DELIVER ALSO TO THE RIGHT OR STRAIGHT AWAY.

Harvesters were used to bring in the crop. But it was estimated that farm machinery was a century behind the progress in industrial machinery. Left: More than a score of horses stand hitched to a harvester, as farmers pause for the camera. Right: An 1880 trade card shows the farmer how a machine could speed up his labor and make life easier.

meeting each region's peculiar climate. For example, Kansas and Nebraska pioneers in the 1880s planted corn. This was what they and their ancestors had done farther east, where rainfall was more abundant. They persisted in trying to raise corn even though the hot winds of July and August usually burned and destroyed the crop. There was simply not enough rainfall in most years to grow corn successfully on the Great Plains. It was years before farmers broke their old habits.

Gradually, however, after the severe droughts of the late 1880s, farmers shifted to wheat as the main grain crop on the plains. Wheat also dried out and failed in some years, but the chances of getting a satisfactory wheat crop were much better than those of corn. Consequently, in western Kansas wheat acreage increased fivefold between 1889 and 1896, while corn acreage dropped by one-third. The facts of geography had forced farmers to adjust to new and different conditions.

Farmers on the plains also relied increasingly on livestock. The abundant and nutritious grasses provided excellent pasturage and hay. As periodic droughts ruined grain crops, farmers came to see that livestock production was a much better bet. During the late 1880s and 1890s, cattle numbers increased. The ideal farm operation on the plains was a combination of live-

stock and those crops which were most drought resistant. These included grain sorghums and Turkey Red wheat. Farmers also adopted new dry farming techniques which would get the greatest value from the limited rainfall. By the 1890s, farmers in western Kansas and Nebraska were experimenting with summer fallowing. This permitted part of the land to lie unused every other year in order to store up moisture. Thus, the successful farmer on the Great Plains found that he had to adjust, reorganize, and adopt new techniques if he was to succeed in that forbidding and unfriendly region.

As farmers enlarged their operations, they bought more machinery to plow, cultivate, and harvest the greater acreages. By the 1880s, the twine grain binder was being used extensively to harvest wheat and other small grains. Other machines which more and more came into use were cultivators, mowing machines and hay rakes, grain drills and seeders, corn planters and threshing machines. The farms in the Red River valley of North Dakota were the most highly mechanized. Operated on modern corporate principles, they had thousands of dollars invested in machinery. One observer in 1889 estimated that a 10,000 acre wheat farm needed 60 gang plows, 60 seeders, 150 wagons, 50 to 60 grain binders, 10 threshing machines, and

10 steam engines. Steam engines were used both for pulling plows and for furnishing power for threshing machines. However, even by 1890, the ordinary plains farmer had only a modest amount of machinery, which was probably worth less than $500.

Coping with Hardships

At times, natural conditions became so bad on the western prairies and plains that farmers experienced not only bankruptcy but untold physical and emotional suffering. Prairie fires and hail, drought and grasshoppers wreaked havoc with plains settlers. In 1874 much of the frontier from Kansas to Dakota was visited by hoards of ravenous grasshoppers and searing drought. Describing this plague in Kansas in the summer of 1874, the editor of the Wichita City *Eagle* wrote: "they came upon us in great numbers, in untold millions, in clouds upon clouds, until their fluttering wings looked like a sweeping snowstorm in the heavens, until their dark bodies covered everything green upon the earth. In a few hours many fields that had hung thick with long ears of golden maize were stripped of their value and left only a forest of bare yellow stalks that in their nakedness mocked the tiller of the soil. . . ."

A farmer from Council Grove, Kansas, wrote in August that "there has been no rain here of consequence for a couple of months, and between the drought, the chinch bugs, and the grasshoppers, we will be forced to go to Egypt or somewhere for our corn."

In Hamilton County, Nebraska, according to one report, the grasshoppers and drought had destroyed everything except hay and some squash. No longer did people say "come to dinner"; instead they said "come to squash" because that was all there was to eat. Major N. A. M. Dudley reported that in Red Willow County in western Nebraska, at least two-thirds of the people were in dire want. Of 544 needy citizens in the county, he wrote, "100 had either no food or less than a five day supply." Both private and state aid brought some relief. The United States Army distributed surplus clothing and food to settlers. But the help was entirely inadequate to alleviate the suffering from hunger and cold on much of the frontier in the winter of 1874–75.

There were periods of drought following 1875, but the most prolonged period of hardship resulting from crop failure occurred in the late 1880s and early 1890s. In 1889 corn and wheat averaged only four bushels an acre in much of southwestern Kansas. By fall many settlements in western Kansas and Nebraska had been starved into oblivion. One Grant County, Kansas, citizen wrote in November that "most all of the people here that could leave have done so." Only those too poor to get away still remained. In December 1889 the governor of South Dakota found that in three counties in his state there were six hundred farm families "almost absolutely destitute." Some people were actually on the verge of starvation on the plains in the winter of 1889–90.

Conditions were even worse in 1894, the driest year on record up to that time. Only eight to nine inches of rain fell on large sections of the Great Plains. Thousands of farmers experienced total and complete crop failure. Letters written by destitute residents reveal the pitiful situation. In June 1894, one housewife in western Kansas wrote to Governor L. D. Lewelling: "I take my pen in hand to let you know that we are starving to death. It is pretty hard to do without anything to eat here in this God forsaken country . . . I haven't had nothing to eat today and it is 3 o'clock." Another Kansan wrote that two-thirds of the people in his community had to depend on cow chips for fuel in temperatures of 16° below zero. But since families had been forced to sell their cattle because of lack of feed, some citizens were traveling thirteen miles to get even this kind of fuel. An elderly Nebraska woman wrote that she and her grandchildren had been living on bread and butter and boiled weeds. Again, private and public relief were provided to the needy, but many families suffered terrible hardships.

Despite these reversals, production of both crops and livestock rose remarkably, if somewhat erratically, on the Great Plains. For example, in 1869 Kansas, Nebraska, and the Dakotas produced less than 5 million bushels of wheat. Thirty years later the crop amounted to over 185 million bushels when production in Oklahoma Territory is added. Between 1870 and 1900 their share of wheat production increased from less than 2 per cent of the total national output to nearly 30 per cent. The number of cattle jumped from 466,362 to about 13 million during the same period. By 1900 four plains states and Oklahoma Territory had about 20 per cent of the nation's cattle. The region produced large amounts of other grains and livestock as well. Despite a seemingly hostile climate, the Great Plains became a highly productive region.

There was some effort to increase output even further by introducing irrigation. It was vigorously promoted in the 1880s, and again during and after the dry years of the 1890s, but only modest progress occurred before 1900. Some farmers irrigated along the Arkansas River in Colorado and Kansas, and the Platte River in Nebraska, but the total acreage remained small. In 1889 only 32,562 acres were under ditch in western Kansas and Nebraska.

Great Plains farmers also faced difficult economic problems. Isolated and far from the nation's financial centers, they suffered from heavy transportation charges, high interest rates, and excessive marketing costs.

Their distance from central markets for grain and

livestock meant large outlays for transportation. Farmers complained about high and discriminatory railroad rates which ate heavily into their profits. For instance, it cost more to ship a bushel of corn 150 miles from central Nebraska to Omaha than from Omaha to Chicago, a distance more than twice as great. The rate between Chicago and the Missouri River was only about one-third as much per ton-mile in 1880 as it was west of the river. The cost of things which farmers had to buy was also higher because of the transportation charges from the factories to the distant plains.

Farmers in the West also paid higher interest rates than those farther east where agricultural production was more reliable. Anything from 8 to 12 per cent interest on real estate mortgages was common in the plains states in the 1870s and 1880s. Chattel mortgages (loans on machinery and livestock) often carried interest costs of as much as 2 to 3 per cent a month. As one farmer wrote in 1890, Nebraska had three crops—"one is a crop of corn, one a crop of freight rates, and one a crop of interest."

Plains farmers also faced difficult marketing problems. There was little competition in the purchase of farm products. Four meat packing concerns pretty well controlled the price of livestock. The elevators, often owned by the railroads and other distant corporations, established grain prices. Farmers charged that they were penalized by short weights, unfair grading of products, and excessive dockage. For example, to downgrade wheat from number one to number two or three meant the loss of several cents a bushel to the farmer. Some wheat purchased from local farmers in North Dakota as number two sometimes miraculously became number one by the time it arrived in Minneapolis. Formation of the beef trust in the 1880s effectively eliminated competition in livestock markets. Farmers accused the middlemen who handled their products of making huge profits. They were also convinced that machinery dealers and other local retailers exploited them by charging excessive markups on the things farmers bought. The middleman came to symbolize "the heartless monopolies and soulless corporations." The general decline of farm prices in the late nineteenth century intensified the problems confronting the plains dwellers.

Faced with such difficulties, plus frequent crop failures, many farmers on the Great Plains could not remain financially solvent. Initially, most farmers in the Dakotas, Nebraska, and Kansas owned their land. In the 1870s and 1880s however, an increasing number mortgaged their farms to obtain necessary operating capital. Then, unable to meet principal and interest payments, thousands of farmers lost their land through foreclosure. Between 1889 and 1893 some 11,000 farm mortgages were foreclosed in Kansas alone. Between 1880 and 1900 tenancy more than doubled in Nebraska and Kansas, rising from 18 to 37 per cent in Nebraska and 16 to 35 per cent in Kansas. In the Dakotas the percentage increase was even greater. It is no wonder that the demands for economic reform advocated by the Populists received such enthusiastic support in those states by 1890. The Populist call for government ownership of the railroads and control of other monopolies and inflation seemed to be striking at real and vital problems facing farmers.

Family and Social Life

Hard work characterized daily existence for most farmers and their families, as it did in most rural areas in the nineteenth century. The round of planting and harvesting, along with the usual chores connected with tending livestock, kept farmers busy from early morning until late night during much of the year. Most of the work was dull and monotonous. Diaries kept by farmers record for days on end such statements as "plowed today," "hoeing corn," or "cradled wheat." While men were in the fields, housewives pursued a daily grind of washing, baking, sewing, garden work (in the summer), and raising children. In 1873 a woman in northwestern Kansas recorded in her diary: "done my housework then made fried cakes, squash pies, baked wheat bread and corn bread, cut out a night dress and partly made it." A common comment at the end of the day was, "am very tired." Women also worked in the fields, milked the cows, and tended the chickens. Children, too, had their daily responsibilities: herding cattle, milking, gathering fuel, and helping at other tasks.

Conditions of life were made worse by shortages of cash. One Kansas housewife wrote to her relatives in Indiana in 1876 and explained why she had not written sooner. "We have been very busy," she said, "and most of the time out of stamps and money." There was an almost constant struggle to get enough money to buy the bare necessities of life. This was especially true in the early years of settlement. Gifts from relatives sometimes brought joy, if only temporary financial relief. A settler in southwestern Nebraska in the 1880s related that a visit by his father and mother from Illinois had been "a red letter day." Upon departing the parents gave the farmer and his wife $20 each.

Despite the hard work, deprivation, isolation, and loneliness during the initial period of settlement, within a relatively short time enough neighbors had settled nearby so that social intercourse was frequent and enjoyable. The common idea is erroneous that families on the plains were so far apart that they went for weeks without seeing anyone. With families settling on each quarter section of land, or even a full section, it meant that farmers were seldom more than a mile or two from

Forest St. Avenue
PARSONS. KANSAS. AUGUST 4 1873

their neighbors except during the first two or three years of settlement.

Farmers went to town often, especially when there was no field work. Traveling by buggy or wagon eight or ten miles was usual and not considered difficult. As a woman in Nebraska wrote in the 1870s, it "does not take long to drive 20 or 25 miles here." The settlers' diaries reveal that it was not uncommon for them to go to town two or three times a week in the fall and winter. In December 1876, a Nebraska farmer's diary reveals that he and his family traveled to town, entertained company at home, or attended some community social function thirteen out of the thirty-one days.

Literary and debating societies existed in many farm communities. Sometimes outside speakers discussed topics of interest. On other occasions local residents engaged in debates. Such lively topics as, "Resolved that man will do more for the love of money than he will for the love of woman" were discussed. A victory for the negative no doubt flattered the ladies. On another occasion the subject was "there is more enjoyment in poverty than in riches." The judges again awarded victory to the negative.

After a few years of settlement, churches were organized in both town and country. Within six years of settlement in Phillips County in northwestern Kansas, the Presbyterians, Congregationalists, Baptists, Methodists, and Catholics all had congregations. Sometimes services were held in country schoolhouses and were conducted by itinerant ministers or a local lay preacher. The church became a focal point for many social activities.

By 1900 there were approximately half a million farms in the Dakotas, Nebraska, Kansas, and Oklahoma Territory. There were still large parts of the Great Plains in western Dakota, eastern Montana, Wyoming, New Mexico, western Texas, and Oklahoma yet to be settled. Those areas, however, except where irrigation or the most advanced techniques in dry farming could be applied, were more suitable for livestock production than for grain farming. But even before the turn of the century, plains farmers had added greatly to the nation's growing agricultural production. This increasing output boosted the country's economic strength. These farmers, like those in other parts of the country, played an important role in the economic development of the United States.

Farmers and their families went to town as often as possible—for business and for pleasure. Left: A watercolor painted in 1873 of Forest Avenue, the main street of Parsons, Kansas.

Settling the Great Plains was an arduous task, but for many it was the gateway to a secure and prosperous future. Below: An artist's impression of the Douglas Knox Ranch as it appeared in 1882.

Chapter 10

THE INDIAN TRAGEDY

"As long as the stars shall shine and the rivers flow," the government promised, the rights of the Indians would be preserved. The treaty commissioners acted in good faith, but the westward push of the frontier could not be halted. And whenever white men coveted Indian lands, the US Army was there to ensure that dispossession was "peaceful." The Indians fought to preserve their homelands, with occasional success—notably at the Battle of the Little Bighorn. But their struggle was doomed to failure. And the loss of their homes ultimately led to an even greater loss, for Indian culture declined radically as well-intentioned government agents tried to turn the braves into imitation white men.

Subjugation of a People

From the beginning of their history on the American continent, European settlers always faced an Indian problem. Between the white man's urge to expand into a boundless West, and the red man's resolve to stay where he was and live as he had, an irreconcilable conflict existed. Until the final defeat of the Indians and their confinement on reservations, the conflict was played out in warfare. The ultimate result never varied. After each military defeat the red men agreed, by treaty or some other formal means, to cede the lands at issue, and white expansion continued westward.

In 1865, at the end of the Civil War, the Indian barrier extended over most of the trans-Mississippi West. Over the next two decades, a combination of military might, economic disaster, and persistent government pressure drove the Indians from the warpath to reservations, thus opening the West to the conquering white civilization.

Conflict between whites and Indians of the trans-Mississippi West was not new in 1865. Forty years earlier, Apaches in the far Southwest had killed twenty fur trappers along the Gila River. Traders along the Santa Fe Trail in the 1830s encountered difficulties with Comanche and Kiowa Indians. Attacks increased during the great migrations to California after gold was discovered there in 1848. More trouble erupted in 1854 between soldiers and Sioux Indians near Fort Laramie, in present-day Wyoming. Late in the 1850s there were repeated clashes on the southern plains with Comanches, and in 1860 soldiers and settlers confronted Paiute Indians in the Nevada desert. Finally, in 1862, an uprising of the Santee Sioux in southwestern Minnesota brought a month of carnage and destruction to settlers, militiamen, and Indians alike, and depopulated the area for a generation.

Continually exposed to the dangers of Indian hostility, white frontiersmen came to hate the red men with an intensity which Americans elsewhere could not understand. To the settlers there seemed only two possible solutions. Either the army must conquer the savages, then put them under close guard on reservations, where they could never again make trouble; or the cause of civilization demanded that they be exterminated. The withdrawal of troops from much of the West during the Civil War left many citizens without protection. For some, extermination seemed the quickest and the most certain means of overcoming the Indian menace. In Arizona in 1864, King S. Woolsey, a rancher and Indian fighter, massacred twenty-four Apaches during a peace council with them. The territorial legislature congratulated him, gave him the rank of colonel, and sought to raise a militia to wipe out the hostile Indians altogether.

The late autumn of the same year saw an engagement which, in fame if not in treachery, far outshone Woolsey's massacre. Northern Cheyenne and Arapaho Indians had fought settlers during the summer in

An idyllic view by Albert Bierstadt of an Indian encampment in the Rockies. Such abstract admiration for the noble savage did not stop pioneers from pushing Indians off their land.

western Kansas and eastern Colorado. But in September, at a peace conference outside of Denver, a number of chiefs and their followers agreed to make peace with the whites. In return, they received assurances of safety if they agreed to camp near Fort Lyon, a military post where a small regular army garrison still remained. Army and civilian militia officers, however, proved more anxious to punish the Indians than to encourage their peaceful intentions. In October, Major Scott Anthony, the post commander, ordered the bands of peaceful Indians to move away, saying that the army could not feed them. About 700 Cheyennes under Chief Black Kettle, and Arapahos under Left Hand, moved northeast and camped on Sand Creek, forty miles away. Six hundred more Arapahos went farther east down the Arkansas River to stay for the winter.

Late in November, Colonel John Chivington, commanding a regiment of Colorado Volunteers, arrived at Fort Lyon, where Anthony and a detachment of regulars joined him. With about 750 men under arms, Chivington started out for Sand Creek, where he arrived, after an all-night march, at dawn on November 29. The force fell savagely upon the camp, taking it completely by surprise. Over 150 peaceful Indians were killed, most of them women and children; only nine soldiers died. Chivington and his men returned to Denver, bringing a

hundred scalps, and the citizens greeted them as conquering heroes.

But the Sand Creek Massacre, far from ending Indian hostilities, intensified them. Northern Cheyennes and Arapahos banded together with Oglala and Brulé Sioux in the north, and terrorized settlers and travelers until the following summer. To the south, survivors of Sand Creek allied with Kiowas and Comanches, the lords of the southern plains. They would have made the same sort of war as their friends in the north had not the government made every effort to keep the peace. Finally, in October 1865, as part of a general pacification, commissioners made treaties with the bands of Black Kettle and others. The whites admitted responsibility for the "gross and wanton outrage" of the massacre, and provided indemnities for the widows and orphans.

The end of the Civil War in the spring of 1865 had a profound effect on the character and extent of Indian hostilities. With the nation again united, westward expansion resumed in force. Before the end of the decade, the railroads would span the country from sea to sea. As farmers, miners, and cattlemen moved west, the army came too, to provide protection. On every frontier where pioneers ventured to wrest a living from the new land, small military garrisons were posted to guard them against the hostility of the red men. The conflict between

In 1862 when the government failed to honor its agreement with the Sioux, members of that tribe attacked settlers in Minnesota. Left: Survivors of the raids pause for rest on the prairie. They were on their way to safety in eastern cities. Bottom: Captured Sioux camped at Fort Snelling on the banks of the Minnesota River. Right: Chivington and his men storm Black Kettle's village. Over a hundred Indians were killed—mostly women and children—and the incident became known as the Sand Creek Massacre.

Minnesota Historical Society

Indian and settler was inevitable, shaped by the fact that each wanted the land for his own purposes. Equally inevitable was the pattern of Indian warfare which emerged, and which characterized these conflicts until they finally ceased in 1886.

A New Type of Warfare

The Indian wars were unlike those which United States soldiers had fought in Mexico and the American South so recently. While many of the battles in the Mexican and Civil wars had been large, involving thousands of troops on either side, most Indian engagements numbered no more than a hundred soldiers and warriors all told. Soldiers soon learned, too, that the red men had different ideas of bravery than those to which whites had been schooled. Most Indians saw no glory in dying nobly for a doomed cause when it was possible to get away and resume the battle elsewhere under better conditions. Unless pressed, they would not fight except where terrain favored their side, and where they were able to profit from the element of surprise. Usually, too, the Indians enjoyed a mobility and speed in attack and retreat which white soldiers, mounted on slower animals and heavily encumbered with packs and field gear, could not match. Astride fast war ponies and, more often than not,

armed as well or better than their adversaries, the Indians proved formidable enemies. They fought swift, small-scale actions foreshadowing the commando tactics of modern warfare.

But if many circumstances seemed to favor the Indians in war, the white men also enjoyed substantial advantages. Of these, one of the most significant was the mutual enmity of many Indian groups. The backbone of countless expeditions against hostile tribesmen all over the West was native scouts. These were recruited by the army from tribes or bands which hated their Indian foes more than they did white men, and therefore stood ready to join the soldiers in war in an attempt to defeat a common foe.

The troops also soon learned to capitalize on the weaknesses inherent in the Indian war system. Indian wars were seasonal. During the winters, snows were heavy on the Great Plains from the Canadian border to central Texas, drastically restricting the mobility of the warriors. As a result, hostilities generally were suspended during this season. The idle Indians sought to stay alive on the foods stored during the previous summer. Thus winter was the ideal time for the army to attack hostile bands. Although such campaigns wrought great hardship upon the soldiers, they were devastatingly effective against the Indians. The tribes frequently lost not only warriors killed and women and children captured, but also saw their tepees, blankets, robes, and food burned,

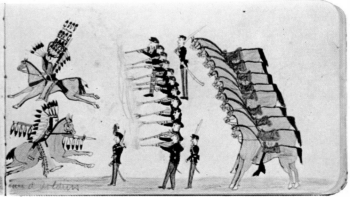

Indian braves were skilled horsemen and employed hit-and-run tactics. Soldiers, however, usually outnumbered the Indians and were highly regimented. Above: Sometime between 1875 and 1878, the imprisoned Squint Eyes, a Cheyenne, painted this version of the Battle Between Cheyennes and Soldiers, *and it illustrates the different methods of fighting.*

and their horses run off. Such economic devastation forced many a hostile band to accept peace.

Moreover, the extermination of the huge buffalo herds on the Great Plains from the late 1860s on permanently undermined the way of life of all the plains tribes. It weakened first their power, then their resolve to fight. Finally, the army gained an increasing technological superiority over the Indians which, by the 1880s, had become a significant advantage. As railroads spanned

238

Above: Remington's Indian Warfare. *While the cavalry fires from the distance, war-painted braves ride off with the body of a fallen brother. Right: An Indian listens to* The Song of the Talking Wire, *in the painting by Henry Earney. The telegraph destroyed the Indians' advantage of quick surprise attacks.*

the continent, it became possible to move large numbers of troops to remote places with a speed unknown in the West a decade before. With the instant communication made possible by the telegraph, they could be summoned as soon as trouble erupted. Progressively, too, the army built military posts in and around the Indian country, and from these installations soldiers could constantly police the conduct of defiant tribesmen. By the mid-1880s, the red men had come to realize that they could nowhere be secure from the vigilance and punishment of the army. A combination of economic disaster and certain military defeat at last brought peace.

Between 1865 and 1886, however, Indian wars flared in the West. Prior to 1875, warfare on the southern plains was almost constant. A treaty, negotiated in 1867 with 5,000 Indians on Medicine Lodge Creek, in Kansas, provided reservations in the Indian Territory for the nomadic tribes. But the army had to subdue them before peace could be attained. A winter campaign the following year established the reputation of Lieutenant Colonel George A. Custer as an Indian fighter. With troops of the Seventh Cavalry, he attacked and destroyed the village of Black Kettle—of Sand Creek fame—on the Washita River in the Indian Territory. The chief himself was peaceful, but he was encamped off his reservation and hostile parties had come and gone from his village, so the attack was not as completely unjustified as Custer's critics claimed it to be. If nothing else, it helped convince the Cheyennes and their friends the Arapahos that the army was inflexible, and other actions during the same campaign reinforced the impression. By the summer of 1869 these tribes were at peace, and remained so until the final abortive war on the southern plains in 1874–75.

The Kiowas and Comanches posed a far more difficult problem. Both tribes held an enmity generations old toward Mexicans and Anglos in Texas, and their raiding

had an important economic function as well. It required years of campaigning, as well as the arrest and imprisonment of two of the most important Kiowa chiefs, before these Indians could be effectively subdued and made to accept reservation life. In the end, the most prominent war leaders of the southern plains tribes were sent to prison in Florida for two years, and their followers, confined on reservations in the Indian Territory, at last resigned themselves to following the white man's road.

The Sioux Fight Back

The warfare on the southern plains found parallels in other parts of the West. To the north, a protracted struggle by Sioux warriors under the Oglala chief Red Cloud forced the government in 1868 to withdraw soldiers from the Powder River country of Wyoming and Montana, and to close the Bozeman Trail which had passed through it to the Montana gold fields. It was a rare triumph for the Indians who, though they might win battles, generally lost the wars. The conclusion of the conflict saw the United States promise the Sioux a reservation comprising all of present-day South Dakota west of the Missouri River. The government also agreed to regard the vast land between the Platte and Yellowstone rivers, where the tribes traditionally hunted, as unceded Indian country from which whites were to be excluded. These concessions quieted the Sioux for eight years. Had the United States continued to honor its word, they might have ended Indian conflict on the northern plains. But the inevitable advance of the frontier and the pressure of white settlers made this impossible, and war with the Sioux and other northern tribes erupted again in the mid-1870s.

Smithsonian Institution/Western Americana

Above: Chief Red Cloud of the Oglala tribe. He and his followers managed to gain for the Indians most of South Dakota including the Black Hills region. It was a major triumph for the Indians. Right: Colonel George A. Custer offers terms of surrender to defeated warriors. In the 1868–69 campaign, Custer gained a glowing reputation as an Indian fighter.

The cause of renewed trouble was the discovery of gold in the Black Hills of South Dakota, an area sacred in Sioux tradition and religion—and a part of their reservation. After an army expedition led by Colonel Custer confirmed the existence of gold deposits there in 1874, whites flocked in. The government, finding it impossible to prevent this influx, decided late the next year to restore the Black Hills to the public domain. At the same time, citizens in the territories of Montana and Wyoming applied pressure on the national government to restrict the Indians' use of the unceded country. The Sioux, however, refused to surrender either land or rights. The War and Interior departments in Washington then demanded that all Indians leave the unceded territory and return to the agencies where they were fed by January 31, 1876, or else be considered hostile. This order reached the Sioux country in December 1875, too late—as government officials probably realized—for the Indians to comply if they wished to avoid war. The end of January arrived, and large numbers remained away from their agencies. The army then planned an extensive campaign to drive the tribesmen in, and so clear the disputed areas for white occupation.

The war which followed, probably the most famous in the history of the American West, resulted in a series of disasters for the army but, in the long run, brought defeat for the Indians. It included the defeat of Custer and his men at the Little Bighorn in July 1876. But this "massacre" resulted only in a nationwide demand for the defeat of the Sioux, and the army resumed its campaign at once. Although Sitting Bull and Gall, two of the most prominent of the Sioux chiefs, fled to Canada and there found safety, the army forced the rest of the hostile Indians to surrender at their agencies in Dakota Territory early in 1877. The Sioux lost their rights to the unceded country, which white men then progressively occupied, and their reservation was cut down and divided, eliminating the Black Hills. The Sioux had won a battle, but lost the war.

The War with the Modocs and Nez Percés

Other wars disturbed remote areas of the West. In the early 1870s, the Modoc Indians, whom the government had compelled to share a reservation in southern Oregon with their enemies, the Klamaths, had rebelled. Under a chief known as Captain Jack, the Modocs had returned to their own country. The army gave chase, but the Modocs took refuge in a wild country with huge lava beds, and the soldiers could not dislodge them. Finally, in 1873, the government sent a commission to treat with them. The Modocs murdered two of the commissioners (including a Civil War hero, General Edward R. S. Canby), and wounded another. It was a hollow victory. The

Some captured Indian braves were charged with murder, tried, and sentenced to death. Left: Leaders of the Modoc War, Schonchin John and Captain Jack, in chains. They were hanged at Fort Klamath on October 3, 1873.

Smithsonian Institution National Anthropological Archives

following year renewed army campaigning forced the Modocs' surrender. Captain Jack and three of his confederates were tried, convicted, and hanged for murder. The Modocs were removed from their country to the Indian Territory. They were exiles in a strange land.

Even as the Modoc difficulties ended, another source of trouble was brewing in the Northwest. The Nez Percé Indians, whose native range spanned eastern Washington and northern Idaho, had been dispossessed of much of their country by gold miners who had invaded the region during the Civil War. By a spurious treaty, to which the Indians had never agreed, but which the United States Senate nevertheless had ratified, the tribe lost all its land save a small reservation around Fort Lapwai, Idaho. When ordered to this reserve, the Nez Percés split into two factions, the treaty Indians, who complied with the order, and the non-treaty Indians, who did not. The latter group, captained by a young chief named Joseph, led the army on an epic chase through 1,300 miles of country in Idaho, Wyoming, and Montana. The pursuit was punctuated by a succession of battles in which Joseph outshone his opponents. But the engagements thinned the Nez Percé ranks, and the Indians, refused sanctuary by other tribes, failed to reach safety in Canada. Brought to bay at last only thirty miles below the border in October 1877, the great chief and his little band surrendered.

"I am tired," Joseph told his followers in the last war council; "my heart is sick and sad. From where the sun now stands I will fight no more forever." He counted upon returning to Lapwai as his military pursuers had

The cavalry pursued Chief Joseph over more than a thousand miles before he was finally captured. After years of internment on various reservations, many of the Nez Percés finally returned to the Northwest. Joseph himself was not allowed to join them.

Smithsonian Institution National Anthropological Archives

BATTLE OF THE LITTLE BIG HORN

Along the banks of the Little Bighorn River in June 1876, thousands of Sioux, with their Cheyenne and Arapaho allies, were encamped for the annual sun dance. Their tepees stretched for miles along the river. This gathering of the tribes in southeastern Montana, thought to be the largest ever, was defended by an estimated 2,500 braves. As part of the campaign to rout the Sioux from their hunting grounds and move them to reservations, the army planned a three-pronged offensive against them.

Cavalry was to converge on the camp from the east, the west, and the south. Colonel John Gibbon, coming from Fort Ellis near the gold fields in the west, halted when he met up with Brigadier General Alfred Terry, the campaign commander who had come from the east. But General George Crook, advancing from the south, was turned back by a force of 1,000 or more on the Rosebud River. Terry sent Lieutenant Colonel George Armstrong Custer with about 600 officers and men from the Seventh Cavalry to locate the Indians on the Little Bighorn River. This was the only column to reach the Indian camp.

Custer's military career was checkered at best. After graduating last in his West Point class in 1861, the fiercely ambitious Ohioan managed to dis-

Indian fighter and glory hunter, George A. Custer His military reputation had slipped since the Civil War, and critics accused him of using the Indian wars as a means to further his own career.

tinguish himself as a daring and reckless commander of cavalry during the Civil War. In June 1863, when only twenty-three years old, Custer was promoted to a brevet brigadier general of volunteers, and before the war's end he held the rank of brevet major general.

After the Civil War, this "boy general," known for his long golden hair, dashing manner, and flamboyant dress, rode with General Philip Sheridan as a lieutenant colonel in the reorganized Seventh Cavalry. He took part in offensives against the Indians of the Southwest. In 1867 his career met a serious setback when he was court-martialed for deliberately deserting his company. He was suspended without rank or pay for a year but was reinstated after only ten months. Thereafter Custer took part in the 1868 winter campaign against the Indians and earned a widespread reputation as an Indian fighter. He was to have an important command in the 1876 campaign against the Sioux but shortly found himself in trouble again.

In testimony in Washington, he implicated President Grant's relatives and even the president himself in a scandal involving the sale of post traderships at forts in the West. Grant ordered his removal from the Indian campaign but the intercession of General Terry succeeded in restoring him to active duty in the Great Plains of Montana. Custer was given written orders only to reconnoiter the area of the Little Bighorn River and not to attack until Gibbon could supply him with reinforcements.

"Don't be greedy, Custer," said Gibbon as the young officer rode off. "Save some for us."

"I will," Custer replied.

Using classic bad judgment, Custer pushed his command so hard that his men and their horses were completely exhausted by the time they reached the Indian camp on June 24. When Custer's scouts informed him that his trail of dust betrayed the cavalry's presence and that he was hopelessly outnumbered, Custer nevertheless ordered an attack.

Following his standard battle plan designed to confuse and divide the enemy, Custer split his unit into three wings. The initial attack, from the southeast, was designed to draw the main Indian force into battle. Custer could then surprise and decisively attack the enemy from the northeast. But the first charge, led by Major Marcus Reno,

was dispatched in such a way that it was impossible to provide close support for it. After crossing the Greasy Grass River (as the Indians called the Little Bighorn River), Reno was beaten back. He made a hasty retreat which left Custer exposed to bear the brunt of the camp's entire force of warriors.

As Custer tried to organize his men north of the camp, Chief Gall's braves who had just repulsed Reno attacked from the southeast, while chiefs Crazy Horse and Two Moon led a charge from the southwest. Together they hit and wiped out Custer's entire battalion, the exact number of which is not known but thought to be about 225. The only

Below: The only painting of the battle by an eyewitness. Custer lies at left center. Standing in the center are: (left to right) Sitting Bull, Rain-in-the-Face, Crazy Horse, and Kicking Bear, the artist.

Custer Battlefield Museum/Western Americana

survivor of the slaughter was Captain Keogh's horse, "Comanche." The victorious Indians retired from the field the next day, leaving the gruesome evidence of defeat for Terry and Gibbon to find when they reached the battlefield on June 27.

No whites survived to tell of Custer's Last Stand. But Sitting Bull's account of the battle indicates that Custer and his men were all extremely tired. He said some of them were staggering under the weight of their guns. But Sitting Bull acknowledged the bravery of the whites under "Long Hair" and called him a "mighty chief."

Sitting Bull described Custer as standing like a "sheaf of corn with all the ears fallen around him," a pistol in hand, laughing because he had just fired his last round of ammunition. Because of the respect the Sioux had for him, Custer was not scalped (as were so many of his comrades).

Right: Chief Sitting Bull, medicine man of the Hunkpapa Sioux, whose braves won the stunning victory at the Little Bighorn. Following the battle, the chief escaped to Canada but returned to the United States in 1883 after the government granted him amnesty in 1879. The fifty-six-year-old chief was killed in 1890 near Fort Yates, North Dakota, while "resisting arrest."

Above: Apaches on their way to imprisonment
in Florida after their abortive uprising
in Arizona. Right: Geronimo surrendered
on condition that he could join his
family in Florida. He was, however,
sent to Oklahoma, where he died in 1909.
Bottom: Apache braves photographed with
their weapons.

promised. But the government, afraid of a general Indian war such as the Sioux had carried out the year before, ordered the Nez Percés to the Indian Territory. Joseph's plight, his skill in war, and his gallantry in defeat had aroused great sympathy across the nation, however, and the tribe's sufferings in their new homes aroused such an outcry that they were allowed to return to the Northwest (though not to the country they had lost) in 1885.

The Final Struggle

The far Southwest provided the scene for the last Indian conflicts. Vigorous campaigning during the Civil War had subdued the powerful Navajos, but the Apaches remained untamed. Under a remarkable chief named Cochise, the Chiricahuas, one subgroup of the tribe, terrorized southeastern Arizona and southwestern New Mexico for more than a decade before the government sent a special peace commissioner from the East to negotiate an end to the war. Undefeated, the Chiricahuas accepted a reservation in their own country in 1872, and ceased their attacks, at least in United States territory. By this time the army had coaxed and coerced most of the other Apache bands onto reservations, and it appeared by the mid-1870s that Indian troubles in the Southwest might be at an end.

After 1877, however, the government concentrated all the Apaches west of the Rio Grande on the sprawling San Carlos Reservation in central Arizona. There traditional enmities between several of the subgroups threatened the peace, and encroachments on the reservation by whites eager to exploit its metals and other resources increased instability. The autumn of 1881 saw a major outbreak by the Chiricahuas, who had been moved to San Carlos five years earlier. Led by the formidable chief and medicine man Geronimo, warriors kept the army busy much of the time until 1886, when the last hostiles surrendered. They were sent into exile and imprisonment in Florida, never again to disturb the peace of the Southwest. With their departure the Indian wars of the West came to an end.

An isolated epilogue occurred in 1890. For a decade the Sioux, peaceful on their South Dakota reservations, had seen the traditional patterns and values of their lives erode before the assault of white ways, and a deep despair gripped them. There was fear, also, that the government would take still more of their land, and that they would lose the rations which treaty commissioners had promised them long ago. They had many other grievances too. Some bands had lost their ponies to the army years before, even though they had been at peace, and they had received no compensation. Agents displaced traditional chiefs with others whom they could easily control, thus undermining both the political and the social structure of the tribe. And the buffalo, central to the Sioux religion, way of life, and economy, had virtually disappeared from the northern plains.

Discontented, wretched, and frightened, the Sioux in 1890 fell easy prey to a new Indian revivalist religion. The cult of the ghost dance had originated a year earlier in Nevada with a Paiute Indian named Wovoka, but it had spread among the tribes like fire across a parched prairie. Wovoka preached that a great cataclysm would soon

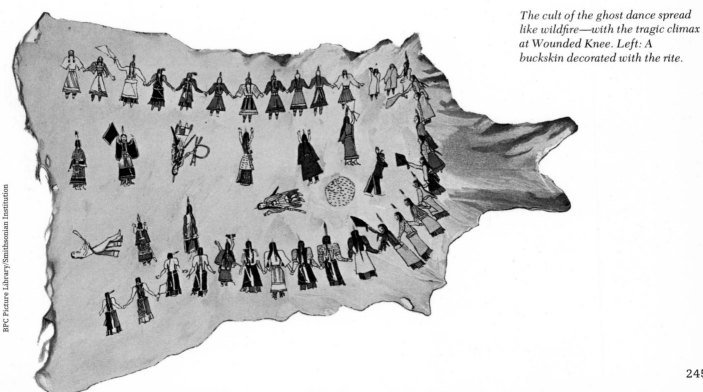

The cult of the ghost dance spread like wildfire—with the tragic climax at Wounded Knee. Left: A buckskin decorated with the rite.

Kicking Bear

National Archives

National Archives

The last battle of the Indian wars involved the Sioux. Far left: Kicking Bear. Left: Short Bull—both Sioux chiefs. Right: A military column returns from Wounded Knee where whites and Indians battled in the winter of 1890.

come, renewing the earth and removing all whites across the sea once more. Dead Indians'from all ages would return, and the earth would be again as it had been in the dimly remembered time before the foreigners had come. Indians could prepare for this millennium by dancing the ghost dance, a frenzied ritual to put them in contact with the Great Spirit and to glimpse the life to come.

The Sioux eagerly espoused a doctrine which promised the imminent return of the old days, but they perverted its meaning from peaceful inevitability to a message of militancy. Throughout the summer of 1890, tension increased on the reservations. In the autumn the ghost dancing commenced. Too late, Indian service officials recognized the deep hostility of the new ritual. Armed with good weapons, and secure in the belief that the ghost shirts they wore had the power to repel white men's bullets, the Sioux became increasingly militant. Sitting Bull, the great chief and medicine man, lent his prestige to the movement; he was killed on his reservation in December "while resisting arrest." The inevitable explosion followed two weeks later at Wounded Knee Creek, on the Pine Ridge Reservation, when warriors under a chief named Big Foot provoked a bloody and destructive battle with soldiers who were disarming them. The result was at least 153 tribesmen killed, with probably another 50 wounded. Military casualties, though far fewer, were nonetheless heavy. It was a tragic and unnecessary battle, but it discredited the ghost dance in Sioux eyes, and so broke their spirit of resistance. Wounded Knee was the last major engagement between Indians and whites.

The Debate in Washington

As the drama of warfare on the plains, mountains, and deserts of the West had been played out, federal Indian

246

Above: The body of Chief Big Foot lies half buried in the snow after the Battle of Wounded Knee. The slaughter brought an abrupt end to the cult of the ghost dance.

policy had evolved no less painfully in Washington. The debate commenced soon after the Civil War ended. Army officers, many influential men in the East, and western frontiersmen in general were arrayed against a growing number of humanitarians concerned with the treatment of American Indians. The dispute between the two sides did not concern long-range objectives, but rather the question of what immediate tactics should be used to pacify the red men and control them thereafter.

At the close of the Civil War, Americans in general believed that the army could quiet Indian hostilities. The Fetterman Massacre, an incident in the Sioux War of 1866 which saw an entire army command of eighty men ambushed and killed by the Indians, destroyed the optimism of many, and led directly to a reappraisal of government policy. For the first time, men in and out of Congress began to speak of the need to find a peaceful solution to the Indian problem. The quest for peace and justice for the Indian became the rallying cry for a group of reformers. Their efforts in and out of government had as wide-ranging effects on the tribesmen as did the wars by which the army subdued them. Nevertheless, the reformers' antimilitary bias involved the nation in a major dispute over the question of Indian control even while the conquest of the hostile Indians continued.

To army men and their supporters, it seemed clear that there could be no peace until the Indians were decisively defeated in war. It followed logically that the military should be left unhampered by civilian interference in its quest for victory over the tribes. Once victorious, moreover, the army must retain control over the Indians. Civil officials, appointed under the spoils system for political reasons, could not be relied upon to deal justly and honorably with the red men, the army felt. Their bungling and graft would keep the Indians unsettled, continually jeopardizing the peace and threatening to make the prairies and plains again crimson with blood.

Other men and women, no less sincere in their quest

for peace with the Indians, disagreed violently. Military contact with the red men could result only in brutalization, they argued. Disease and vice would spread, and the army would encourage the Indians' warlike character, rather than their nobler instincts for a useful life. It followed that civilians must manage Indian affairs. They alone could lead the savages out of darkness toward the light of Anglo-Saxon civilization.

An early and major disagreement between the reformers and the army thus centered upon the question of which branch of government should control the Indians. Since early in the nineteenth century there had existed a Bureau of Indian Affairs, which, in theory, controlled all matters relating to the red men. When first created, this office had been under the War Department, and had continued there until 1849. The Congress assigned it to the Department of the Interior, newly created in that year.

Both before and after this change in jurisdiction, the Indian Office suffered from a reputation of gross inefficiency and grosser corruption. This bad name was substantially undeserved. Given the nature of political appointments, the Indian service was probably no worse than any other branch of the government. Nevertheless, army officers and other opponents of civilian control seized upon the stories of graft, fraud, and costly inefficiency. They demanded that the bureau be purified by placing it once again under the War Department. The opponents of the military stoutly resisted, adamant that such a change would result in incalculable damage to the Indians. At the same time it would be fatal to the policy of absorbing Indians into white society. Between 1865 and 1879, the transfer issue came up before every session of Congress, provoking heated debate and calling forth strong emotions. In the latter year the army finally lost the struggle. The Indian Office remained under the control of the Interior Department.

During the years when the transfer question vexed the nation, federal Indian policy underwent a significant change in direction. The aftermath of the Fetterman Massacre had seen a commission, composed of three prominent civilians and four high-ranking army officers, appointed to secure peace with the warring plains tribes. This Peace Commission was responsible, by 1868, for negotiating the treaties of Medicine Lodge which pacified most of the Indians of the southern plains, and for bringing the Sioux War to a close in the north. The following year, the beginning of President Grant's Indian Peace Policy marked a still more significant development in the government's handling of the tribesmen.

The Peace Policy had two objectives. First, it sought to assure the honesty and efficiency of the Indian service. In 1869 Congress created a Board of Indian Commissioners, composed of nine prominent men, whose task it was to exercise joint supervision with the secretary of the interior over the expenditure of appropriations for the Indians. Members of the board were also authorized to be present at the letting of all contracts for Indian supplies and rations, to inspect the goods purchased, and to pass on all vouchers submitted for payment to the Indian Office. Bureaucratic bungling and Interior Department jealousy prevented the full execution of these duties. But the board remained a power for reform within the government.

The second focus of the peace policy was the intent to improve the quality of men who served the government as agents and employees among the Indians. The government sought to infuse a spirituality into the Indian service which had previously been lacking. To promote the employment of honest, conscientious, and Christian men, President Grant offered control of the agencies on the northern and southern plains to the Quakers in 1869. This denomination had long been interested in working with the Indians and was distinguished by its commitment to peaceful means of dealing with them. Within the two superintendencies over which they had control, the Quakers would be responsible for the nomination of all people working with the Indians. Implicit in the arrangement also was the supposition that the Quakers would undertake missionary and educational work among the natives.

So successful was the experiment of Quaker control over the plains agencies that President Grant expanded it in 1870. He invited other Protestant groups, and the Roman Catholic Church, to assume responsibility for different superintendencies and agencies. By 1872, thirteen denominations controlled seventy-three agencies in all parts of the West, and had charge of nearly 250,000 Indians. Of the churches some, such as the Episcopalians and Roman Catholics, were very active in the missionary and educational fields. Others contented themselves with simply nominating agents and trying to secure from the Indian Office the help and supplies they requested. Where denominations were active, missionary rivalries frequently undid the efforts of the churches, leaving the Indians confused and unhappy. Uneven participation in the goals of the Peace Policy was reflected in limited accomplishment. Moreover, as was the case with the Board of Indian Commissioners, the Interior Department and the Indian Office often failed to give full cooperation to the churches. All too frequently, especially after the mid-1870s, the government obliged the denominations to accept appointees chosen in Washington for political reasons. Church responsibility declined as a result. By the end of the decade the Quakers had withdrawn from participation in Indian management, and early in 1882 the government formally abandoned the system of church nominations. It had been a notable experiment, but its success in improving the quality of the Indian service had been limited.

However uneven the success of reform, the 1870s saw a

national consensus emerge as to the proper objectives of Indian policy. Its overall goal was to save the red men from the extinction which seemed to threaten them both by the onward thrust of the frontier and by their own inability to survive in a land completely dominated by whites. The first requirement, therefore, was that the Indians be removed from areas of settlement, and given reservations where they could be safe from white trespassing and the corruption of frontiersmen. There, at least, they would have land on which to survive and homes secure from their foes. The next priority was the pacification of the tribes which remained warlike, lest their inevitable defeat at the hands of the army result in their extermination. Once these Indians also were on reservations, the work of adapting them to the ways of Anglo-Saxon Americans could begin.

A New Way of Life

Government policy, and the most advanced humanitarian thought of the age, called for the systematic wiping out of Indian culture and its replacement with the values of nineteenth-century rural Americans. The Indian man, it was held, must be brought to understand the dignity of honest labor, rather than leaving menial tasks to his women. He must learn to support himself by agriculture, or such other occupations as stockraising and wagon freighting. To instill the ambition to labor, he had to learn the value of property. Greed would then keep him work-

ing and prevent him from indulging in the prodigal generosity which characterized many native cultures.

To educate the Indian in the techniques of self-support, and to wean him away from the barbarisms of his culture, reformers declared that he must attend school. Here, in "industrial" classes, he could learn useful crafts by which he could contribute to his support. Here, too, he would learn to use a plow, seed a furrow, and build an irrigation ditch. At the same time he would learn English, and so, it was hoped, be brought to forget his native tongue, a major link with his savage past. Simple arithmetic and elementary spelling and writing would complete the curriculum. Such education as this seemed most appropriate at boarding schools, preferably far from the reservations, where young students could be isolated for years at a time from their parents and the influences of an uncivilized environment.

Significant as the school was in preparing the Indian for absorption into white society, government officials hoped that other factors would be scarcely less important. On the San Carlos Reservation, an agent in the mid-1870s discovered that he could maintain order among the Apaches and other tribesmen with a native police force.

For many Indians "Americanization" began in a schoolroom, where tribesmen learned English and new agricultural methods. The government encouraged them to abandon their ancient heritage and adopt the white man's ways. Below: In Indian Territory in 1872, Ottawas pose outside a Quaker schoolhouse.

So successful was his experiment that in 1878 Congress appropriated funds to establish Indian police corps at all agencies. Five years later the Interior Department ordered the creation of Courts of Indian Offenses, at which native judges tried their fellow red men accused of a wide variety of crimes. Reformers hoped that such experiences as these would accomplish a multiple purpose. They would familiarize Indians with American justice, encourage responsibility among them, and foster the individualism which seemed essential to acculturation.

Breaking Tribal Bonds

Men and women concerned with the Indian problem generally agreed that tribalism was the greatest enemy of Indian progress. Tribal life, they believed, provided an environment in which backwardness and superstition necessarily flourished, excluding the eternal truths of Christianity upon which American civilization rested. In the tribe, a man could remain indolent except when he was at war, training his children in no useful arts, living off the public dole but resisting progress, and so perpetuating the darkness of barbarism. Polygamy, too, was associated with the tribal existence. Most nineteenth-century Americans saw the monogamous family as the indispensable training ground for morality, individual development, and the work ethic. Since in the tribe the Indian was part of a communal society, reformers hoped that the encouragement of individualism might prove a powerful weapon against this bastion of Indian backward-

At their reservations, Indians were given rations by the government. This compensated for the food they could no longer hunt. Above: Apaches line up at the San Carlos Reservation in Arizona.

ness. Thus schools, police corps, and native courts were established for ideological as well as practical reasons.

For the most part, the men and women active in the cause of Indian policy reform in the decades after the Civil War were idealists. Of their leaders, many, like Wendell Phillips, William Lloyd Garrison, and Lucretia C. Mott, had been involved in the antislavery movement before the war. They had seen the Negroes emancipated, and their concern spread to the achievement of equal rights for all men. The postwar reform movement, properly speaking, began in 1868. In that year, reporting to Congress and the nation, the Indian Peace Commission had remarked that Americans seemed unconcerned about the Indians, except when it was a question of getting their lands. If these intrusions ceased, the commissioners declared, frontier warfare could be eliminated. Then, through educational and missionary work, the Indians could be "civilized." The reformers accepted the challenge to involve themselves on behalf of the red men, and the new movement took shape.

Reformers demanded that the government begin programs which would lead to justice, equality, assimilation, and finally citizenship for the Indians. In works such as *Our Indian Wards,* by George W. Manypenny, and Helen Hunt Jackson's *A Century of Dishonor,* they denounced the entire past course of federal dealings with the

Indian, and insisted on the need for a radical change of policy. Treaties must be honored. Where graft and corruption characterized relations between the races, it must be completely eliminated. Indians had a full right to protection under federal and state laws, and to an end to all forms of discrimination in courts. Race prejudice must be eliminated as a factor determining official policy. Indians must be separated from their tribal allegiances, Christianized by missionaries dedicated to their improvement, then educated to live and work like white men. When all of this was done, they could be absorbed into white society and finally made citizens of the nation.

In their thinking about the Indians, the reformers showed considerable naiveté. They revered the red man's nobility, yet sought to undo the culture which had fostered it. Even as they decried warfare and called for peace, they praised the Indian's will to resist the white invasion. They excused atrocities which, if committed by soldiers or settlers, they would have bitterly denounced. Without understanding the nature of tribal warrior culture, they assumed that Indian hostilities resulted only from hunger and the loss of land. The reformers proposed a program of feeding and clothing the natives without making any further provision for stopping their warfare and raiding. These views provoked the scorn of frontiersmen, who rightly branded them as impractical and visionary. Nevertheless, in publicizing the plight of the Indian and demanding

just treatment for him, the reformers gave valuable service to the nation.

The long-term objectives of humanitarian reformers remained constant, but the means by which they sought to achieve them changed by the late 1870s. During the first decade of reform, they had urged the establishment and continuance of reservations for the Indians. They also had supported the government's program, during the peace policy years, of removing and concentrating the red men on a few large reserves. By this means, they hoped not merely to insulate the Indians from contact with whites, but to fill up the land so that further white invasion would be impossible. Finally, the reformers' emphasis during the early part of the decade had been more spiritual than secular. They underlined the prime importance of missionary work, as opposed to economic or educational advancement.

By 1879 the situation had changed. Convinced that the solution to the Indian problem lay in the rapid absorption of the red man into white society, reformers came to oppose the reservation system. They now saw that the system prevented the interracial contacts which led to

Remington's Battle of Warbonnet Creek.
In 1879, sixty-four Cheyennes were killed by the army when they refused to move south to Indian Territory.

The government initiated a program to distribute parcels of land to individual Indians. But with a few exceptions the experiment was a failure. Above: Apaches delivering hay in 1893.

assimilation. The same logic caused them to play down spiritual objectives in favor of urging programs leading toward greater material improvement. They also advocated the education of young Indians to bring economic self-sufficiency and independence.

The Growing Pressure for Reform

In the late 1870s and early 1880s, reformers joined together in several organizations whose strength enabled them to exert a strong influence on government policy. Of these, three of the most important were the Boston Indian Citizenship Committee, the Women's National Indian Association, and the Indian Rights Committee. The work of these organizations, and of others less prominent, was coordinated, from 1883 onward, at the Lake Mohonk Conferences of the Friends of the American Indian. These annual meetings were the idea of Albert K. Smiley, a Quaker member of the Board of Indian Commissioners. He invited leading reformers to his rural New York resort for three days each year to discuss the

direction of policy. The minutes of their conferences, with resolutions and recommendations, were printed and widely distributed, and they had a profound influence on a government ready to listen to these humanitarians.

By the early 1880s, the most important objective of government thinkers and reformers was the enactment of a law to grant lands to Indians individually. The idea was not new. Missionaries and government agents had experimented with it since the early nineteenth century, always with an eye to fostering the Anglo-Saxon property system among the tribesmen. Where the land had been divided, however, the results had been unfortunate. All too often the Indians sold their holdings for a pittance to ambitious whites. They then squandered what they received and became more dependent than ever on the public dole. Nevertheless, as the emphasis of reform turned increasingly toward assimilation, individual land tenure seemed a necessary condition for the "Americanization" of the Indians, as well as a potent weapon against the tribalism which held them in bondage.

Fortunately for the cause of the reformers, but unfortunately for the Indians, the concept of individual grants appealed both to humanitarians and to land-hungry westerners. Reformers saw in it a cure-all for Indian backwardness, as tribesmen at last could be secure in their ownership of land. Allotments made to Indians would be collectively far smaller than the lands they had occupied previously. The humanitarians held this to be an advantage, as they believed the availability of too much space encouraged nomadic habits. After allotments were made, the reservations would cease to exist. The Indians would then come into closer contact with whites, and the process of assimilation would be speeded. As for white frontiersmen, they found another cause to support the policy. Indians would receive allotments of a quarter-section (160 acres) per family. Why should not the government dispose of the rest of the tribal lands as public domain? The hope of possessing large tracts of previously unavailable land made westerners in general enthusiastic about the idea of individual Indian grants. Thus unselfish reformers and frontier boomers joined in an improbable alliance to support a policy which each group desired for its own reasons.

The General Allotment Act, known as the Dawes Act for its leading congressional sponsor, Senator Henry L. Dawes of Massachusetts, became law in February 1887. It authorized individual land tenure for all American Indian families except those of the Five Civilized Tribes of the Indian Territory and a few other tribes who already had titles to their lands. Allotments would be made at the president's discretion; Indian consent was unnecessary. Once the lands were allotted, individual grants were to be held in a trust status, untaxed and incapable of being disposed of for a period of twenty-five years. After all eligible Indians had chosen lands, the surplus from each reservation would be purchased by the government from the tribes, then restored to the public domain for sale to white settlers. All Indians receiving allotments would automatically become citizens of the nation and

The Indian's native culture was fast disappearing, while a new one loomed on the horizon. Below: Wohaw, a Kiowa, symbolizes the red man's dilemma. Turning from the buffalo, Wohaw faces the farm and rests his foot on plowed land, as if accepting the new way of life.

the state or territory in which they resided.

The Indians in general were dismayed by the provisions of the Dawes Act. As clearly as the reformers, they realized the effect it would have on their tribal life. They understood that the law would rob them of most of their remaining lands, and irrevocably alter the patterns of their existence. Many also saw that the allotments were not large enough for profitable or even marginal farming or ranching in a dry land. Protests against the law came from Indians in all parts of the West, but they were unavailing. In the end, only those of the far Southwest were wholly exempt as the act was amended to include even the tribes initially excepted from its provisions.

The operation of the Dawes Act made possible land-grabbing from the Indians on a grand scale. Whites married into many Indian tribes in order to become eligible for allotments. In other cases it frequently proved easy to rent or lease allotted Indian lands for a token sum. Many of the owners thus lost their allotments in everything except title. Trust provisions could be evaded without difficulty, too. Lands which legally were inalienable were signed away by their owners for the payment or promise of a paltry sum. In almost every case, the best reservation lands were included in the "surplus" which reverted to the public domain, and thus passed into the hands of whites.

The overall effect of the Dawes Act, therefore, was vastly different from what its humanitarian sponsors had hoped. Far from creating a sturdy class of yeoman Indian farmers, proud of their holdings and eager to copy their industrious white neighbors, the law pauperized the red men. It created a large and ever-increasing class of landless men and women with no means of survival. Perhaps still worse was the cultural effect of the law on the Indians, for it weakened the tribes, often fatally, without giving the tribesmen any viable social organization to take its place. Much of the despair of Indians in the twentieth century, and the concurrent problems of alcoholism and suicide, can be traced to the social disintegration created by the Dawes Act.

With the Indian wars at an end, and with the enactment of individual land tenure, the reformers considered the Indian problem solved. Their confidence mirrored the blindness of men and women who, with the best of motives, were too wedded to a single point of view to see the dangers it entailed. Yet such was the climate of race prejudice and moral bigotry that, quite possibly, no better solution could have been found. Government and reformers alike were unwilling to leave the Indian alone to develop along lines dictated by his own culture; the object of their policy was to make him a white man with a dark skin. No one, except perhaps the Indian himself, believed the task of assimilation to be impossible. Therefore the law undermined his tribal existence and the culture which accompanied it, confident that enlightenment and "civilization" would follow. The fact that it did not bespoke the blindness of good intentions. It also constituted the most enduring tragedy of the Indian.

Fierce Apache warrior Geronimo was one of the most famous survivors of the Indian wars. Here the chief, accompanied by three ceremoniously dressed braves, enjoys a ride in a Locomobile in 1905.

Chapter 11

THE CLOSING OF THE FRONTIER

The census of 1890 declared that the frontier no longer existed: the West had been settled. Railroads and the telegraph spanned the nation; the army had subdued the Indians; buffalo—and other wildlife—were on the verge of extinction. But there were those who realized that the complete loss of the West's distinctive character would impoverish all America. The conservationist movement sought to preserve some vestige of the wilderness for relaxation and reflection. At the same time, an eager public snapped up the sensational books and romantic paintings that perpetuated—and expanded— the myths and legends of the West.

Preserving the Wilderness

Conservation came late to the American West because it was the last region of the forty-eight states to surrender its frontier character. This meant that westerners still subscribed to the myth of inexhaustibility long after it bowed to reality in the East. In most western eyes it seemed that the abundance of the virgin land could never be depleted. Run out of resources? Nonsense. Consider the buffalo. The herds seemed endless—square miles of solid animals—and they poured past a given point for half a day. By 1890 the original herds of perhaps 30 million had declined to 900 animals, and Americans found it difficult to believe. As for timber, the forests of the Far West appeared limitless. They extended, ridge after ridge, as far as a man could see. The supply of timber was apparently sufficient for every conceivable need for all time. And the giant redwoods of the Pacific Coast were trees beyond men's wildest imaginings. These trees were over one hundred yards tall and ten yards in diameter. When the bark of a redwood was peeled and reassembled in the East and in England, crowds praised the showman for a colossal hoax. When he protested that whole forests of such trees existed in the American West, incredulity increased. A timber shortage? Someone must be joking. Up to the twentieth century, in short, Americans in the West enjoyed a population-to-resources ratio which made conservation seem unnecessary.

But, inevitably, reality caught up with the West just as it had with the Old World and the Eastern Seaboard. Toward the end of the nineteenth century some Americans began to discover that limits existed, even in the fabled West. It was these individuals who moved beyond such a realization to the concept of conservation. They had the wisdom to understand that in the long run it was not the natural abundance of the West that would ensure America's prosperity, but rather the care with which the natural heritage was managed.

Many, of course, were not convinced. For them conservation was entirely unnecessary as well as an infringement on freedom and free enterprise. Exploitation of natural resources seemed to be a natural right. But then the frontier vanished. The official end came in the census of 1890 which simply declared that in view of the spread of settlement the West could no longer be considered as having a frontier line. The sudden absence of the frontier was profoundly shocking. Americans could not help but wonder if the growth of cities and industry that was transforming their environment would also transform their values and institutions. Perhaps the nation had seen its greatest days.

In this transformed context conservation made increasing sense. It would extend the continent's remaining abundance, deny the chilling implications of the census pronouncement, and lessen the anxiety over the growth of cities, industry, and population. Conservation, to be sure, was not the only beneficiary of America's end-of-the-century malaise. Imperialism and the movement for immigration restriction also reflected the nation's anxiety. But conservation had special appeal because it directly attacked the problem which was, at

On fields where herds of buffalo had once roamed, only their hides remained. Below: At Dodge City buffalo skins are piled high before they are moved east by railroad.

root, environmental. Conservation would *be* the new frontier. It would keep the middle-aged nation youthful, vigorous, prosperous, democratic. America would remain full of opportunity for the individual and, because of its relation to nature, wholesome and moral. These had once been the frontier's functions. For a civilization that had by the twentieth century begun to notice its first gray hairs, conservation was welcome tonic, for the land as well as for the minds of its inhabitants. As a result when President Theodore Roosevelt's chief forester, Gifford Pinchot, coined the term "conservation" in 1907, a large proportion of the American people were prepared to understand its meaning and its importance.

The Importance of the Wilderness

One of the earliest applications of the conservation idea to the Far West concerned national parks. The idea and implementation of a national park—defined as large-scale wilderness preservation in the public interest—was an American invention. Parks had previously existed, but generally as the private nature preserves of wealthy land-holders. The idea of a socially owned park or forest awaited the fortunate combination of the American democratic tradition and the vacant spaces of the Far West. Another characteristic of pre-American parks was their pastoral or semicivilized character. European and Asian parks were, in effect, gardens. The idea of a *wild* park was something of a contradiction before America began to preserve wilderness in its primeval condition.

The roots of the national park idea can be traced to the writings of George Catlin, a notable painter of Indians and Western scenery. In the spring of 1832 Catlin arrived at Fort Pierre, South Dakota, with paints and brushes in hand. He found a large number of Sioux camped near the fort and observed them trading fourteen hundred fresh buffalo tongues for whiskey. The grisly spectacle confirmed his suspicions that the extinction of both was imminent. The typical westerner might well have rejoiced in this prospect, but Catlin's perspective was different. "Many are the rudenesses and wilds in Nature's works," he mused, "which are destined to fall before the deadly axe and desolating hands of cultivating man." Catlin, however, was convinced that the primitive in both man and nature was "worthy of our preservation and protection." Keeping the wilderness was important because "the further we become separated from that pristine wildness and beauty, the more pleasure does the mind of enlightened man feel in recurring to those scenes."

A few others had said as much, but Catlin's 1832 reflections went further. He held the idea that the Indians, the buffalo, and the wilderness might not yield completely to civilization if the federal government would

Inspiring forests of redwoods—the world's tallest tree—deceived many into thinking that America's supply of timber was inexhaustible. Above: A stand of redwoods in California.

protect them in "*a magnificent park*." Fascinated with the idea, Catlin spread a map of North America on a hill near Fort Pierre and contemplated the prospect of a wilderness reserve extending along the front range of the Rocky Mountains from Canada to Mexico. "What a beautiful and thrilling specimen for America to preserve and hold up to the view of her refined citizens and the world, in future ages! A *nation's Park*, containing man and beast, in all the wild[ness] and freshness of their nature's beauty!" Catlin closed his journal with the thought that he would ask no other monument than the reputation of founding such a park.

Similar recognition of the value of the American wilderness led others to call for its preservation. In the late 1840s Thomas Cole, another artist who had seen the fate of wilderness in the Old World, proposed to write a book concerning "the wilderness passing away, and the necessity of saving and perpetuating its features." Cole never wrote the book, but his landscape paintings helped publicize the beauty of the primeval American

257

environment. Contact with Europe also prompted Horace Greeley to implore Americans "to spare, preserve and cherish some portion of your primitive forests." If these vanished, he warned, they could not easily be replaced. The more he traveled in England, the more Greeley's thoughts ran back to the "glorious . . . still unscathed forests" of America which he had "never before prized so highly." Europe, in short, was a mirror in which Americans could see their own environmental future. While some civilization was, of course, desirable, a few individuals began in the mid-nineteenth century to realize that there could be too much of a desirable thing. The nation could become *over* civilized.

The philosopher from Concord, Massachusetts, Henry David Thoreau, had the most refined rationale for saving America's vanishing wildness. The disappearance of wild country made him uneasy. Even the Far West was succumbing to the attack of the pioneer army. "It is a thorough process, this war with the wilderness," Thoreau lamented. The problem, in Thoreau's view, was that when wildness vanished so did the physical and intellectual energies that nourished a great civilization. In company with many of his contemporary intellectuals he was obsessed with the legend of Rome being founded by the twins Romulus and Remus who had been suckled by a wolf. These wild beginnings explained Rome's rise to world dominance. But, in time, the Roman Empire became civilized and then over civilized and decadent. Finally, Rome was overrun by barbarians from the northern forests, people who had retained their wild roots and, consequently, their vitality. The problem for the United States was to avoid a fate similar to Rome's, not to lose contact with the wildness that blessed its beginnings. One solution was the maintenance in the American environment of what Thoreau called "a certain sample of wild nature, a certain primitiveness." Like Catlin, Thoreau saw the preserves as offering protection for animals and Indians, but he also understood them as sanctuaries for civilization. "Let us keep the New World *new*," he pleaded.

Along with sentiment for saving wilderness, the idea of government responsibility in this respect was a necessary prelude to national parks. One precedent came in 1832, when the Arkansas Hot Springs were set aside as a national reservation. More important was the 1864 federal grant of Yosemite Valley in California's Sierra Nevada range as a park "for public use, resort and recreation." The reserved area was only about ten square miles, and a flourishing tourist business soon altered its wild character. But the preservation of part of the public domain for scenic and recreational values created a significant precedent for national parks.

The world's first national park came into being early in March 1872 when President Ulysses S. Grant signed an act of Congress designating over 2 million acres of

northwestern Wyoming as Yellowstone National Park. At the time only a handful of trappers, prospectors, and explorers had seen this spectacular high mountain region with its geysers, hot springs, waterfalls, and lakes. But two men who had—Nathaniel P. Langford and Cornelius Hedges—came away from their 1870 expedition convinced that such natural wonders should not be exploited by private speculators. Instead it should be set aside as the common possession of the American

Thomas Gilcrease Institute, Tulsa, Oklahoma

Artist and photographers played an important role in the early conservation movement. Their pictures showed untouched nature. But such scenes would be despoiled unless the government stepped in to prevent economic exploitation. Thomas Moran's work was a major influence in convincing Congress to preserve the wilderness. Above: His painting Lower Falls on the Yellowstone.

people. Along with Ferdinand V. Hayden, director of the Geological and Geographical Survey of the Territories, Langford and Hedges publicized the Yellowstone country and petitioned Congress to accord it protection while it was still part of the public domain. Thomas Moran, a landscape artist, and William Henry Jackson, a pioneer outdoor photographer, supplied important visual documentation of Yellowstone's splendor. Their efforts bore fruit when the president approved an act declaring that the Yellowstone region "is hereby reserved and withdrawn from settlement, occupancy, or sale . . . and set apart as a public park or pleasuring ground for the benefit and enjoyment of the people."

It took little effort to declare Yellowstone a national park, particularly since in 1872 no private land claims or businesses existed in that remote region. No one, in fact, lived there at all. But maintaining the park in the decades that followed was another matter. Congress had not provided for supervision of the new park, and without it timber thieves and game poachers ran rampant. Railroad and mining interests also demanded access to Yellowstone. Moreover, there was a sizable segment of Congress unsympathetic to the whole idea of a national park. As one congressman put it, why should the government enter into "show business"? Another asked if the demands of prosperity and progress were to yield to the eccentric demands of "a few sportsmen bent only on the protection of a few buffalo."

Earlier the West's virgin character had always succumbed to arguments such as these. But in the 1880s, when Yellowstone National Park faced the severest challenges to its existence, its friends mustered a counterargument. The park, they said, represented an assertion of national pride and aesthetic taste in the face of private greed. Yellowstone, they charged, should be preserved for the long-term pleasure of posterity, not the immediate profits of a few exploiters. Another weapon in their arsenal was the idea of Thoreau and Ralph Waldo Emerson that contemplation of unspoiled nature brought mankind into closer communion with the deity. Let us "prefer the beautiful and the sublime," Representative William McAdoo of New Jersey declared, instead of "heartless mammon and the greed of capital." At length such arguments prevailed. Congress appropriated a few dollars to maintain Yellowstone, and the United States Army was called upon to police the national park. Organized professional management by rangers was still decades away, but the nation had expressed its intent to prevent all the virgin West from vanishing.

Yellowstone laid the groundwork for the expansion of the national park concept to other parts of the American West. But further preservation depended on public acceptance of the idea that wilderness had value for civilization. In the late nineteenth century wild country needed a champion, and it found one in John Muir.

Below: The Geological and Geographical Survey of the Territories was led by Ferdinand Hayden— a strong conservationist and lobbyist. This trail stretched between the Yellowstone and East Fork rivers.

Starting in the 1870s Muir made exploring wilderness and extolling its values a way of life. Many of his ideas merely echoed those of earlier men like Thoreau and Emerson, but he articulated them with an intensity and enthusiasm that commanded widespread attention. As a publicizer of the vanishing wilderness Muir had no equal.

John Muir was born in Scotland in 1838. Eleven years later, his family emigrated to a farm in central Wisconsin not far from the Mississippi River. Muir attended the University of Wisconsin for a time in the 1860s but dropped out to enter what he called "the University of the Wilderness." A near-disaster helped him reach this decision. Late one evening in March 1867 while Muir was working at his part-time job in a factory, his usually sure hands slipped and drove a sharp file into the cornea of his right eye. As he stood silently by a window the aqueous humor fell out into his cupped hand. Soon his other eye became blind from sympathetic shock. Reduced to an invalid's bed in a darkened room, Muir contemplated a life without sight. After a month, however, he recovered his vision—fully in one eye, partially in the other. Immediately he vowed to waste no more time abandoning civilized ways for those of the wilderness. "God has to nearly kill us sometimes," he concluded, "to teach us lessons."

As his first project Muir elected to wander "just any-

Mansell Collection

Above: John Muir, naturalist and writer.
When Ralph Waldo Emerson visited Yosemite,
Muir served as his guide. Emerson
said of Muir, "He is more wonderful than Thoreau."

where in the wilderness southward," and eventually walked a thousand miles to the Gulf of Mexico. His journal for the trip contained most of the ideas he used to defend wilderness the rest of his life. Wild nature was full of "Divine beauty" and "harmony." A "spiritual power" emanated from the landscape. If man would only seek the wilderness he could purge himself of the distractions of civilization and become a "new creature." Muir intended to pursue his interests in the wilds of South America, but a bout with malaria forced him to seek the colder climate of northern California. Arriving in San Francisco in March 1868 he allegedly inquired of the first man he met the way out of town. Asked to specify his destination, he replied, "any place that is wild." His trail led across San Francisco Bay and the flower-strewn San Joaquin Valley and, finally, to the Sierra. There amidst 14,000-foot peaks capable of satisfying his enthusiasm he found a permanent home.

For the next forty years John Muir used both literary and political means to advance the cause of wilderness preservation in the West. His essays describing the Sierra and later the Grand Canyon and Alaska made these far-flung places come alive for eastern audiences. His books were minor best sellers, and the nation's best journals competed for his articles. One of the places Muir described most enthusiastically was the portion of the Sierra surrounding Yosemite Valley and its pocket-sized state park. Along with Robert Underwood Johnson, an editor of the leading literary magazine, *Century*, and the tourist-minded Southern Pacific

National Archives

Railroad, Muir brought pressure on Congress to protect this high country. He succeeded on October 1, 1890, when President Benjamin Harrison signed a bill creating the 1,500-square mile Yosemite National Park. In 1906 Muir led another battle to persuade California to transfer its state park in Yosemite Valley to the federal government for inclusion in the surrounding national park. Currently one of America's most popular national parks, Yosemite is proof that if enough people cared, parts of the virgin West could be preserved.

Conservation: Successes and Problems

Yosemite National Park marked a great triumph, but John Muir knew from experience that without close supervision even legally protected wilderness was not safe from utilitarian pressures. Consequently he welcomed Johnson's 1891 idea for "a Yosemite and Yellowstone defense association." At the same time a group of professors at the University of California and at Stanford University were discussing plans for an alpine club. Muir saw the connection and took the lead in planning an organization which would "be able to do something for wildness and make the mountains glad." On June 4, 1892, twenty-seven men formed the Sierra Club and dedicated it to "exploring, enjoying and rendering accessible the mountain regions of the Pacific Coast." They also proposed "to enlist the support of the people and government in preserving the forests and other features of the Sierra Nevada Mountains." Muir was the obvious and unanimous choice for president, an office he held for twenty-two years until his death in 1914. Meanwhile the Sierra Club became a mecca for those interested in wilderness and its preservation.

For John Muir and the Sierra Club "conservation" meant preserving nature in an unspoiled condition without any lumbering, grazing, or mining. But many of his contemporaries subscribed to a different definition of the term. In their estimation conservation signified the wise *use* of resources and necessarily entailed some economic development. The profession of forestry, for example, was based on the concept of sustained yield—the provision of a continuous supply of timber and other forest products for centuries. In the late nineteenth century, forestry was almost exclusively a European practice. In the United States, where trees seemed so numerous as to constitute a liability rather than an asset, forestry had little appeal. Even the government acted in ways calculated to deplete rapidly the West's forest resources. Millions of acres of the best timberlands in the world were virtually given to private exploiters who operated on a short-sighted "cut-out-and-get-out" basis. In the 1870s and 1880s the Northern Pacific Railroad alone received more land than the area of Pennsylvania, New Jersey, and Rhode Island combined.

Under the Timber and Stone Act of June 3, 1878, a citizen could obtain up to 160 acres of forest land supposedly "unfit for cultivation" at a price of $2.50 per acre. The law was intended to help the humble settler, but it invited abuse. Lumber companies lined up stooges whose individual claims quickly became part of sprawling timber empires ready for exploitation. Other entrepreneurs took advantage of loopholes in the Homestead Act of 1862 which required that improvements such as a house be placed on unappropriated land as a requirement for ownership. Some timber thieves circumvented the law by building a doll house a foot square. Another ploy was to construct a standard-sized house on a wagon and move it from lot to lot in the presence of witnesses who swore they had seen a "house" on the land in question. Once the land became the possession of the lumbering interests, the doctrines of individualism, free enterprise, and property laws combined to permit abuse of the environment. Ownership was absolute and often ecologically irresponsible.

The American attitude toward forest fires typified this preconservation perspective. Millions of acres of choice timberland burned every year—12 million in 1891 alone —and the fact elicited only yawns. When 1,500 people died in a forest inferno that enveloped northern Wisconsin in 1871 there was concern, but only for the human lives involved. The lives of trees had no significance. At that time waste seemed immaterial to the national interest.

Against this background of irresponsible abuse and vanishing resources, a few Americans spoke up on behalf of forest conservation. A Vermonter named George Perkins Marsh, fluent in twenty languages, was one of the first. On his many travels in the 1840s and 1850s, some as an American diplomat in the Near East, Marsh saw land that centuries of careless exploitation had reduced to barren dust. It occurred to Marsh that part of the reason for the fall of Greece, Persia, and Rome might have been the exhaustion of their environment's supporting ability. In particular, Marsh deplored the loss of forests surrounding the Mediterranean and the consequent cycle of drought, flood, and erosion of vital soil.

Back in the United States, Marsh saw widespread and alarming evidence of the same practices that had destroyed sections of the European and Near Eastern environments. In 1864 he reacted, publishing *Man and Nature; or Physical Geography as Modified by Human Action.* It was an angry book. Marsh lashed Americans for their environmental irresponsibility and presented dramatic evidence of its consequences. On the positive side, he argued that technology's power to transform the environment should entail a commensurate sense of stewardship. At stake was the existence of civilization itself. "Let us be wise in time," Marsh pleaded, "and profit by the errors of our older brethren." Another statement, remarkable for the era in which Marsh wrote, held that "man has too long forgotten that the earth was given to him for usefruct alone, not for consumption, still less for profligate waste." In Marsh's view "usefruct" entailed husbanding the wealth of the earth and maintaining a continuous supply of vital resources like forests. The woodlands, he pointed out, served not only as suppliers of wood, but as giant sponges which soaked up water during rainy seasons (preventing floods) and released it slowly (preventing droughts).

One of the men who was impressed by Marsh's arguments was in a position to do something about federal policy. Carl Schurz served as secretary of the interior from 1877 to 1881. An immigrant from Germany in 1852, Schurz understood the Old World view of natural resources with its emphasis on sustained yield. During his tenure as secretary, his primary concern was the condition and future of the nation's forests. "The rapidity with which this country is being stripped of its forests," he wrote in his annual report for 1877, "must alarm every thinking man." Within twenty years, Schurz predicted, the United States would face a timber shortage unless it adopted conservation measures. Schurz went on to suggest that the federal government should begin to preserve the western forests by retaining title to the land and leasing cutting rights to private lumbermen. In this way effective regulation could be obtained. If a lumberman proved irresponsible, his lease could be revoked. Schurz's 1877 proposals contained the seeds of the idea of "national forests" and of the United States Forest Service. They had the immediate

effect of encouraging Franklin B. Hough to prepare a report on the application of European management methods to the American forests.

To be sure, the recommendations of Carl Schurz fell on a good many deaf ears. To a large number of his contemporaries in the 1870s and 1880s they smacked of socialism and represented a threat to cherished principles of free enterprise and private control. But Schurz received support from social philosophers like Lester Frank Ward, who questioned the wisdom of free-for-all competition. In its place Ward proposed cooperative social and environmental engineering, a method by which man carefully shaped the kind of future he wanted. Schurz's ideas also had the backing of another German immigrant, Bernhard E. Fernow. In 1886 Fernow assumed direction of the recently expanded federal Division of Forestry. At this time Fernow had no actual forests to manage. The role of his bureau was supervisory and, usually, ineffective. Consequently Fernow, along with Secretary of the Interior John W. Noble, agitated for federal ownership of forest lands. They got their wish on March 3, 1891, when Congress passed the Forest Reserve Act whereby the president by executive order could create "forest reserves" (later renamed "national forests") from the unappropriated public domain. President Benjamin Harrison took immediate advantage of the new power by proclaiming fifteen reserves in the Far West totaling more than 13 million acres.

At first the new forest reserves received only paper

The Bettmann Archive

The European practice of forestry was virtually unknown in America. Settlers and lumbermen believed the forests of the West to be limitless and squandered their resources.

263

protection. In practice exploitation was not halted. Also disconcerting was the general confusion over the purpose of the reserves. Muir regarded them as wilderness that would be forever protected from all commercial use in the manner of national parks. But professional foresters like Bernhard E. Fernow and Gifford Pinchot had other ideas. In their viewpoint the forest reserves had to do with economics, not aesthetics. Accusing the preservationists of wishing to "lock up" the forests, they agitated for a utilitarian definition of the purpose of the reserves. Supporting the foresters were western congressmen. Many of their constituents were outraged at the land withdrawals, particularly 21 million acres set aside by President Grover

Loggers escort a visitor on the Gallatin River in Montana. The rivers of the Northwest provided a convenient method of moving the logs from the forest to the mill.

Cleveland in the closing days of his administration. A movement to repeal the Forest Reserve Act in its entirety was thwarted only by passage (June 4, 1897) of the Forest Management Act which left no doubt that the reserves would not be wilderness. In response to the demands of foresters and most westerners, the act made clear that one of the primary purposes of the reserves was "to furnish a continuous supply of timber for the use and necessities of citizens of the United States." The Forest Management Act also opened the reserves to grazing and mining. Henceforth there was to be a clear distinction between the national parks (administered by the Department of the Interior) and the national forests (administered by the Department of Agriculture).

With the purpose of the forest reserves defined, the United States was prepared to launch conservation in a major way. To lead the effort the nation turned to Gifford Pinchot who, in 1898, took over the reins of the federal

Division of Forestry from Bernhard E. Fernow. Pinchot was young, rich, well educated, and energetic. After graduating from Yale in 1889, he went to France and Germany for instruction in forestry since no American university at the time could provide such training. Impressed with the accomplishments of Europeans in maintaining a forest's productivity over hundreds of years, Pinchot then set about convincing Americans that they could do the same. At first, the nation was less than eager to listen. At length Pinchot found employment on the private forest estates of several individuals and proved that the land could produce timber without impairment of its long-term capacity for such production. This was the essence of forestry.

When Gifford Pinchot began his association with the government in 1898, he had a two-room office, a staff of eleven men, a tiny budget, and no forests in his jurisdiction. Ten years later his United States Forest Service was one of

the most powerful bureaus in Washington, and Pinchot, as chief forester, was the leading figure in a movement that made "conservation" a household word. Explaining this meteoric rise was Pinchot's close friendship with President Theodore Roosevelt. Another factor was the 1905 transfer of 86 million acres of forest reserves to Pinchot's office. The West was still suspicious of the whole forestry endeavor, but Pinchot worked hard to dispel fears that he intended to lock up resources. His objective, he explained at the highly-publicized 1908 White House Conservation Conference of Governors, was to promote the greatest good of the greatest number over the longest time. "Conservation," by this time, extended beyond forests to include the

Workers stand amid the logs about to be loaded at the Gallatin River rail yard in Montana. The Forest Management Act of 1897 ensured a regular supply of timber.

National Archives

John Hillers, photographer with the John Wesley Powell survey team, examines a negative at the camp on Aquarius Plateau, Utah Territory. His photographs provide a historic record of the West.

efficient management of soil, water, wildlife, grassland, and minerals. Its chief principles were the elimination of waste and the protection of the right of the people, both present and future, to the natural resources they shared. The major villain from the conservationists' perspective was the wasteful exploiter who placed his immediate personal gain ahead of the long-term welfare of the nation as a whole. Obviously, conservation was good politics as well as good environmental stewardship, and Pinchot made it a key component of the Progressive reform crusade.

Water equaled forests as an important ingredient of the western environment. In regard to this resource the central figure was a one-armed veteran of the Civil War named John Wesley Powell. Powell had a passion to explore the mysteries of the natural world. After his service in the Civil War, he penetrated one of the most uncharted regions remaining in the American West—the Grand Canyon of Arizona. In 1869, with ten companions, Powell led the first descent of the Colorado River from Wyoming, through the Grand Canyon, to the vicinity of Las Vegas, Nevada. Two years later he made part of the

thousand-mile voyage again, carefully mapping and recording scientific data. Powell followed these river trips with overland explorations of the Great Basin between the Rocky Mountains and California's Sierra Nevada. He published some of his findings in 1878 in his *Report on the Lands of the Arid Regions of the United States.*

Powell's book described the region as neither an agrarian paradise nor a Great American Desert. Rather he portrayed it as an environment capable of a limited amount of cultivation. The key was federal involvement in what came to be called "reclamation" projects. In the arid West this meant irrigation. The desert could be reclaimed for agriculture, Powell argued, if the government would sponsor large-scale dam and irrigation projects. Powell also proposed radical changes in land laws to suit the environmental conditions of the West. The apportionment of land, he insisted, should conform to its geography and water supply rather than to an arbitrary grid of 160-acre squares. The overriding importance of Powell's work was the way it illustrated that man need not be at the mercy of the environment provided he went about the task of environmental management with realistic objectives and scientific methods. But Powell's ideas for water management ran afoul of traditional American suspicion of too much government involvement. Like most of the early conservationists, he was a person at least a generation ahead of both popular thought and congressional support. During his lifetime Powell made little headway with his concept of a planned, controlled, federally-financed development of western water resources. But in 1902, the year he died, Congress passed the Reclamation Act. A monument to Powell and to his disciples like Frederick H. Newell and William John McGee, the act accepted the principle of federal management of the West's major rivers and created a mechanism for paying for it through the sale of land and of water rights. Within a few years the Bureau of Reclamation was involved in a number of water conservation projects in the West. Some of these were harbingers of multipurpose dam and reservoir complexes that later transformed the Colorado and Columbia river areas.

Between 1870 and 1900 the native western environment melted under the heat of civilization's spread like a snowbank in the May sunshine. Reacting in alarm, the first American conservationists all had the courage to challenge the dominant conception of the land's purpose and to expose the myth of inexhaustibility. They were also prepared to question the dogma of free enterprise and the competitive economy which balked at the prospect of government regulation—even when that regulation was in the long-term interest of society. Finally, a few of the pioneer conservationists made so bold as to suggest that growth and prosperity were not the only criteria for progress and happiness. The *kind* of life lived amid abundance also had its claims and sometimes, as in the case of national parks, demanded that limits be set to civilization's expansion.

The West: Myth and Reality

From the earliest days of the Republic, the West has occupied a special place in the American consciousness. It has not merely been recognized as a separate region with a distinctive heritage of its own. The West has at the same time been identified by successive generations of Americans with the past and future history of the nation *as a whole.* In other words, western history has had a symbolic quality. It has tended to become, in the words of one historian, "an allegory of ideals unfulfilled or unattainable elsewhere."

To be sure, the empty continent beyond the frontier has always existed in the popular imagination on more than one plane. For most of the nineteenth century it was generally seen in tangible, material terms, as a virgin land which awaited settlement and exploitation in fulfillment of Manifest Destiny. But the West was never merely that. To a greater extent than the other regions into which the United States can be divided, the West existed in the realm of folklore and myth. In the nineteenth century it provided the backdrop for some of the nation's best-known folk heroes and heroines, real and fictional: Daniel Boone, Leatherstocking, Kit Carson, Wild Bill Hickok, Calamity Jane, Buffalo Bill, Annie Oakley, Deadwood Dick, Billy the Kid, George A. Custer. In the twentieth century motion pictures and television have played a vital role in keeping alive the western-hero tradition. The continued appeal of western themes is also demonstrated by the huge sales of Zane Grey's novels and the success of musicals like *Annie Get Your Gun* and popular songs like "Home on the Range."

The varied, and sometimes contradictory, images of the West conjured up in the popular mind have not always squared with the facts. On the contrary, the realities of frontier life have regularly given way to the requirements of myth. But the significance of what Americans thought about the West did not depend upon its historical accuracy. Popular conceptions and misconceptions alike reflected the ideas the American people held about themselves as a nation and the view they had of what constituted the Good Society.

The West which was to exercise the greatest fascination upon the popular mind was the untamed region in which Buffalo Bill and his fictional counterparts performed their exploits. But a much earlier myth about the West was that of an agrarian Eden. Americans had a vision of a vast, thriving, agricultural empire occupying the heartland of the continent. This dovetailed nicely with Thomas Jefferson's agrarian dream—the notion that the independent yeoman was the ideal American. Only he, according to Jefferson, had the independence of mind and

Library of Congress

Above: The West was often portrayed as an Eden. President Jefferson believed that a nation of yeoman farmers—innocent of big-city corruption—would best preserve American democracy.

means necessary to shoulder the responsibilities of democracy. Walt Whitman would go further and argue that the West was "the real genuine America."

As the tide of settlement moved westward, this agrarian ideal was applied to successive frontiers. Then when it reached the Great Plains it had to contend with—and overcome—the opposing myth of the Great American Desert. That the Great Plains were at the same time the Wild West of popular imagination was, of course, true, but this was merely another example of the ambiguity and contradiction so characteristic of American ideas about the West. In any case, such ideas did not need to be tied down to a particular place in order to be effective.

The tendency to harbor contradictory notions about the West—and cling to them despite their failure to correspond with the facts—was early demonstrated by the legends that gathered around the name of Daniel Boone. The image of Boone as the archetypal frontier figure started with the publication in 1784 of his "autobiography." This celebrated Boone's achievements in planting civilization in Kentucky—how he blazed the Wilderness

Far left: Daniel Boone, the legendary frontiersman. Left: Kit Carson, who guided travelers along the Oregon Trail and helped to organize Union scouts during the Civil War.

Trail, led the first settlers to Boonesborough, and defended that outpost against the Indians during the Revolution. All of these were distinctions to which Boone could properly lay claim, but later biographers went much further. They claimed that he was the discoverer of Kentucky, its first explorer, its first settler, even The First White Man in the West. These exaggerations did, however, serve to create the image of Boone as an empire builder.

Nevertheless, at the same time a conflicting image developed of a child of nature who fled into the wilderness at the first sound of the backwoodsman's ax. In fact,

Boone's successive migrations westward were the result of his difficulty in securing and holding land grants. But the picture was built up of a noble savage fleeing the corruptions of civilization. The two legendary Boones could, and did, exist side by side.

All the same, the Boone cult which flourished after 1820 tended to emphasize only one of the two images—that which depicted him as a symbol of anarchic freedom. A similar emphasis was to be found in the character of Leatherstocking, the hero of several of James Fenimore Cooper's novels and the best-known fictional symbol of western adventure in the early nineteenth century. The similarities between the legendary Boone and Leatherstocking were close and probably not accidental. Just as Boone was supposed to have done, Leatherstocking had "been driven by the increasing and unparalleled advance of population, to seek a final refuge against society in the broad and tenantless plains of the West. . . ." Both heroes wore buckskin, loved the freedom of the forest, delighted in hunting, and spurned the day-to-day pursuits of civilized men. Both were depicted as patriarchal figures of great age, which Boone certainly was not. Moreover, a straw in the wind pointing to the future development of the fictional western hero was the fact that Boone and Leatherstocking were shown as enemies of law and order. Until about 1850 most fictional Wild West heroes could in some sense be described as the lineal descendants of Boone and Leatherstocking. That is to say, they were generally represented as having fled to the wilderness to

James Fenimore Cooper's novels provided nineteenth-century readers with a glimpse of life on the frontier. Left: A youthful Leatherstocking, the hero of The Deerslayer, offers help to an Indian. Right: The cover of a Buffalo Bill 1894 Beadle novel.

Buffalo Bill's Most Remarkable Story!

BEADLE'S
Dime
New York Library

Copyrighted, 1301, by BEADLE AND ADAMS.   ENTERED AS SECOND CLASS MATTER AT THE NEW YORK, N. Y., POST OFFICE.   April 11, 1894.

No. 807.   Published Every Wednesday.   *Beadle & Adams, Publishers,* 98 WILLIAM STREET, NEW YORK.   Ten Cents a Copy. $5.00 a Year.   Vol. LXIII.

BY BUFFALO BILL.—(Gen. Wm. F. Cody.)

WILD BILL, THE WILD WEST DUELIST;

Or, THE GIRL MASCOT OF MOONLIGHT MINE.

N. ORR—N.Y.

"READY!—RIGHT-ABOUT WHEEL!—FORWARD!—MARCH!"

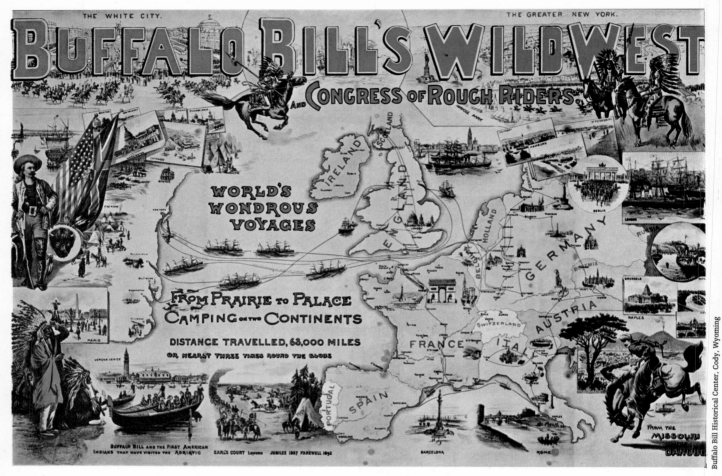

Buffalo Bill's Wild West show traveled all over Europe and the eastern United States. Its stylish cowboys and amazingly costumed Indians thrilled audiences wherever the show appeared.

escape the restrictions of organized society. But in the 1830s and 1840s there came a different conception of the typical Wild Westerner. As the scene shifted beyond the Mississippi, he ceased to be a benign forest hunter and became instead a Rocky Mountain fur trapper. Popular literature now created a semi-savage figure who, to a far greater extent than the pioneers east of the Mississippi, had adopted Indian ways—in costume, speech, outlook, and behavior.

There was a further development in the 1840s: the Mexican War and the huge gain in territory that resulted from it stimulated popular interest in the settlement of the Far West. This meant that the half-savage mountain man had to be changed back into just such a symbol of civilization and progress as Boone had been originally. It was neatly done by depicting an already well-known trapper and guide, Kit Carson, as a character of infinite purity, nobility, and refinement. According to one of his biographers, Carson drew from communion with nature a

genuine simplicity and a generosity of spirit which were rare in organized society. Nature was said also to have endowed him with "a delicacy which never allowed him to use a profane word, to indulge in intoxicating drinks, to be guilty of an impure action." This extravagant nonsense was a far cry from the real Kit Carson. But it did no more violence to the truth than did the daredevil Kit Carson who made his appearance simultaneously in western adventure stories. This was anything but a genteel Kit. Instead, one is given an heroic Indian fighter and bear slayer, a crack shot and consummate horseman, the epitome of bravery, hardihood, and self-reliance.

From the daredevil Kit Carson of midcentury thrillers, it was but a short step to the rip-roaring heroes of the dime novel. Advances in printing technology, notably the introduction of the rotary steam press, led to a revolution in American publishing in the 1840s and 1850s. Mass circulation periodicals made their appearance, among them cheap weeklies specializing in popular adventure stories. The pioneers in this field were the Boston firm of Gleason and Ballou, but the man who came to capture the market for cheap fiction was a New Yorker, Erastus Beadle. The weekly series of dime novels he began publishing in 1860 were patterned on the Gleason and

Ballou stories but tended more often to be set in the Far West. The writers needed, and indeed possessed, only a minimum of imagination or inventiveness; all they had to do was to write to a formula. The result was a standard product whose huge circulation—nearly 5 million copies sold by 1865—testified to its appeal.

That the Beadle "Westerns" derived mainly from Cooper's Leatherstocking novels is plain from the frequency with which they featured an aged, buckskin-clad hunter carrying a long rifle and displaying great prowess as a marksman and Indian fighter. Such a character was the hero of the most famous of the Beadle stories, Edward S. Ellis's *Seth Jones: or, The Captives of the Frontier,* published in 1860. Running a close second were the young, handsome, genteel trappers who were obviously the literary descendants of Kit Carson.

A more complicated pedigree belonged to the character of Deadwood Dick, created by Edward L. Wheeler in 1877. Located originally in the Black Hills of South Dakota during the gold rush of the 1870s, Deadwood Dick inherited all the skills and accomplishments that previous writers had ascribed to western heroes. But he also possessed some distinctive attributes of his own. There was a flavor of lawlessness from a criminal past, a certain slickness that went with his customary role of detective, and a remarkable attraction to women that resulted in a complicated love life. Deadwood Dick's appeal to readers was due less to his remarkable array of talents than to the fact that he personified the popular ideal of the self-made man.

The most celebrated dime novel hero of all was Buffalo Bill. Ned Buntline succeeded in transforming an obscure army scout, William F. Cody, into an epic hero worthy to rank with Boone and Carson. This transformation opened up a sizable gap between fact and fiction, but Cody succeeded in closing it again by adopting on the stage and in *Buffalo Bill's Wild West* show the flamboyant appearance of his fictional counterpart. Wearing top boots, a velvet suit, gauntlet gloves, and a wide sombrero, sporting a goatee and a moustache, he enacted episodes which were crude parodies of his real life on the plains—or pure inventions.

The Visible West

Throughout the nineteenth century popular conceptions of the West were powerfully shaped by pictorial representations as well as by the written word. The western wilderness had an obvious appeal to the artist: it was full of spectacular natural wonders as well as being rich in dramatic themes—the buffalo chase, the Indian attack, the cattle drive. Literally scores of artists sought to record the western scene on canvas or paper, sometimes on the

basis of firsthand experience, but all too frequently from the vantage point of an eastern studio.

In the former category was George Catlin, the young Philadelphia portrait painter who lived for eight years among the Plains Indians in the 1830s and whose widely-exhibited collection of paintings provided a vivid pictorial record of Indian life. But it was not until the 1880s, when the frontier was about to close, that the three most celebrated painters of the western scene made their appearance. Charles M. Russell was himself a product of the open range; on the other hand, Frederic Remington and Charles Schreyvogel were both easterners who spent

Buffalo Bill Historical Center, Cody, Wyoming

Right: The popular star of Buffalo Bill's Wild West *show, Annie Oakley, displays the medals earned by her marksmanship.*

271

time in the West studying and sketching their subjects before executing their paintings in their eastern studios.

A great many illustrations of the West came, however, from artists who had never been there—in particular many who contributed pictures of western life to the immensely popular series of lithographic prints produced by Currier and Ives. Thus two immigrant artists, Louis Maurer and Arthur Fitzwilliam Tait, relied upon knowledge gained in New York's Astor Library when tackling such western themes as a buffalo chase or an encounter with a grizzly bear. Not surprisingly, lack of familiarity with the West sometimes led to error, one of the commonest being the representation of the Great Plains as a sea of tall grass. But accuracy was less important than the capacity to appeal to strong emotions—and at this the Currier and Ives artists excelled.

Some of the best known prints in the series were the work of an Englishwoman, Fanny Palmer. One of her most famous was *Across the Continent* which contained many of the images which Americans associated with the West—the grandeur of the landscape, the line of covered wagons heading for the far horizon, the mounted Indian warrior, the locomotive belching smoke as it chugged westward, the log cabin of the settler, the school and the church located alongside the railroad tracks. In such fashion was a vast historical drama recalled for the benefit of countless Americans in towns and villages throughout the land.

Above: The four horsemen of Frederic Remington's bronze Comin' Through The Rye. *The sculptor-painter lived for many years in the West and brilliantly portrayed its way of life. Right: The Cassily Adams version of Custer's last stand. There were no white survivors—and Indian accounts of the battle varied widely.*

One of Currier and Ives most famous prints, Across the Continent. *The painting by Fanny Palmer contains many elements of the Western legend.*

For all their huge popularity, the Currier and Ives prints contributed less to myth-making than did two paintings of Custer's last stand. These works, by John Mulvany and Cassilly Adams, have, in the opinion of one art historian, been seen and discussed by more Americans than any other paintings. Both date from the 1880s and in both the scene is totally imaginary, since no white witness survived the Custer tragedy. Mulvany's picture, *Custer's Last Rally*, was completed in 1881 and for the next ten or twelve years was constantly displayed throughout the country. Before starting the work, which was painted chiefly in Kansas City, Mulvany visited the battlefield on the Little Bighorn and also observed Sioux on a reservation. Probably for that reason the scene he depicts contains no obvious historical inaccuracies.

The Adams version is far more dramatic and is clearly intended to contribute to the Custer legend. Although there is no hard evidence how or at what point in the battle Custer was killed, Adams shows him as the last survivor, holding an empty pistol in one hand and with the other fighting off his Indian assailants with a saber. In fact no sabers were carried in the engagement. Nor was Adams correct in depicting Custer in a short jacket, an enormous red tie, and long red hair flowing over his shoulders. But this is the version of the Custer tragedy with which Americans are most familiar. This is because a lithograph

of the Adams painting was published by a St Louis brewery in 1896 and was widely distributed to advertise its product. Over the next half century, 150,000 copies were distributed, and copies are still to be seen in barrooms, taverns, hotels, and restaurants.

The romantic legends surrounding the West were to a remarkable degree manufactured in the East, particularly in the established cultural centers of the Eastern Seaboard, around the turn of the century. It was at this time that Frederic Remington rose to a position of artistic prominence as an interpreter of western life, and Theodore Roosevelt demonstrated his love of the outdoors and the wilderness by publishing *The Winning of the West* and numerous accounts of his Dakota ranching experiences. Then Owen Wister conferred literary respectability upon the cowboy in *The Virginian*, the most widely read American novel of the first decade of the twentieth century. Remington, Roosevelt, and Wister were all from eastern upper-class families of established wealth and social position and, having each lived for a time in the West, chose to emphasize those western qualities which seemed threatened by the conformity of eastern business civilization—manliness, individualism, self-reliance. In so doing they captured the nostalgia for a simpler America which many of their contemporaries shared.

The emotional responses elicited by such people owed

Left: The historian Frederick Jackson Turner. The existence of the frontier, he claimed, explained many of the differences between the American and European characters.

most, however, to their capacity to make the West the image of American society as a whole. The same factor also helped to explain the appeal of an interpretation of American history put forward in the same period by a young historian, Frederick Jackson Turner, who saw the moving frontier as the key to the American past.

The notion that the West was a formative influence in American life had been current since the earliest days of the republic, but it was Turner who gave classical expression to the idea. In a paper he read to a gathering of fellow-historians in Chicago in 1893 on "The Significance of the Frontier in American History," Turner put forward what became known as the frontier hypothesis. What explained American development, according to Turner, was "the existence of an area of free land, its continuous recession, and the advance of American settlement Westward." Each move westward, he declared, meant "a return to primitive conditions on a continually advancing frontier line," a "perennial rebirth."

Turner saw the frontier as "the meeting point between savagery and civilization." First the wilderness environment mastered the colonist, stripping him of the garments of civilization, arraying him in "the hunting shirt and the moccasin," and reducing him to a state of near savagery akin to that of the Indian. Little by little the colonist transformed the wilderness and succeeded in planting civilized institutions. But the society he created was different from that he had known in the East; it was a new product, less European, more distinctively American. One result was that the frontier "promoted the formation of a composite nationality." More important, however, was the promotion of democracy and individualism. Frontier conditions bred antipathy to control and a tendency to confuse individual liberty with the absence of all government.

Turner's frontier thesis was to revolutionize historical thought in the United States. Within a decade or so his ideas were almost universally accepted by the historical profession, and the frontier interpretation came to dominate the writing and teaching of American history. Nor was Turner's influence limited to historians. His ideas were taken over by magazine editors, popular authors, public lecturers, and politicians, and thus became the common property of the American people.

Eighty-odd years after it was put forward, the frontier thesis remains the most widely-known interpretation of American history, but few scholars would accept it without serious qualifications. It was a distortion of the facts, for example, to assert that the inhabitants of America's successive frontiers generally reverted to barbarism. Disorder and savagery were typical only of certain notorious centers, such as cow towns and mining camps.

The true frontiersmen were the small farmers, ranchers, artisans, and merchants who formed the bulk of the settlers on every frontier. These people did not go west in order to escape from civilization; they wanted rather to keep in touch with it. Admittedly the primitive social environment and the preoccupation with material tasks were hardly suited to the development of culture. But in scores of frontier settlements an educated minority made heroic efforts to transplant their cultural heritage intact. From the very beginning they established newspapers and magazines, founded schools, churches, and theaters, and patronized literary societies and subscription libraries. These cultural institutions tended, moreover, to duplicate traditional forms though they sometimes functioned in incongruous surroundings, as when literary societies met on the sod-house frontier in Nebraska and when Italian opera was performed to an audience of miners in Virginia City.

Or take Turner's assertion that frontier conditions promoted democracy. If he had political democracy in mind then the evidence is strongly against him. The western states simply adopted the political ideals and contitutional practices long established in the older states. Turner's claim that frontier society was free from class divisions was similarly contrary to fact. On every frontier a social elite emerged which felt little affinity with the mass of the common people and which sought every opportunity to demonstrate its superiority. But however much the "better sort" might stand aloof, it is true that there was a closer approximation to economic equality than in the East and a greater degree of social mobility.

Of all the myths wrapped up in the Turner thesis, that which expressed a belief in frontier individualism was probably the most persistent. The fact that the pioneer supposedly fled to the wilderness to escape social controls and that, once there, he was forced to rely upon his own efforts in the fight against nature, was believed to have contributed to a spirit of self-reliance and to a disregard of the interests of others. But the realities of frontier life were more suited to collective than to individual action. Cooperation with neighbors was essential for defense against Indians, the accomplishment of essential pioneering tasks, and the successful functioning of economic life. Hence the "cabin raisings" and "logrollings" that provided newcomers with a home; hence, too, the "corn huskings" and "quilting bees" that came to charac-

All over the world, films about the American West draw millions of customers to the box office. Right: A Hollywood version of a Western town, erected on a studio back lot.

terize frontier community life. So pervasive was the community spirit that social conformity and standardized behavior became the norm. In practice, the frontier exemplified not individualism but interdependence.

But for all the criticism leveled at the theory, Turner had portrayed an American past which the average citizen found both recognizable and psychologically satisfying. It was not merely that an interpretation which glorified democracy and nationalism as American virtues and which stressed American rather than European influences corresponded perfectly to the mood of the 1890s. More important was the fact that Turner expressed ideas and attitudes which had long been essential ingredients of the folklore of American expansion. And it is not surprising that with the closing of the frontier and the rise of industrialism, a thesis which reasserted old values and symbols should have struck a responsive chord.

That these yearnings have persisted into our own times is shown both by the continued appeal of the Turner thesis and, on a different level, by the enormous popularity of the "Western"—a term which, significantly enough, is universally understood to mean a story, novel, or motion picture dealing with life on the Great Plains, especially cowboy life. In the earliest days of the American cinema the frontier was simply a picturesque locale for movie dramas. But by the time of the First World War the Western had become what it has remained ever since—a morality play, in which democratic feeling and moral standards are forcefully asserted.

The United States is not the only part of the world with a frontier past. Canada, Australia, Brazil, Argentina, Siberia, were all settled at about the same time. But nowhere else did the empty land that lay beyond the margin of settlement exercise such a profound pull on the popular consciousness. The reason was only in part that on other frontiers either the environment or the prevailing cultural traditions were unfavorable to repeated pioneering.

Americans themselves were not put off by discrepancies between the myth and the reality. Americans believed about the West not so much what *was* true but what they thought *ought* to be true. This was largely the result of their preoccupation with the question of national identity. Lacking the common heritage that bound other nations together, they were forced to look elsewhere for the basis of their national existence. They found it in the West.

Bibliography

GENERAL

*Billington, Ray A., *The Far Western Frontier, 1830–1860* (New York, 1956)

*De Voto, Bernard, *The Year of Decision, 1846* (Boston, 1943)

*Goetzmann, William H., *When the Eagle Screamed: The Romantic Horizon in American Diplomacy, 1800–1860* (New York, 1966)

Goodwin, Cardinal, *The Trans-Mississippi West, 1803–1853: A History of its Acquisition and Settlement* (New York, 1922)

*Graebner, Norman A., ed., *Manifest Destiny* (Indianapolis, 1968)

*Merk, Frederick, *Manifest Destiny and Mission in American History: A Reinterpretation* (New York, 1963)

Merk, Frederick & L. B., *The Monroe Doctrine and American Expansion, 1843–1849* (New York, 1966)

*Turner, Frederick Jackson, *The Frontier in American History* (New York, 1921)

*Turner, Frederick Jackson, *The United States, 1830–1850* (New York, 1935)

Wright, Louis B., *Culture on the Moving Frontier* (Bloomington, 1955)

Chapter 1: WESTWARD TO THE PACIFIC

Bannon, John F., *The Spanish Borderlands Frontier, 1513–1821* (New York, 1970)

Chittenden, H. M., *The American Fur Trade of the Far West* (3 vols., New York, 1902)

Cleland, Robert G., *This Reckless Breed of Men: The Trappers and Fur Traders of the Southwest* (New York, 1950)

De Voto, Bernard, *Across the Wide Missouri* (Boston, 1952)

Favour, Alpheus H., *Old Bill Williams, Mountain Man* (Chapel Hill, N.C., 1936)

Goetzmann, William H., *Exploration and Empire: The Explorer and the Scientist in the Winning of the American West* (New York, 1966)

*Goetzmann, William H., *Army Exploration in the American West, 1803–1863* (New Haven, 1959)

Morgan, Dale L., *Jedediah Smith and the Opening of the West* (Indianapolis, 1953)

Nevins, Allan, *Fremont, Pathmarker of the West* (rev. edn., New York, 1955)

Vestal, Stanley, *Jim Bridger, Mountain Man* (New York, 1946)

Wallace, Edward S., *The Great Reconnaissance: Soldiers, Artists and Scientists on the Frontier, 1848–1861* (Boston, 1955)

Wood, Richard G., *Stephen Harriman Long, 1784–1864: Army Engineer, Explorer, Inventor* (Glendale, Cal., 1966)

Chapter 2: THE SPANISH PRESENCE

Adams, Ephraim D., *British Interests and Activities in Texas, 1838–1846* (Baltimore, 1910)

Barker, Eugene C., *Mexico and Texas, 1821–1835* (Dallas, 1928)

Bean, Walton, *California: An Interpretive History* (New York, 1968)

Callcott, Wilfred H., *Santa Anna* (Norman, Okla., 1936)

Chitwood, Oliver P., *John Tyler* (New York, 1939)

Gambrell, Herbert P., *Anson Jones, the Last President of Texas* (Garden City, N.Y., 1948)

Hogan, William R., *The Texas Republic: A Social and Economic History* (Norman, Okla., 1946)

James, Marquis, *The Raven: A Biography of Sam Houston* (Indianapolis, 1929)

Richardson, Rupert N., *Texas: The Lone Star State* (2nd edn., New York, 1958)

Rives, George L., *The United States and Mexico, 1821–1848* (2 vols., New York, 1913)

Siegel, Stanley, *A Political History of the Texas Republic, 1836–1845* (Austin, 1956)

Chapter 3: THE SPIRIT OF EXPANSION

Drury, Clifford M., *Marcus Whitman, M.D., Pioneer and Martyr* (Caldwell, Idaho, 1937)

*Graebner, Norman A., *Empire on the Pacific: A Study in American Continental Expansion* (New York, 1955)

Jones, Wilbur D., *Lord Aberdeen and the Americas* (Athens, Ga., 1958)

Lavender, David, *Westward Vision: The Story of the Oregon Trail* (New York, 1963)

Merk, Frederick, *The Oregon Question: Essays in Anglo-American Diplomacy and Politics* (Cambridge, Mass., 1967)

Merk, Frederick, *Slavery and the Annexation of Texas* (New York, 1972)

Monaghan, Jay, *The Overland Trail* (Indianapolis, 1947)

Paul, James C. N., *Rift in the Democracy* (Philadelphia, 1951)

Pierce, Gerald S., *Texas under Arms, 1836–1846* (Austin, 1969)

Stewart, George R., *The California Trail: An Epic with many Heroes* (New York, 1962)

Stewart, George R., *Ordeal by Hunger: The Story of the Donner Party* (Boston, 1960)

Weinberg, Albert K., *Manifest Destiny* (Baltimore, 1935)

Wiltse, Charles M., *John C. Calhoun, Sectionalist, 1840–1850* (Indianapolis, 1951)

Chapter 4: A CLASH OF REPUBLICS

Bill, Alfred H., *Rehearsal for Conflict: The War with Mexico, 1846–1848* (New York, 1947)

Brauer, Kinley J., *Cotton Versus Conscience: Massachusetts Whig Politics and Southwestern Expansion, 1843–1848* (Lexington, Ky., 1967)

Clarke, Dwight L., *Stephen Watts Kearny: Soldier of the West* (Norman, Okla., 1961)

Dyer, Brainerd, *Zachary Taylor* (Baton Rouge, 1946)

Fuller, John D. P., *The Movement for the Acquisition of All Mexico, 1846–1848* (Baltimore, 1936)

Lavender, David, *Climax at Buena Vista: The American Campaigns in Northeastern Mexico, 1846–47* (Philadelphia, 1966)

Morrison, Chaplain W., *Democratic Politics and Sectionalism: The Wilmot Proviso Controversy* (Chapel Hill, N.C., 1967)

Pletcher, David M., *The Diplomacy of Annexation: Texas, Oregon and the Mexican War* (Columbia, Mo., 1973)

Sellers, Charles G., *James K. Polk, Continentalist: 1843–1848* (Princeton, 1966)

*Singletary, Otis A., *The Mexican War* (Chicago, 1960)

Smith, Justin H., *The War with Mexico* (2 vols., New York, 1919)

*indicates paperback

Chapter 5: THE MORMON TREK TO UTAH

*Arrington, Leonard J., *Great Basin Kingdom: An Economic History of the Latter Day Saints, 1830–1900* (Cambridge, Mass., 1958)

Brooks, Juanita, *The Mountain Meadows Massacre* (rev. edn., Norman, Okla., 1962)

Creer, Leland H., *The Founding of an Empire: The Exploration and Colonization of Utah, 1776–1856* (Salt Lake City, 1947)

Flanders, Robert B., *Nauvoo: Kingdom on the Mississippi* (Urbana, Ill., 1965)

*Furniss, Norman F., *The Mormon Conflict, 1850–1859* (New Haven, 1960)

Hansen, Klaus J., *Quest for Empire: The Political Kingdom of God and the Council of Fifty in Mormon History* (East Lansing, 1967)

Hirshson, Stanley P., *The Lion of the Lord: A Biography of Brigham Young* (New York, 1959)

Mulder, William, *Homeward to Zion: The Mormon Emigration from Scandinavia* (Minneapolis, 1957)

*O'Dea, Thomas F., *The Mormons* (Chicago, 1957)

Taylor, Philip A. M., *Expectations Westward: The Mormons and the Emigration of their British Converts in the Nineteenth Century* (Edinburgh, 1965)

West, Ray B., Jr. *Kingdom of the Saints: The Story of Brigham Young and the Mormons* (New York, 1957)

Chapter 6: ELDORADO ON THE PACIFIC

Caughey, John W., *Gold is the Cornerstone* (Berkeley, 1948)

Caughey, John W., ed., *Rushing for Gold* (Berkeley, 1949)

Goodwin, Cardinal, *The Establishment of State Government in California, 1846–1850* (New York, 1914)

Grivas, Theodore, *Military Governments in California, 1846–1850* (Glendale, Cal., 1963)

Hafen, Leroy, *Overland Routes to the Gold Fields* (Glendale, Cal., 1942)

Hawgood, John A., "John C. Frémont and the Bear Flag Revolution: A Reappraisal." *Historical Society of Southern California. Quarterly,* XLIV (1962)

Howe, Octavius T., *Argonauts of '49: History and Adventures of the Emigrant Companies from Massachusetts, 1849–1850* (Cambridge, Mass., 1923)

Lewis, Oscar, *Sea Routes to the Gold Fields: The Migration by Water to California in 1849–1852* (New York, 1949)

Lewis, Oscar, *Sutter's Fort: Gateway to the Gold Fields* (Englewood Cliffs, N.J., 1966)

*Paul, Rodman W., *California Gold* (Cambridge, Mass., 1947)

Shinn, C. H., *Mining Camps* (New York, 1948)

Stewart, George R., *Committee of Vigilance: Revolution in San Francisco, 1851* (Boston, 1964)

White, Stewart E., *The Forty-Niners* (New Haven, 1921)

Chapter 7: ACROSS THE CONTINENT
Western Panorama

*Andrist, Ralph K., *The Long Death: The Last Days of the Plains Indians* (New York, 1964)

*Athearn, Robert G., *High Country Empire: The High Plains and the Rockies* (New York, 1960)

Brandon, William, *The American Heritage Book of Indians* (New York, 1961)

Debo, Angie, *A History of the Indians of the United States* (Norman, Okla., 1970)

Fenneman, Nevin M., *Physiography of the Western United States* (New York, 1931)

*Gard, Wayne, *The Great Buffalo Hunt* (New York, 1959)

*Hagan, William T., *American Indians* (Chicago, 1961)

Hollon, W. Eugene, *The Great American Desert, Then and Now* (New York, 1966)

*Josephy, Alvin M., Jr., *The Patriot Chiefs: American Indian Leadership* (New York, 1961)

La Farge, Oliver, *A Pictorial History of the American Indian* (New York, 1956)

Malin, James C., *The Grassland of North America* (Lawrence, Kan., 1956)

Pomeroy, Earl S., *The Pacific Slope* (New York, 1964)

Wissler, Clark, *North American Indians of the Plains* (New York, 1920)

Ribbons of Steel

Athearn, Robert G., *Rebel of the Rockies* (New Haven, 1962)

Chapman, Arthur, *The Pony Express* (New York, 1932)

Fogel, Robert W., *Railroads and American Economic Growth: Essays in Econometric History* (Baltimore, 1964)

Frederick, James V., *Ben Holladay, the Stagecoach King* (Glendale, Cal., 1940)

Galloway, John D., *The First Transcontinental Railroad* (New York, 1950)

Hafen, Leroy R., *The Overland Mail, 1849–1869* (Cleveland, 1926)

Hedges, James B., *Henry Villard and the Railways of the Northwest* (New Haven, 1930)

Lewis, Oscar, *The Big Four: The Story of Huntingdon, Stanford, Hopkins and Crocker, and of the Building of the Central Pacific* (New York, 1938)

Overton, Richard C., *Burlington Route* (New York, 1965)

Riegel, Robert E., *The Story of the Western Railroads* (New York, 1926)

*Stover, John F., *American Railroads* (Chicago, 1961)

Taylor, George R., & Neu, Irene D., *The American Railroad Network, 1861–1890* (Cambridge, Mass., 1956)

Waters, Leslie L., *Steel Rails to Santa Fe* (Lawrence, Kan., 1950)

Winther, Oscar O., *The Transportation Frontier: Trans-Mississippi West, 1865–1890* (New York, 1964)

Chapter 8: THE CATTLE KINGDOM
"Head 'em North"

Adams, Andy, *Log of a Cowboy: A Narrative of the Old Trail Days* (New York, 1903)

Atherton, Lewis, *The Cattle Kings* (Bloomington, Ind., 1961)

Brisbin, James S., *Beef Bonanza* (Norman, Okla., 1959)

Dale, Edward E., *The Range Cattle Industry* (Norman, Okla., 1930)

Dykstra, Robert R., *The Cattle Towns: A Social History of the Kansas Cattle Trading Centers* (New York, 1968)

Frantz, Joe B., & Choate, Julian E., Jr., *The American Cowboy: The Myth and the Reality* (Norman, Okla., 1955)

Gard, Wayne, *The Chisholm Trail* (Norman, Okla., 1954)

*Gressley, Gene M., *Bankers and Cattlemen* (New York, 1966)

McCallum, F. T. & H. D., *The Wire That Fenced The West* (Norman, Okla., 1965)

*Osgood, Ernest S., *The Day of the Cattleman* (Minneapolis, 1929)

Pelzer, Louis, *The Cattleman's Frontier* (Glendale, Cal., 1936)

Wellman, Paul I., *The Trampling Herd* (New York, 1939)

The Wild West

Bennett, Estelline, *Old Deadwood Days* (New York, 1928)

Faulk, Odie B., *Tombstone: Myth and Reality* (New York, 1972)

Gard, Wayne, *Frontier Justice* (Norman, Okla., 1949)

Lyon, Peter, "The Wild, Wild West," *American Heritage,* II (1960)

Raine, William McL., *Guns of the Frontier* (Boston, 1940)

Raine, William McL., *Famous Sheriffs and Western Outlaws* (Garden City, N.Y., 1929)

Rosa, Joseph G., *They Called Him Wild Bill: The Life and Adventures of James Butler Hickok* (Norman, Okla., 1964)

Russell, Don, *The Lives and Legends of Buffalo Bill* (Norman, Okla., 1960)

Settle, William A., Jr., *Jesse James Was His Name* (Columbia, Mo., 1966)

*Shirley, Glenn, *Law West of Fort Smith: A History of Frontier Justice in the Indian Territory, 1834–1896* (New York, 1957)

Sollid, Roberta B., *Calamity Jane: A Study in Historical Criticism* (Helena, Mont., 1958)

Chapter 9: RICHES OF THE LAND
The Mining Bonanza

Greever, William S., *The Bonanza West: The Story of the Western Mining Rushes, 1848–1900* (Norman, Okla., 1963)

Hafen, Leroy R., *Colorado Gold Rush: Contemporary Letters and Reports, 1858–1859* (Glendale, Cal., 1941)

Jackson, W. Turrentine, *Treasure Hill: Portrait of a Silver Mining Camp* (Tucson, 1963)

*Paul, Rodman W., *Mining Frontiers of the Far West, 1848–1880* (New York, 1963)

Rowe, John, *The Hard-Rock Men: Cornish Immigrants and the North American Mining Frontier* (Liverpool, 1974)

Smith, Duane A., *Rocky Mountain Mining Camps: The Urban Frontier* (Bloomington, Ind., 1967)

Smith, Grant H., *The History of the Comstock Lode, 1850–1920* (Reno, Nev., 1943)

Spence, Clark C., *British Investments and the American Mining Frontier, 1860–1901* (Ithaca, N.Y., 1958)

Spence, Clark C., *Mining Engineers and the American West: The Lace Boot Brigade (1849–1933)* (New Haven, 1970)

*Twain, Mark, *Roughing It* (Hartford, 1872)

The Farmer on the Plains

Dick, Everett, *The Sod-House Frontier, 1854–1890* (New York, 1937)

*Fite, Gilbert C., *The Farmers' Frontier, 1865–1900* (New York, 1966)

*Gates, Paul W., *Fifty Million Acres: Conflicts Over Kansas Land Policy, 1854–1890* (Ithaca, N.Y., 1954)

Gates, Paul W., "The Homestead Act in an Incongruous Land System," *American Historical Review*, XLI (1936)

*Hibbard, Benjamin H., *A History of the Public Land Policies* (2nd edn., Madison, 1965)

*Lamar, Howard R., *Dakota Territory, 1861–1889: A Study of Frontier Politics* (New Haven, 1956)

Overton, Richard C., *Burlington West* (Cambridge, Mass., 1941)

*Pomeroy, Earl S., *The Territories and the United States, 1861–1890* (Philadelphia, 1947)

*Robbins, Roy M., *Our Landed Heritage: The Public Domain, 1776–1936* (Princeton, 1942)

Chapter 10: THE INDIAN TRAGEDY

Athearn, Robert G., *William Tecumseh Sherman and the Settlement of the West* (Norman, Okla., 1956)

*Beal, Merrill D., *'I Will Fight No More Forever': Chief Joseph and the Nez Perce War* (Seattle, 1963)

Beaver, R. Pierce, *Church, State and the American Indians* (St. Louis, 1966)

Ellis, Richard N., *General Pope and U.S. Indian Policy* (Albuquerque, 1970)

Faulk, Odie B., *The Geronimo Campaign* (New York, 1969)

Fritz, Henry E., *The Movement for Indian Assimilation, 1860–1890* (Philadelphia, 1963)

*Jackson, Helen Hunt, *A Century of Dishonor: The Early Crusade for Indian Reform* (New York, 1881)

Mardock, Robert W., *The Reformers and the American Indian* (Columbia, Mo., 1970)

Olson, James C., *Red Cloud and the Sioux Problem* (Lincoln, Neb., 1965)

Priest, Loring B., *Uncle Sam's Stepchildren: The Reformation of United States Indian Policy, 1865–1887* (New Brunswick, N.J., 1947)

Rahill, Peter J., *The Catholic Indian Missions and Grant's Peace Policy, 1870–1884* (Washington, D.C., 1953)

Rister, Carl C., *The Southwestern Frontier, 1865–1881* (Cleveland, 1928)

Utley, Robert M., *The Last Days of the Sioux Nation* (New Haven, 1963)

Vestal, Stanley, *Sitting Bull* (Norman, Okla., 1932)

Wellman, Paul I., *Death on Horseback: Seventy Years of War for the American West* (Philadelphia, 1947)

Wellman, Paul I., *The Indian Wars of the West* (Garden City, N.Y., 1954)

Chapter 11: THE CLOSING OF THE FRONTIER
Preserving the Wilderness

Clepper, Henry E., ed., *Leaders of American Conservation* (New York, 1971)

Graham, Frank, Jr., *Man's Dominion: The Story of Conservation in America* (Philadelphia, 1971)

Greeley, William B., *Forest Policy* (New York, 1953)

Ise, John, *Our National Park Policy: A Critical History* (Baltimore, 1961)

Jones, Holway R., *John Muir and the Sierra Club: The Battle for Yosemite* (San Francisco, 1965)

Lowenthal, David, *George Perkins Marsh, Versatile Vermonter* (New York, 1958)

*Nash, Roderick, ed., *The American Environment: Readings in the History of Conservation* (Reading, Mass., 1968)

*Nash, Roderick, *Wilderness and the American Mind* (New Haven, 1967)

Pinkett, Harold T., *Gifford Pinchot: Private and Public Forester* (Urbana, Ill., 1970)

*Stegner, Wallace E., *Beyond the Hundredth Meridian: John Wesley Powell and the Second Opening of the West* (Boston, 1954)

*Tilden, Freeman, *The National Parks* (New York, 1968)

The West: Myth and Reality

Allen, Harry C., *Bush and Backwoods: A Comparison of the Frontier in Australia and the United States* (East Lansing, Mich., 1959)

Billington, Ray A., *Frederick Jackson Turner: Historian, Scholar, Teacher* (New York, 1973)

Carter, Harvey L., *'Dear Old Kit': The Historical Christopher Carson* (Norman, Okla., 1968)

Kraenzel, Carl F., *The Great Plains in Transition* (Norman, Okla., 1955)

Noble, David W., *Historians Against History: The Frontier Thesis and the National Covenant* (Minneapolis, 1965)

Shannon, Fred A., "A Post-Mortem on the Labor-Safety-Valve Theory," *Agricultural History* (1945)

*Smith, Henry Nash, *Virgin Land: The American West as Symbol and Myth* (Cambridge, Mass., 1950)

Steckmesser, Kent L., *The Western Hero in History and Legend* (Norman, Okla., 1965)

*Turner, Frederick J., *The Frontier in American History* (New York, 1921)

Utley, Robert M., *The Custer Legend* (New Haven, 1962)

Index

Page references in *italics* refer to captions

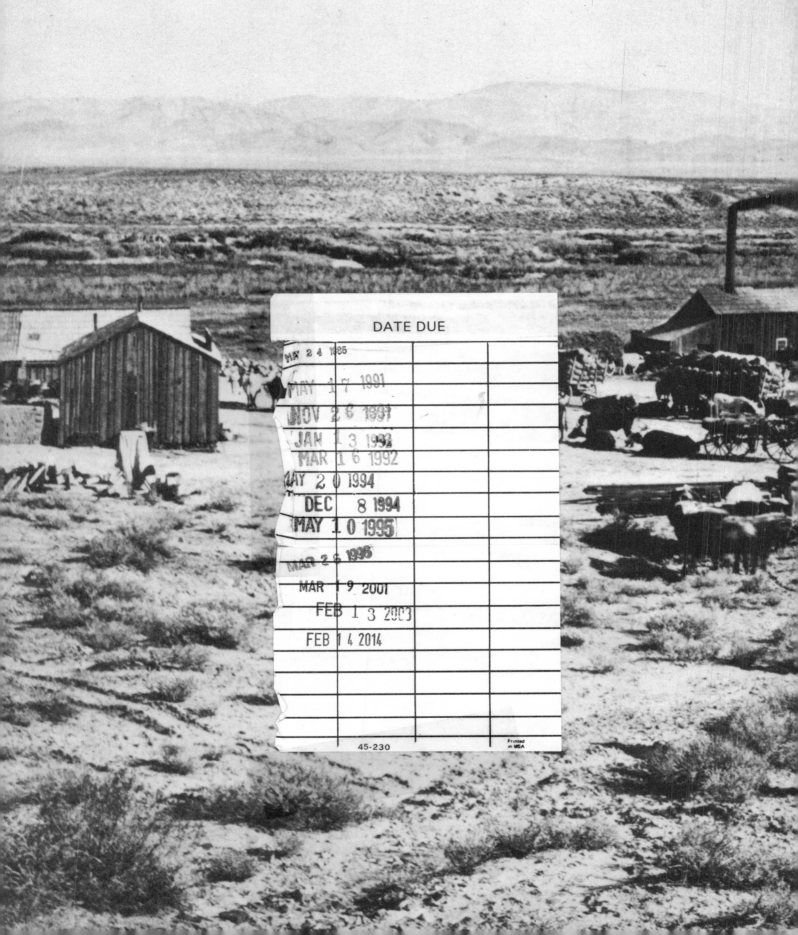